Light Locomotives

Tenth Edition

H K Porter Company

©2010 PERISCOPE FILM LLC
ALL RIGHTS RESERVED
ISBN 978-1-935700-18-0
WWW.PERISCOPEFILM.COM

Light—— Locomotives.

Compliments of H. K. Porter Co.

H K Porter Company

Builders of

Light Locomotives

Steam and Compressed Air

HENRY KIRKE PORTER President
WILLIAM ENSIGN LINCOLN Vice-President
HOBART BENTLEY AYERS General Manager
WILLIS ELIPHALET MARTIN Treasurer
CHARLES LAWRENCE McHENRY Secretary
DAVID EDWARD FERGUSON Purchasing Agent

Office 12th Floor Union Bank Building Fourth Ave and Wood St
Works on Pennsylvania Railroad B & A V Div Forty-ninth St

Pittsburgh Pa

Cable Address Porter Pittsburgh

Codes Used

A B C Code Fourth Edition   A B C Code Fifth Edition   Lieber's Code
Western Union Code   A 1 Code   Business Telegraph Code
H K Porter Company Code (Beginning page 204 of this Catalogue)

©2010 Periscope Film LLC
All Rights Reserved
ISBN 978-1-935700-18-0
www.PeriscopeFilm.com

The above illustration shows a portion of the erecting floor. A 40-ton, 36-inch gauge engine is hanging from the electric cranes ready to load on the car. On the floor are locomotives for steel works, coke ovens, mines, etc., and also plantation locomotives for Hawaii, and an industrial locomotive for Spain.

Light Locomotives

Our exclusive specialty is the manufacture of Light Locomotives—**Steam and Compressed Air**—in every variety of size and design, and FOR ANY PRACTICABLE GAUGE OF TRACK, WIDE OR NARROW.

By "Light Locomotives" we do not mean lightly constructed machines, but locomotives of smaller sizes than are used on main lines of road. Our "Light Locomotives" as compared with usual construction are built heavier and stronger. They are specially adapted to severe requirements and difficult conditions for which ordinary railroad locomotives are unsuitable and too costly.

The business was begun in 1866 by the firm of Smith & Porter; they were succeeded in 1871 by Porter, Bell & Company; in 1878 by H. K. Porter & Company; and in 1899 by the H. K. Porter Company. The annual capacity of the first shop, which was destroyed by fire in 1871, was 15 to 25 locomotives; of our earliest shops on the present 49th Street site, from 1872 to 1880, about 75 locomotives; of our enlarged shops, 1881 to 1893, about 125 locomotives; and our present shops have an annual capacity of 400 locomotives.

Our first catalogue, printed in 1874, comprised 59 small pages and described 17 locomotives. This Tenth Edition describes 559 locomotives and contains 224 pages. **All of the designs herein described and illustrated are original with us and are the growth of our more than forty years' experience in this specialty.** The interval between the Ninth Edition Catalogue and this Tenth Edition marks a greater progress in the efficiency and quality of our locomotives, as well as the amount of output, than any equal period in our history. Our present designs are practically equivalent in power and efficiency to the next size larger cylinders as described in the previous catalogue.

Our Guaranty

Every one of our locomotives, whether expressly so stipulated in the contract or not, is guaranteed by us to be in accordance with the specifications; to be of the best workmanship and material; accurately constructed to our duplicate system; and to develop the tractive force stated in the catalogue.

This guaranty appears to us to cover everything for which a manufacturer can be considered accountable.

Between one-half and two-thirds of our sales are repeated orders, and of the remainder the majority are for neighbors or acquaintances of customers.

Our Duplicate and Stock System

By means of original and duplicate classified drawings and records, and of standard gauges and templets and special tools, each locomotive is made duplicate and interchangeable with all others of the same size and class.

One extremely valuable feature of our duplicate system is original with us, and so far as we know has not been adopted by any other locomotive shop, viz.: We always keep on hand, independent and ahead of locomotives under construction, a large stock of duplicate parts completed and under way for all of our standard designs and sizes, enabling us to fill orders for repairs promptly or immediately. On receipt of an order for repairs the parts ordered are taken from the proper rack or shelf and shipped. This saves from several days to several weeks time over the ordinary way of starting to make the parts upon receipt of the order. It ties up a considerable amount of our money, but avoids tying up our customers' business and saves them money. Necessarily our stock system cannot cover departures from standard designs or odd gauge parts varying with gauge of track.

Completed Locomotives on Hand in Stock

It has been our practice for over thirty-five years to keep on hand in stock a number of sizes and designs of completed locomotives both for **thirty-six and fifty-six and one-half inches gauge of track.**

Correspondents needing immediate delivery of locomotives for contractor's use, industrial service, mine and logging roads, shifting, steel-works, etc., can usually find something suitable on our erecting floor ready for shipment as soon as the couplings can be adjusted to the required height and the locomotive lettered.

While we do not deal in **second-hand** locomotives, we often are able to refer such inquiries to customers having locomotives for sale. Second-hand locomotives—unless the history of the machine is known—may be expected to be of old-style, light machinery, light boiler pressure, and of less power than modern designs; they are liable to need more repairs than they are worth. A second-hand locomotive without the builder's name plate is open to suspicion as the year of its construction is given on the missing plate.

Many buyers do not appreciate the difference in power and value between modern and old-style locomotives of the same size cylinders and general design. As an illustration, we note below the weight, boiler pressure, and power of two types of locomotives at different dates.

Locomotive Code Word Kirwan, 7x12 Cylinders, Class B-S

		Weight.	Boiler Pressure.	Tractive Force.
First	Edition Catalogue (1874).	12,000 lb.	120 lb.	2,495 lb.
Sixth	" " (1889).	15,000 "	140 "	2,915 "
Ninth	" " (1900).	16,500 "	140 "	2,915 "
Tenth	" " (1907).	17,500 "	160 "	3,330 "

Locomotive Code Word Kizloz, 10x16 Cylinders, Class B-S

		Weight.	Boiler Pressure.	Tractive Force
First	Edition Catalogue (1874).	28,000 lb.	120 lb.	5,005 lb.
Sixth	" " (1889).	29,000 "	140 "	5,775 "
Ninth	" " (1900).	32,000 "	140 "	5,775 "
Tenth	" " (1907).	36,500 "	160 "	7,250 "

The increase of weight and power of other sizes and designs has progressed at a similar rate, and locomotives of our latest designs may be reckoned about ten to fifteen per cent more efficient than those built about five years ago.

Overhauling and Repairing Locomotives

We have the best facilities for making general repairs of locomotives, and do such work as promptly as contracts on hand will admit. If a locomotive is considered worth general overhauling we recommend that the work be done thoroughly, and we will use our best judgment to keep the cost as low as may be consistent with a satisfactory job. It is not possible to make any accurate estimate of cost of overhauling in advance of doing the work. **Locomotives for repairs should be shipped to us to reach Pittsburgh by Pennsylvania Railroad or Pennsylvania Company Lines.**

Shipment of Locomotives

Locomotives for points accessible by rail are shipped on flat cars, well loaded and secured, and set up ready for fuel and water excepting that small parts liable to injury or loss en route are removed and boxed, and bright work is protected from rust. This applies to all locomotives of narrow or unusual gauges of track, and to standard gauge locomotives excepting sizes large enough to make shipment on own wheels preferable. Unless otherwise agreed, our delivery is free on car or track at our shops. We are prepared to secure lowest possible freight rates.

Orders for Export

We have exported locomotives for over thirty-five years and are acquainted with the preferences and requirements of foreign countries. Our locomotives are in use throughout the United States and Territories, including Alaska and our West India Islands, the Canal Zone, Hawaii, and the Philippines; also in the various divisions of Canada, and in Mexico, Nicaragua, San Salvador, Honduras, Guatemala, Yucatan, Republic of Colombia, Venezuela, Guiana, Brazil, Uruguay, Argentine, Chile, Peru, Ecuador, Cuba, Haiti, San Domingo, Spain, Italy, Austria, Finland, Russia, Sweden, South Africa, Zanzibar, Korea, Formosa, and Borneo, and we were the first American builders to ship locomotives to Japan. Since our designs are the evolution of home conditions of excessive grades and curves, light rails, rough track, hard service, and poor care, our locomotives are better adapted for export to countries where similar conditions prevail than are English and Continental machines. Repeated orders from foreign customers have been a feature of our business for many years.

For foreign shipment our locomotives, after being thoroughly tested by their own steam on friction rollers, are taken apart and the various pieces marked to show their proper position and to facilitate setting them up again on arrival at destination. All bright work is carefully protected from rust by a coating of white lead and tallow, which can be removed readily with naphtha or turpentine rubbed on with rags or waste. The various parts are carefully packed, and secured by cleats, to prevent damage by shifting or chafing, in strong, tight boxes, well fastened and hooped. Boilers are completely protected by boards and hoops. Driving wheels and other items not requiring complete boxing are wrapped and protected from injury at the journals. All boxes and packages are distinctly and permanently marked with the proper shipping marks and numbers, dimensions and weights. An experience of many years enables us to conform to the requirements of different countries in the manner of boxing and packing, and to insure safety from injury during ocean voyages and the frequent transfers often necessary. A detailed list of boxes and packages, with weights, dimensions, and contents, is furnished. We are also prepared to include in proposals for export the delivery of boxed locomotives to the vessel's tackle in New York harbor, or delivery at any other port in this country. For customers' convenience in estimating ocean freights we will furnish, when desired, a memorandum, based on actual shipments, of the approximate weights and dimensions of boxes and packages, and the total measurement in cubic feet, for locomotives of the required design, size of cylinders, and gauge of track. If a supply of extra duplicate parts is needed we will quote promptly on such parts as may be desired, or if preferred we will submit for approval, with estimate of cost, a list of such parts as our experience would lead us to suggest.

Standard Specifications

With every proposition for a locomotive we are prepared to furnish DETAILED SPECIFICATIONS with the various dimensions fully noted.

The STANDARD SPECIFICATIONS of our LIGHT LOCOMOTIVES include axles, crank-pins, guides, rods, and other forgings of open-hearth steel; oil-tempered half-elliptic steel springs; links of skeleton style to facilitate taking up wear, links and blocks of case-hardened forged mild steel with extra large bearings; valve gear and other working joints with removable case-hardened steel pins and bushings; locomotive frames of best quality hammered iron with pedestals and braces forged in solid, or of steel castings if so desired; bumper and drawbar connections at front and rear extra solid and strong; cylinders of special close metal, as hard as can be worked, with raised valve face; driving-wheel centers of special hard, close, cast iron (or of steel), with open-hearth steel tire; tender and truck wheels (if any) of iron with chilled flange and tread (unless otherwise specified); crossheads of steel castings with babbitted or brass gibs; all journals and wearing surfaces of ample size; wearing brasses of ingot copper and tin or of approved alloy of new metals; all movable nuts case-hardened; all bolts to U. S. standard thread; all cocks to standard gas-taps.

Boiler of homogeneous open-hearth steel plates, tested for chemical analysis and physical properties, "best flange" and "best firebox" grades; flanging done by hydraulic flanging press; firebox with crown-bars stayed to dome, or with radial stay-bolts; stay-bolt holes tapped by pneumatic tools; lap-welded iron or seamless steel flues set with copper ferrules at the firebox ends; all caulking done with pneumatic blunt tool on beveled edges; all rivets driven by hydraulic power where possible; tested by hydraulic pressure before lagging, to a pressure of 33% over the working pressure of 160 to 180 pounds, according to the class of locomotive. Boiler throughout constructed to conform to Boiler Insurance Companies' requirements. Tank of homogeneous open-hearth "flange" steel plates. Water supplied by two injectors of approved make and of ample capacity; or, if preferred, one injector and one full-stroke pump operated from the right-hand crosshead.

Our locomotives are furnished with sand-box; bell (except mine and other special designs); safety valves; steam gauge; cab-lamp; double or triple sight-feed lubricators; cylinder cocks; blow-off, gauge, blower, heater, and other cocks; tool-box and cushion; tools, including two screw-jacks, tallow and oil cans, monkey-wrench; flat wrenches to fit all bolts and nuts; steel and copper hammers; chisels, pinch-bar, poker, scraper, and torch.

Special attention is given to secure for all of our locomotives thorough fitness in all details for the service required; durability for hard service, and ease of repairs, also compactness and accessibility of machinery; and convenient and perfect control of all working levers, gauges, handles, and cocks by the engineer.

Before shipment each locomotive is placed upon friction rollers, fired up and worked by its own steam to test the adjustment of the valve gear, alignment of bearings, and satisfactory working in all respects.

Every locomotive is built to our duplicate system, by which like parts of all engines of the same class are interchangeable, and these duplicate parts are always kept on hand.

The following items may be furnished as extras, but are not included in our standard specifications: head-lights; driver brakes, operated by hand, steam, or air; steam syphon, with hose for filling tanks from streams below track level; snow-plow; copper firebox, brass or copper flues; steel-tired truck or tender wheels; steel wheel centers; steel cab, and other special features.

The various locomotives illustrated and described in this catalogue may be constructed with smoke-stacks, fireboxes, and grates and bunkers or fuel space arranged for the kind of fuel desired.

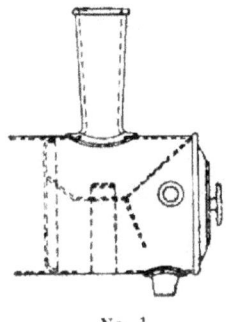
No. 1

For coal fuel we recommend the taper stack with extension boiler front, as shown by annexed outline sketch (No. 1). The exhaust steam is wholly unobstructed; the sparks are arrested by a steel wire netting and steel plate in the smoke-box until they are churned fine enough to pass through the netting, or if the quality of the coal or the conditions of service allow sparks to accumulate they are withdrawn through a hopper.

If preferred, we furnish instead of the taper stack a straight stack with cast top finish (No. 2).

No. 2

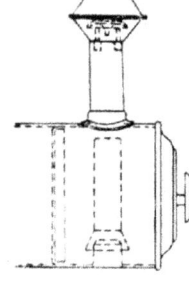

The old-style diamond stack with cast cone and wire netting, and petticoat pipe, is generally used with short boiler front (No. 3).

No. 3

For wood fuel, and especially for pitch pine, we recommend, as the safest smoke-stack, our balloon-shaped stack with spiral cone (No. 4). This stack is very efficient and interferes very little with the draft, as there is no wire netting for the exhaust steam to pass through. The spiral cone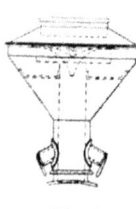

No. 4

imparts a rotary motion to the sparks by which they are ground fine before escaping or are deposited in the space between the inner barrel and the outer part of the stack, from whence they may be removed through hand-holes.

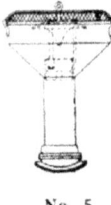

No. 5

If preferred, we furnish for wood fuel the "sunflower" style of stack with cast cone, and projection of inside barrel arranged to break up the sparks, and with a fine steel wire netting over the top to prevent the escape of anything but very small cinders (No. 5). This stack is efficient for hardwood fuel, but not well adapted for pitchy woods.

We are prepared to construct locomotives with apparatus for burning crude oil.

Physical Tests of Materials

All materials used shall be of the best quality of their respective kinds, carefully inspected and tested, conforming to the requirements adopted by the American Society for Testing Materials. If, after acceptance any material shows mechanical defects in working, it will be rejected.

Boiler Shell and Firebox Steel

All plates must be rolled from open-hearth steel and be true to gauge and free from laminations, seams, and other defects.

All shell plates shall have a tensile strength of not less than 55,000 or more than 65,000 pounds per square inch; elongation not less than 25 per cent in 8 inches; sulphur not to exceed 0.05, phosphorus not to exceed 0.04 per cent.

All firebox plates shall have a tensile strength of not less than 52,000 or more than 62,000 pounds per square inch; elongation not less than 26 per cent in 8 inches; sulphur not to exceed 0.04, phosphorus not to exceed 0.04 per cent.

Tank Steel

The plates to be rolled from soft, homogeneous steel billets, and must be of good surface finish, free from defects and hard scale. The steel to be of such quality that test pieces cut lengthwise from any plate selected shall show no sign of fracture when bent double cold over a mandrel of diameter one and one-half times the thickness of plate so tested.

Firebox Copper

Copper plates for fireboxes must be rolled from best quality Lake Superior ingots; they must have a tensile strength of not less than 30,000 pounds per square inch, and an elongation of at least 30 per cent in 8 inches. Test strips must be furnished with each firebox for testing.

Copper Stay-Bolts

Copper for stay-bolts to contain not less than 99.5 per cent of pure copper, and to be free from defects. Tensile strength must not be less than 30,000 pounds per square inch, with an elongation of not less than 30 per cent in 8 inches.

Stay-Bolt Iron

Iron for stay-bolts must be double refined, with an ultimate tensile strength of not less than 46,000 pounds per square inch, and an elongation of not less than 28 per cent in section 8 inches long. Iron must show a good fibrous fracture and be free from crystallization. Pieces 24 inches long must stand bending double both ways without showing fracture or flaws. Iron must be free from seams, true to gauge, and take a good, clean, sharp thread with dies in good working order.

Boiler Tubes, Seamless Steel or Charcoal Iron

A careful examination will be made of each tube, and those showing pit-holes or other defects will be rejected. Each tube must be tested by the manufacturer to an internal hydraulic pressure of not less than 500 pounds per square inch. Tubes must be straight and true to size, and must expand and bend over tube-sheet without flaw, crack, or opening.

All tubes must stand the following test: A section $1\frac{1}{4}$ inches long, taken at random, to stand hammering down vertically until solid without cracking or splitting.

Charcoal-iron tubes to be lap-welded, seamless-steel tubes to be open-hearth.

Bar Iron

Must be thoroughly welded, free from seams, blisters, and cinder spots, with a fibrous fracture free from crystallization. Iron will not be accepted if tensile strength falls below 46,000 pounds, nor if elongation is less than 20 per cent in 8 inches, nor if it shows a granular fracture. Iron 1 inch thick or less to bend double over a bar equal to its thickness; sizes above 1 inch to bend to 120 degrees without flaw.

Steel for Forgings

All blooms to be of open-hearth steel, not exceeding 0.05 per cent in phosphorus. A test piece cut from forging 4 inches diameter hammered from the bloom must conform to the following test: For axles, main and parallel rods, tensile strength of not less than 75,000 pounds per square inch, and elongation of 18 per cent in section originally 2 inches long. For crank-pins, piston-rods, etc., tensile strength of 80,000 pounds per square inch, with elongation of not less than 18 per cent in section originally 2 inches long. Limits of tensile strength, 5,000 pounds below or above the amounts given.

Steel Castings

All steel castings must have uniform surface, free from blow-holes, slag, and shrinkage cracks. Test pieces cut from casting should show a tensile strength of not less than 60,000 pounds, and elongation of 22 per cent in 2 inches. Castings badly warped or distorted, which will not true up properly to drawing, will be rejected.

Steel Shapes, Angles, Channels, Tees, etc.

Must be of open-hearth steel, free from injurious seams, etc., and variation from estimated weight not to exceed 5 per cent. Tensile strength not less than 52,000 nor more than 62,000 pounds, and elongation of not less than 25 per cent in 8 inches. Specimens must stand bending through 180 degrees and an inner diameter equal to its own thickness, without crack or flaw.

Spring Steel

All spring steel must be free from any physical defects. The metal desired has the following composition:

Carbon................1.00 per cent	Silicon, not over 0.15 per cent
Manganese.........0.25 " "	Sulphur, " " 0.03 " "
Phosphorus, not over.0.03 " "	Copper, " " 0.03 " "

Steel will not be accepted which shows on analysis less than 0.90 or over 1.10 per cent of carbon, or over 0.50 per cent of manganese, 0.05 per cent of phosphorus, 0.25 per cent of silicon, 0.05 of sulphur, and 0.05 of copper.

Classification of Locomotives

For sake of convenience in classifying our numerous designs of locomotives we have adopted a very simple system.

The **size** of the locomotive is designated by the diameter and stroke of its cylinder in inches; thus, 9 x 14 means a locomotive with cylinders nine inches diameter by fourteen inches stroke.

The **number of driving wheels** is expressed by:
A for two driving wheels.
B for four driving wheels.
C for six driving wheels.
D for eight driving wheels.

The **number and position of locomotive truck wheels** is expressed by a figure **2** for two-wheel, or **4** for four-wheel truck; for a rear truck, this figure is placed to the left, and for a front truck placed to the right, of the letter denoting the number of driving wheels, and separated by a hyphen. (The locomotive is supposed to be headed toward the observer's right hand.) Thus, **2-B** denotes a locomotive with a two-wheel rear truck and four driving wheels; **4-C-2** a locomotive with a four-wheel rear truck, six driving wheels, and a two-wheel front truck.

The arrangement of **water-tank** is denoted by:
T for tender-tank with eight wheels.
T4 for tender-tank with four wheels.
T6 for tender-tank with six wheels.
S for saddle-tank.
SS for two side tanks alongside of boiler.
R for rear tank.
RR for two tanks, one each side at rear.

K denotes a locomotive with **sheet-steel open canopy** for cab.
M denotes a **motor-style cab** enclosing the machinery.
I denotes a locomotive with a **steel cab**.
O denotes a locomotive **without cab**.
P denotes **pneumatic or compressed-air** locomotive, with one air-tank, and **PP** one with two air-tanks.

Letters and figures relating to tank, cab, etc., should follow the letter and figures for driving wheels and truck wheels. Thus, 12 x 18-2-B-4-SS-K-T 4 denotes a locomotive with cylinders twelve inches diameter by eighteen inches stroke, four driving wheels, two-wheel rear truck, four-wheel front truck, side tanks, open steel canopy cab, and four-wheel tender—thirteen figures and letters expressing the meaning of twenty-eight words.

Memorandum of Conditions and Requirements of Service to be Furnished by Intending Purchasers

To facilitate the selection in all cases of the sizes and designs of locomotives which will be most thoroughly satisfactory to our customers, we request from intending purchasers as clear a statement as may be practicable of the work the locomotive will be expected to do. This statement should include items as follows:

1. The gauge of track (i. e., space in the clear between rails).
2. Length of road.
3. Description of fuel.
4. Weight of rail per yard.
5. Steepest up-grade for loaded cars, and the length of this grade, and whether trains must be started on the grade. If grades are numerous and steep a memorandum of principal grades is desired.
6. If cars on return trips are empty, the steepest up-grade for return trips with empty cars. Length of this grade.
7. Radius of sharpest curve. Length of track occupied by this curve, and grade, if any, on which this curve occurs.
8. Kind of traffic, and, if freight, the kind of freight.
9. Total amount to be hauled daily in one direction (stating number of hours reckoned as one day).
10. Greatest number of cars to be hauled at one trip. (This should not be exaggerated, as we make a reasonable allowance for surplus power, and if double allowance is made there is liability of selecting too heavy and too expensive a locomotive.)
11. The weight of empty car. (Also, if practicable, a brief description of car, stating number and diameter of wheels and arrangement for oiling.)
12. Weight of load carried on each car.
13. Limitations, if any, of height or width.
14. Any preference as to design or details.

We fully appreciate that where the road has not been completed or fully surveyed it may be impossible to give complete information. In such cases we would request as close estimates of the length of road, grades, curves, daily amount of traffic, etc., as practicable, leaving the weight of rail, and number of cars to be hauled per trip, to be determined.

It is very desirable that the information should be given as fully as possible. Even in cases where intending purchasers have strong preferences as to size or design of locomotives required, an outline of the requirements and conditions of service may enable us to submit suggestions of value. We desire, also, in justice both to ourselves and to our customers, that in making propositions for locomotives we may, in every instance, feel assured that the locomotive will be, beyond doubt, well adapted to the service, economical and satisfactory in all respects, and thus lead to future orders from the purchaser and from his neighbors. If correspondents will kindly go to the trouble of furnishing us the desired information it will enable us to submit propositions, with specifications and photographs, for such sizes or designs as we would feel safe in recommending and guaranteeing.

"American" or "Eight-Wheel Passenger" Locomotive, Class B-4-T

Wide or Narrow Gauge

ILLUSTRATION No. 4, from photograph of 12 x 16 cylinders, coal-burning locomotive, 56½ inches gauge exported to South America.

SEVEN SIZES, each with code word, are described on the opposite page, subject to modifications to suit gauge, fuel, size of locomotive, and requirements or preferences of customers. We are prepared to build additional sizes. The engine truck has pivotal and lateral motion. The driving wheels are connected by side equalizers. See page 10 for general specifications and pages 11 and 12 for choice of stacks.

Correspondents are Requested to Designate Locomotives by Code Word

CODE WORD	HADRIA	HAERAD	HAFSSA	HAGADA	HAGNON	HAKKOZ	HAKSEL
Cylinders { diameter, inches	10	11	12	12	13	14	15
{ stroke, inches	16	16	16	18	18	20	24
Diameter of driving wheels, inches	42	45	48	48	48	48	56
Diameter of truck wheels, inches	18	20	22	22	22	22	24
Rigid wheel-base of engine, feet and inches	6–0	6–0	6–6	6–9	7–0	7–6	8–0
Total wheel-base of engine, feet and inches	15–6	16–0	17–0	18–0	19–4	20–6	21–6
Wheel-base of engine and tender, feet and inches	32–0	33–0	35–0	36–6	39–0	40–2	41–0
Length over all of engine and tender, feet and inches	39–0	41–0	43–0	45–0	46–3	47–9	49–0
Extreme height (head-room not limited), feet and inches	10–6	11–0	11–6	12–0	12–1	12–6	13–0
Weight of engine, exclusive of tender, in working order, pounds	34,000	38,000	42,000	46,000	54,000	70,000	85,000
Weight on driving wheels, pounds	23,500	26,000	28,000	31,500	37,500	48,000	58,000
Weight on four-wheel truck, pounds	11,500	12,000	14,000	14,500	16,500	22,000	27,000
Weight of tender in working order, pounds	20,000	25,000	28,000	28,000	31,500	38,000	45,000
Water capacity of tender-tank, gallons	800	1,050	1,200	1,200	1,400	1,600	2,000
Fuel capacity of tender { coal, pounds	3,000	3,700	4,000	4,000	4,500	6,000	7,500
{ wood, cords	1¼	1⅜	1¼	1¼	2	2½	3
Weight per yard of lightest rail advised, pounds	25	25	30	30	35	45	55
Radius of sharpest curve advised, feet	160	175	180	200	225	250	275
Boiler pressure per square inch, pounds	160	160	160	160	160	160	160
Tractive force, pounds	5,180	5,860	6,530	7,340	8,625	11,100	13,100
Hauling Capacity, in tons of 2,000 pounds (exclusive of locomotive and tender), 6½ pounds per ton resistance of rolling friction:							
On absolute level	770	865	965	1,090	1,280	1,650	1,950
" ½ per cent grade = 26 4/10 feet per mile	285	320	360	405	475	620	725
" 1 " " = 52 8/10 " " "	165	185	210	240	280	360	425
" 2 " " = 105 6/10 " " "	80	90	105	120	140	180	215
" 3 " " = 158 4/10 " " "	50	55	60	70	85	110	130

The **Rule for Calculation** of Hauling Capacity at all rates of resistance of rolling friction and on any practicable grade is given on page 140.

For quick approximate calculation of Hauling Capacity on any practicable grade, and with resistance of rolling friction of 6½ to 40 pounds per ton, refer to **Tables of Percentages** on pages 156 and 157.

For quick selection of **suitable weight locomotive** for stated load, grade and resistance of rolling friction, refer to **Tables I, II, III and IV**, on pages 162 to 169. These tables are also useful for quick comparison of loads that can be handled by locomotives of different weights.

"Six-Wheel Fast Passenger" Locomotive, Class B-2-T

Wide or Narrow Gauge

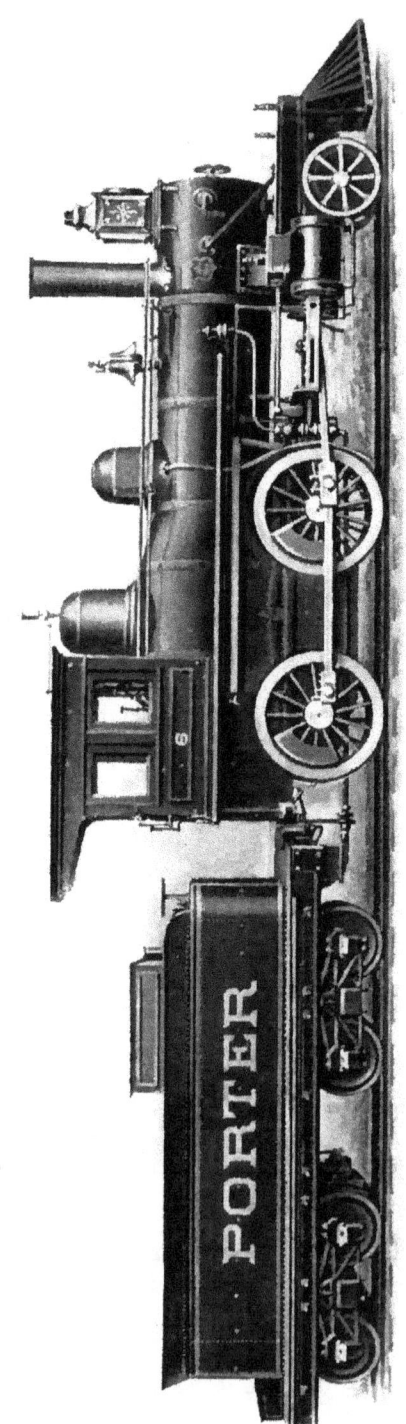

ILLUSTRATION No. 6, from photograph of 11 x 16 cylinders, coal-burning locomotive, 36 inches gauge.

SEVEN SIZES, each with **code word**, are described on the opposite page, subject to modifications to suit gauge, fuel, size of locomotive, and requirements or preferences of customers. We are prepared to build additional sizes. The engine truck has pivotal, lateral, and radial-bar motion. The driving wheels are connected by side equalizers. See page 10 for general specifications and pages 11 and 12 for choice of stacks.

Correspondents are Requested to Designate Locomotives by Code Word

CODE WORD	HALLOO	HALSED	HALYDE	HAMAUX	HAMKIN	HAMOSE	HANANI
Cylinders { diameter, inches	10	11	12	12	13	14	15
{ stroke, inches	16	16	16	18	18	20	24
Diameter of driving wheels, inches	40	42	45	46	46	46	56
Diameter of truck wheels, inches	26	28	28	30	30	30	30
Rigid wheel-base of engine, feet and inches	6–0	6–0	6–6	6–9	7–0	7–6	8–0
Total wheel-base of engine, feet and inches	15–9	16–3	17–0	18–0	19–4	20–6	21–6
Wheel-base of engine and tender, feet and inches	32–3	33–3	35–0	36–0	39–0	40–2	41–0
Length over all of engine and tender, feet and inches	39–5	40–9	43–5	45–5	46–3	47–9	49–0
Extreme height (head-room not limited), feet and inches	10–6	11–0	11–6	12–0	12–3	12–9	13–2
Weight of engine, exclusive of tender, in working order, pounds	33,500	37,000	41,000	44,000	52,000	65,000	81,000
Weight on driving wheels, pounds	25,000	27,500	31,000	33,500	39,500	50,000	60,000
Weight on two-wheel truck, pounds	8,500	9,500	10,000	10,500	12,500	15,000	21,000
Weight of tender in working order, pounds	20,000	25,000	28,000	28,000	31,500	38,000	45,000
Water capacity of tender-tank, gallons	800	1,050	1,200	1,200	1,400	1,600	2,000
Fuel capacity of tender { coal, pounds	3,000	3,700	4,000	4,000	4,500	6,000	7,500
{ wood, cords	1¼	1⅝	1¾	1¾	2	2½	3
Weight per yard of lightest rail advised, pounds	25	30	30	30	35	45	55
Radius of sharpest curve advised, feet	150	160	170	180	200	220	240
Boiler pressure per square inch, pounds	160	160	160	160	160	160	170
Tractive force, pounds	5,440	6,270	6,960	7,665	8,995	11,585	13,910
Hauling Capacity, in tons of 2,000 pounds (exclusive of locomotive and tender), 6½ pounds per ton resistance of rolling friction:							
On absolute level	805	930	1,035	1,140	1,340	1,725	2,075
" ½ per cent grade = 26 4/10 feet per mile	300	345	385	425	500	650	780
" 1 " " = 52 8/10 " " "	175	205	225	250	295	385	460
" 2 " " = 105 6/10 " " "	90	100	115	125	150	195	235
" 3 " " = 158 4/10 " " "	50	60	70	75	90	120	145

The **Rule for Calculation of Hauling Capacity** at all rates of resistance of rolling friction and on any practicable grade is given on page 140.

For quick approximate calculation of Hauling Capacity on any practicable grade, and with resistance of rolling friction of 6½ to 40 pounds per ton, refer to **Tables of Percentages** on **pages 156 and 157**.

For **quick selection of suitable weight locomotive** for stated load, grade and resistance of rolling friction, refer to **Tables I, II III and IV**, on **pages 162 to 169**. These tables are also useful for quick comparison of loads that can be handled by locomotives of different weights.

Light "Six-Wheel Local Passenger" Locomotive, Class B-2-T

Wide or Narrow Gauge

ILLUSTRATION No. 10, from photograph of 7 x 12 cylinders, coal-burning locomotive, 36 inches gauge of track, with steam syphon pump.

THREE SIZES, each with **code word,** are described on the opposite page, subject to modifications to suit gauge, fuel, size of locomotive, and requirements or preferences of customers. We are prepared to build additional sizes. The engine truck has pivotal, lateral, and radial-bar motion. The driving wheels are connected by side equalizers. The 9 x 14 size has horizontal cylinders. The smaller sizes are usually built with four-wheel tender. See page 10 for general specifications and pages 11 and 12 for choice of stacks.

For larger sizes see next page.

Correspondents are Requested to Designate Locomotives by Code Word

CODE WORD	HANGBY	HANGEN	HANNAI
Cylinders { diameter, inches	7	8	9
{ stroke, inches	12	14	14
Diameter of driving wheels, inches	28	30	33
Diameter of truck wheels, inches	14	16	18
Rigid wheel-base of engine, feet and inches	4–8	5–3	5–9
Total wheel-base of engine, feet and inches	8–6	9–5	10–9
Wheel-base of engine and tender, feet and inches	20–2	22–6	24–4
Length over all of engine and tender, feet and inches	25–8	29–8	32–0
Extreme height (head-room not limited), feet and inches	9–6	9–10	10–0
Weight of engine, exclusive of tender, in working order, pounds	16,000	22,000	25,500
Weight on driving wheels, pounds	13,000	18,000	21,000
Weight on two-wheel truck, pounds	3,000	4,000	4,500
Weight of tender in working order, pounds	12,000	12,000	12,000
Water capacity of tender-tank, gallons	500	500	500
Fuel capacity of tender { coal, pounds	2,000	2,000	2,000
{ wood, cords	1	1	1
Weight per yard of lightest rail advised, pounds	16	16	20
Radius of sharpest curve advised, feet	70	75	85
Boiler pressure per square inch, pounds	160	160	160
Tractive force, pounds	2,855	4,055	4,670
Hauling Capacity, in tons of 2,000 pounds (exclusive of locomotive and tender), 6½ pounds per ton resistance of rolling friction:			
On absolute level	425	605	700
" ½ per cent grade = 26 4/10 feet per mile	160	225	265
" 1 " " = 52 8/10 " " "	90	135	155
" 2 " " = 105 6/10 " " "	45	70	80
" 3 " " = 158 4/10 " " "	30	40	30

The **Rule for Calculation** of Hauling Capacity at all rates of resistance of rolling friction and on any practicable grade is given on page 140.

For **quick approximate calculation** of Hauling Capacity on any practicable grade, and with resistance of rolling friction of 6½ to 40 pounds per ton, refer to **Tables of Percentages** on **pages 156 and 157**.

For **quick selection of suitable weight locomotive** for stated load, grade and resistance of rolling friction, refer to **Tables I, II, III and IV**, on **pages 162 to 169**. These tables are also useful for quick comparison of loads that can be handled by locomotives of different weights.

"Six-Wheel Local Passenger" Locomotive, Class B-2-T

Wide or Narrow Gauge

ILLUSTRATION No. 8, from photograph of 10 x 16 cylinders, coal-burning locomotive, 36 inches gauge of track, for a **banana plantation in Central America**.

THREE SIZES, each with **code word**, are described on the opposite page, subject to modifications to suit gauge, fuel, size of locomotive, and requirements or preferences of customers. We are prepared to build additional sizes. The engine truck has pivotal, lateral, and radial-bar motion. The driving wheels are connected by side equalizers. See page 10 for general specifications and pages 11 and 12 for choice of stacks.

For smaller sizes see preceding page.

Correspondents are Requested to Designate Locomotives by Code Word

CODE WORD	HAPJES	HAPSUS	HAPTUK
Cylinders { diameter, inches	10	11	12
{ stroke, inches	16	16	16
Diameter of driving wheels, inches	36	40	42
Diameter of truck wheels, inches	20	24	24
Rigid wheel-base of engine, feet and inches	6-6	6-6	6-6
Total wheel-base of engine, feet and inches	13-3	14-3	14-6
Wheel-base of engine and tender, feet and inches	30-3	33-6	34-6
Length over all of engine and tender, feet and inches	36-8	41-0	42-6
Extreme height (head-room not limited), feet and inches	10-6	11-0	11-3
Weight of engine, exclusive of tender, in working order, pounds	31,000	35,000	40,000
Weight on driving wheels, pounds	26,000	29,000	33,000
Weight on two-wheel truck, pounds	5,000	6,000	7,000
Weight of tender, in working order, pounds	20,000	25,000	25,000
Water capacity of tender-tank, gallons	800	1,050	1,050
Fuel capacity of tender { coal, pounds	3,000	3,700	3,700
{ wood, cords	1¼	1⅝	1⅝
Weight per yard of lightest rail advised, pounds	25	30	35
Radius of sharpest curve advised, feet	125	150	175
Boiler pressure per square inch, pounds	160	165	165
Tractive force, pounds	6,040	6,785	7,695
Hauling Capacity, in tons of 2,000 pounds (exclusive of locomotive and tender), 6½ pounds per ton resistance of rolling friction:			
On absolute level	900	1,010	1,150
" ½ per cent grade = 26 4/10 feet per mile	340	380	430
" 1 " " = 52 10/10 " " "	200	225	255
" 2 " " = 105 6/10 " " "	100	115	130
" 3 " " = 158 4/10 " " "	65	70	80

The **Rule for Calculation of Hauling Capacity** at all rates of resistance of rolling friction and on any practicable grade is given on page 140.

For **quick approximate calculation** of Hauling Capacity on any practicable grade, and with resistance of rolling friction of 6½ to 40 pounds per ton, refer to **Tables of Percentages** on **pages 156 and 157**.

For **quick selection of suitable weight locomotive** for stated load, grade and resistance of rolling friction, refer to **Tables I, II, III and IV**, on pages 162 to 169. These tables are also useful for quick comparison of loads that can be handled by locomotives of different weights.

Light "Mogul" Locomotive, Class C-2-T

Wide or Narrow Gauge

ILLUSTRATION No. 16, from photograph of 15 x 20 cylinders, coal-burning locomotive, 56½ inches gauge of track, for logging railroad.

FIVE SIZES, each with **code word**, are described on the opposite page, subject to modifications to suit gauge, fuel, size of locomotive, and requirements or preferences of customers. We are prepared to build additional sizes. The engine truck has pivotal, lateral, and radial-bar motion. The rear and center driving wheels are connected by side equalizers; the front driving wheels are equalized with the truck; the center driving wheels are flangeless. The double-bar guide is seldom used except on sizes 14 x 20 and larger. See page 10 for general specifications and pages 11 and 12 for choice of stacks.

For larger sizes see next page.

Correspondents are Requested to Designate Locomotives by Code Word

CODE WORD	HARCON	HARHUR	HARIPH	HARIRI	HARLOU
Cylinders { diameter, inches	10	10	11	12	12
{ stroke, inches	14	16	16	16	18
Diameter of driving wheels, inches	33	33	36	36	36
Diameter of truck wheels, inches	20	22	24	24	24
Rigid wheel-base of engine, feet and inches	7–3	7–8	9–0	9–0	9–5
Total wheel-base of engine, feet and inches	12–6	13–0	14–6	14–6	15–1
Wheel-base of engine and tender, feet and inches	29–0	29–4	33–4	33–10	35–4½
Length over all of engine and tender, feet and inches	34–0	36–4	41–2	41–8	43–6
Extreme height (head-room not limited), feet and inches	10–3	10–6	10–10	10–10	11–0
Weight of engine, exclusive of tender, in working order, pounds	30,000	36,000	40,000	44,000	49,000
Weight on driving wheels, pounds	25,000	30,000	33,500	37,000	42,000
Weight on two-wheel truck, pounds	5,000	6,000	6,500	7,000	7,000
Weight of tender in working order, pounds	20,000	20,000	25,000	25,000	28,000
Water capacity of tender-tank, gallons	800	800	1,050	1,050	1,200
Fuel capacity of tender { coal, pounds	3,000	3,000	3,700	3,700	4,000
{ wood, cords	1¼	1¼	1⅜	1⅜	1¾
Weight per yard of lightest rail advised, pounds	20	20	25	25	30
Radius of sharpest curve advised, feet	120	120	135	135	150
Radius of sharpest curve practicable, feet	85	85	100	100	120
Boiler pressure per square inch, pounds	160	160	160	160	160
Tractive force, pounds	5,775	6,585	7,315	8,710	9,800
Hauling Capacity, in tons of 2,000 pounds (exclusive of locomotive and tender), 6½ pounds per ton resistance of rolling friction:					
On absolute level	860	985	1,090	1,305	1,465
" ½ per cent grade = 26 4/10 feet per mile	325	370	410	490	555
" 1 " " = 52 10/10 " "	190	220	240	290	330
" 2 " " = 105 6/10 " "	95	110	120	150	175
" 3 " " = 158 4/10 " "	60	70	75	95	105

The **Rule for Calculation** of Hauling Capacity at all rates of resistance of rolling friction and on any practicable grade is given on page 140.

For **quick approximate calculation** of Hauling Capacity on any practicable grade, and with resistance of rolling friction of 6½ to 40 pounds per ton, refer to **Tables of Percentages** on pages 156 and 157.

For **quick selection of suitable weight locomotive** for stated load, grade and resistance of rolling friction, refer to **Tables I, II, III and IV**, on pages 162 to 169. These tables are also useful for quick comparison of loads that can be handled by locomotives of different weights.

"Mogul" Locomotive, Class C-2-T

Wide or Narrow Gauge

ILLUSTRATION No. 17, from photograph of 16 x 24 cylinders, coal-burning locomotive, meter gauge of track, exported to Spain.

EIGHT SIZES, each with **code word**, are described on the opposite page, subject to modifications to suit gauge, fuel, size of locomotive, and requirements or preferences of customers. We are prepared to build additional sizes. The engine truck has pivotal, lateral, and radial-bar motion. The rear and center driving wheels are connected by side equalizers; the front driving wheels are equalized with the truck; the center driving wheels are flangeless. The double-bar guide is seldom used on sizes smaller than 14x20. The usual construction is two sand-boxes and with dome central. Wheel covers are usually omitted. See page 10 for general specifications and pages 11 and 12 for choice of stacks.

For smaller sizes see preceding page.

Correspondents are Requested to Designate Locomotives by Code Word

CODE WORD	HARPAR	HASHUB	HASPEL	HASPIC	HASRAM*	HATACH	HATANK	HATEAR
Cylinders { diameter, inches	13	14	14	15	15	15	16	16
{ stroke, inches	18	20	24	20	22	24	22	24
Diameter of driving wheels, inches	38	42	45	42	45	48	48	48
Diameter of truck wheels, inches	26	26	26	26	26	28	28	28
Rigid wheel-base of engine, feet and inches	9-10	10-3	11-3	10-6	11-9	11-9	12-0	12-0
Total wheel-base of engine, feet and inches	15-11	16-8	17-8	16-9	18-9	18-9	19-2	19-2
Wheel-base of engine and tender, feet and inches	38-3	38-6	40-0	40-0	40-8	40-8	43-8	43-8
Length over all of engine and tender, feet and inches	45-6	46-0	48-3	48-0	49-0	49-0	53-0	53-0
Extreme height (head-room not limited), feet and inches	11-6	12-0	12-10	12-10	13-3	13-6	13-6	13-6
Wt. of engine, exclusive of tender, in working order, lbs.	56,000	64,500	73,000	74,000	78,000	83,000	87,000	92,000
Weight on driving wheels, pounds	47,000	55,000	63,000	64,000	67,000	71,000	74,000	79,000
Weight on two-wheel truck, pounds	9,000	9,500	10,000	10,000	11,000	12,000	13,000	13,000
Weight of tender in working order, pounds	31,500	38,000	40,000	45,000	45,000	45,000	52,000	52,000
Water capacity of tender-tank, gallons	1,400	1,600	1,800	2,000	2,000	2,000	2,500	2,500
Fuel capacity of tender { coal, pounds	4,500	6,000	6,500	7,500	7,500	7,500	8,000	8,000
{ wood, cords	2	2½	3	3	3	3	3½	3½
Weight per yard of lightest rail advised, pounds	30	35	40	40	40	45	50	50
Radius of sharpest curve advised, feet	165	175	180	180	185	185	200	200
Radius of sharpest curve practicable, feet	140	150	160	155	165	165	180	180
Boiler pressure per square inch, pounds	160	160	160	160	165	170	170	170
Tractive force, pounds	10,885	12,690	14,215	14,590	15,425	16,250	16,955	18,495

Hauling Capacity, in tons of 2,000 pounds (exclusive of locomotive and tender), 6½ pounds per ton resistance of rolling friction:

	HARPAR	HASHUB	HASPEL	HASPIC	HASRAM	HATACH	HATANK	HATEAR
On absolute level	1,625	1,900	2,130	2,180	2,310	2,435	2,540	2,770
½ per cent grade = 26 4/10 feet per mile	615	715	805	820	870	920	955	1,045
1 " " " = 52 8/10 " " "	365	425	480	490	520	545	570	625
2 " " " = 105 6/10 " " "	190	220	245	250	270	285	295	325
3 " " " = 158 4/10 " " "	115	135	150	160	170	180	185	205

The **Rule for Calculation** of Hauling Capacity at all rates of resistance of rolling friction and on any practicable grade is given on page 140.

For quick approximate calculation of Hauling Capacity on any practicable grade, and with resistance of rolling friction of 6½ to 40 pounds per ton, refer to **Tables of Percentages** on **pages 156 and 157**.

For quick selection of **suitable weight locomotive** for stated load, grade and resistance of rolling friction, refer to **Tables I, II, III and IV**, on **pages 162 to 169**. These tables are also useful for quick comparison of loads that can be handled by locomotives of different weights.

"Consolidation" Locomotive, Class D-2-T

Wide or Narrow Gauge

ILLUSTRATION No. 5, from photograph of 12 x 16 cylinders, wood-burning locomotive, 36 inches gauge of track, for logging railroad.

SEVEN SIZES, each with code word, are described on the opposite page, subject to modifications to suit gauge, fuel, size of locomotive, and requirements or preferences of customers. We are prepared to build additional sizes. The engine truck has pivotal, lateral, and radial-bar motion. The driving wheels are equalized together and with the truck. The two center pairs of wheels are flangeless. The double-bar guide is seldom used for the smaller sizes. The design may be built with two sand-boxes and with dome central. See page 10 for general specifications and pages 11 and 12 for choice of stacks.

Correspondents are Requested to Designate Locomotives by Code Word

CODE WORD	HATHOR	HATIFI	HATIJO	HAURAN	HAVIAR	HAUYNE	HAYMOW
Cylinders diameter, inches	11	12	13	14	15	16	17
stroke, inches	14	16	16	18	20	20	20
Diameter of driving wheels, inches	30	33	33	36	38	42	42
Diameter of truck wheels, inches	18	20	22	24	24	26	26
Regid wheel-base of engine, feet and inches	9-0	10-0	10-6	11-3	11-10	12-2	12-8
Total wheel-base of engine and tender, feet and inches	14-0	15-4	16-3	17-6	18-6	19-2	19-8
Wheel-base of engine and tender, feet and inches	33-6	36-6	38-0	39-0	40-3	43-7	44-6
Length over all of engine and tender, feet and inches	40-6	43-6	45-6	47-0	49-0	53-0	54-0
Extreme height (head-room not limited), feet and inches	11-0	11-6	12-0	12-6	13-0	13-0	13-6
Weight of engine, exclusive of tender, in working order, pounds	40,000	49,000	58,000	68,000	82,000	90,000	97,000
Weight on driving wheels, pounds	35,000	43,000	51,000	60,000	73,000	81,000	88,000
Weight on two-wheel truck, pounds	5,000	6,000	7,000	8,000	9,000	9,000	9,000
Weight of tender in working order, pounds	25,000	28,000	31,500	38,000	40,000	45,000	52,000
Water capacity of tender-tank, gallons	1,050	1,200	1,400	1,600	1,800	2,000	2,500
Fuel capacity of tender, coal, pounds	3,700	4,000	4,500	6,000	6,500	7,500	8,000
wood, cords	1⅛	1¾	2	2½	2¾	3	3½
Weight per yard of lightest rail advised, pounds	20	25	25	30	35	40	45
Radius of sharpest curve advised, feet	135	150	165	180	185	200	220
Radius of sharpest curve practicable, feet	100	120	140	160	165	180	200
Boiler pressure, per square inch, pounds	160	160	160	160	160	170	170
Tractive force, pounds	7,680	9,495	11,150	13,330	16,130	17,615	19,885
Hauling Capacity, in tons of 2,000 pounds (exclusive of locomotive and tender), 6½ pounds per ton resistance of rolling friction:							
On absolute level	1,145	1,420	1,670	1,995	2,420	2,640	2,975
" ½ per cent grade = 26.4 feet per mile	430	535	630	755	915	1,000	1,130
" 1 " " = 52.8 " " "	255	315	375	450	545	595	675
" 2 " " = 105.6 " " "	130	165	195	230	285	310	350
" 3 " " = 158.4 " " "	80	100	120	145	180	195	225

The **Rule for Calculation** of Hauling Capacity at all rates of resistance of rolling friction and on any practicable grade is given on page 140.

For **quick approximate calculation** of Hauling Capacity on any practicable grade, and with resistance of rolling friction of 6½ to 40 pounds per ton, refer to **Tables of Percentages** on pages 156 and 157.

For **quick selection of suitable weight locomotive** for stated load, grade and resistance of rolling friction, refer to **Tables I, II, III and IV**, on pages 162 to 169. These tables are also useful for quick comparison of loads that can be handled by locomotives of different weights.

Light Four-Wheel-Connected Locomotive with Tender, Class B-T4

Wide or Narrow Gauge

ILLUSTRATION No. 27, from photograph of 7 x 12 cylinders, wood-burning locomotive, 36 inches gauge of track, exported to Yucatan.

FIVE SIZES, each with **code word**, are described on the opposite page, subject to modifications to suit gauge, fuel, size of locomotive, and requirements or preferences of customers. We are prepared to build additional sizes. A cross equalizer is placed at the front driving wheels. Cylinders 9 x 14 and larger are horizontal. Hanging step-boards or pilots may be used. See page 10 for general specifications and pages 11 and 12 for choice of stacks.

For larger sizes Class B-T see next page.

Correspondents are Requested to Designate Locomotives by Code Word

CODE WORD	HAYUCO	HEADLY	HECATO	HECUBA	HEDONE
Cylinders { diameter, inches	6	7	8	9	10
{ stroke, inches	10	12	14	14	14
Diameter of driving wheels, inches	22	26	30	31	33
Wheel-base of engine, feet and inches	4–0	4–8	5–0	5–3	4–6
Wheel-base of engine and tender, feet and inches	13–9	14–6	17–3	18–0	20–0
Length over all of engine and tender, feet and inches	20–0	22–0	24–6	26–0	29–0
Extreme height (head-room not limited), feet and inches	8–7	8–9	9–4	9–9	9–10
Weight of engine, exclusive of tender, in working order, pounds	11,000	14,000	18,000	22,500	25,500
Weight of tender in working order, pounds	8,000	10,000	10,000	12,000	12,000
Water capacity of tender-tank, gallons	300	400	400	500	500
Fuel capacity of tender { coal, pounds	1,200	1,600	1,600	2,000	2,000
{ wood, cords	½	⅝	⅝	¾	¾
Weight per yard of lightest rail advised, pounds	12	16	20	20	25
Radius of sharpest curve advised, feet	35	40	40	45	40
Radius of sharpest curve practicable, feet	15	16	18	25	20
Boiler pressure per square inch, pounds	160	160	160	160	160
Tractive force, pounds	2,225	3,075	4,055	4,975	5,775
Hauling Capacity, in tons of 2,000 pounds (exclusive of locomotive and tender), 6½ pounds per ton resistance of rolling friction:					
On absolute level	330	460	610	745	870
" ½ per cent grade = 26 4/10 feet per mile	125	170	230	280	330
" 1 " " " = 52 8/10 " " "	70	100	135	170	200
" 2 " " " = 105 6/10 " " "	35	50	70	90	105
" 3 " " " = 158 4/10 " " "	20	30	45	55	65

The **Rule for Calculation** of Hauling Capacity at all rates of resistance of rolling friction and on any practicable grade is given on page 140.

For quick approximate calculation of Hauling Capacity on any practicable grade, and with resistance of rolling friction of 6½ to 40 pounds per ton, refer to **Tables of Percentages** on **pages 156 and 157**.

For quick selection of suitable weight locomotive for stated load, grade and resistance of rolling friction, refer to **Tables I, II, III and IV**, on **pages 162 to 169**. These tables are also useful for quick comparison of loads that can be handled by locomotives of different weights.

Four-Wheel-Connected Locomotive with Tender, Class B-T

Wide or Narrow Gauge

ILLUSTRATION No. 25, from 14 x 20 cylinders, coal-burning shifting locomotive, 56½ inches gauge of track.

NINE SIZES, each with **code word**, are described on the opposite page, subject to modifications to suit gauge, fuel, size of locomotive, and requirements or preferences of customers. We are prepared to build additional sizes. A cross equalizer is placed at the front driving wheels. We are prepared to construct with sloped tank. See page 10 for general specifications and pages 11 and 12 for choice of stacks.

For smaller sizes Class B-T see preceding page.

Correspondents are Requested to Designate Locomotives by Code Word

CODE WORD	HELKAI	HELVIA	HEMESA	HEMMEN	HENAJE	HENBIT	HEPHER	HERIDA	HERJIK
Cylinders { diameter, inches	10	11	12	12	13	14	14	15	16
{ stroke, inches	16	16	16	18	18	20	24	24	24
Diameter of driving wheels, inches	36	36	40	40	42	46	48	50	50
Wheel-base of engine feet and inches	5–3	5–3	5–9	5–9	5–9	6–3	7–0	7–6	8–0
Wheel-base of engine and tender, feet and inches	21–0	22–0	22–6	23–0	24–6	29–0	31–0	33–0	35–0
Length over all of engine and tender, feet and inches	29–6	30–6	31–6	32–0	34–0	38–0	40–0	42–6	45–0
Extreme height (head-room not limited), ft. and in	10–3	10–9	11–6	11–6	12–0	12–6	12–9	13–2	13–6
Weight of engine, exclusive of tender, in working order, pounds	29,000	33,000	36,000	40,000	45,000	52,000	60,000	70,000	80,000
Weight of tender in working order, pounds	20,000	20,000	20,000	20,000	22,000	25,000	28,000	31,500	40,000
Water capacity of tender-tank, gallons	800	800	800	800	900	1,050	1,200	1,400	1,800
Fuel capacity of tender { coal, pounds	3,000	3,000	3,000	3,000	3,000	3,700	4,000	4,500	6,500
{ wood, cords	1¼	1¼	1¼	1¼	1¼	1⅝	1¾	2	2¾
Weight per yard of lightest rail advised, pounds	25	30	35	35	40	45	50	60	70
Radius of sharpest curve advised, feet	45	50	50	55	60	65	75	75	90
Radius of sharpest curve practicable, feet	25	30	30	35	40	40	45	50	70
Boiler pressure per square inch, pounds	160	160	160	160	160	160	160	170	170
Tractive force, pounds	6,040	7,315	7,835	8,820	9,845	11,585	13,330	15,600	17,755
Hauling Capacity, in tons of 2,000 pounds (exclusive of locomotive and tender), 6½ pounds per ton resistance of rolling friction:									
On absolute level	905	1,095	1,175	1,325	1,475	1,740	2,005	2,350	2,670
" ½ per cent grade = 26 4⁄10 feet per mile	340	415	445	500	560	660	760	890	1,015
" 1 " " = 52 8⁄10 " " "	200	245	265	300	335	395	455	535	610
" 2 " " = 105 6⁄10 " " "	105	130	140	160	175	210	240	280	320
" 3 " " = 158 4⁄10 " " "	65	80	90	100	115	135	155	180	205

The **Rule for Calculation** of Hauling Capacity at all rates of resistance of rolling friction and on any practicable grade is given on page 140.

For **quick approximate calculation** of Hauling Capacity on any practicable grade, and with resistance of rolling friction of 6½ to 40 pounds per ton, refer to **Tables of Percentages** on pages **156 and 157.**

For **quick selection of suitable weight locomotive** for stated load, grade and resistance of rolling friction, refer to **Tables I, II, III and IV**, on pages **162 to 169.** These tables are also useful for quick comparison of loads that can be handled by locomotives of different weights.

Light Six-Wheel-Connected Locomotive with Tender, Class C-T

Wide or Narrow Gauge

ILLUSTRATION No. 14, from photograph of 10 x 14 cylinders, coal-burning locomotive, 36 inches gauge of track, exported to Central America for banana plantation.

FIVE SIZES, each with code word, are described on the opposite page, subject to modifications to suit gauge, fuel, size of locomotive, and requirements or preferences of purchasers. We are prepared to build additional sizes. The rear and center driving wheels are connected by side equalizers. A cross equalizer is placed at the front driving wheels. The center driving wheels are flangeless. Cylinders 8 x 14 and smaller are slightly inclined. Sizes 8 x 11 and smaller are usually built with four-wheel tender. See page 10 for general specifications and pages 11 and 12 for choice of stacks.

For larger sizes see next page.

Correspondents are Requested to Designate Locomotives by Code Word

CODE WORD	HERNIE	HEROLD	HERPES	HERTOG	HESTIA
Cylinders { diameter, inches	7	8	9	10	11
{ stroke, inches	12	14	14	14	14
Diameter of driving wheels, inches	24	26	30	30	30
Wheel-base of engine, feet and inches	5–2	5–6	5–10	7–3	7–3
Wheel-base of engine and tender, feet and inches	16–8	20–7	20–11	23–9	26–0
Length over all of engine and tender, feet and inches	25–2	29–6	30–1	32–6	36–0
Extreme height (head-room not limited), feet and inches	9–6	10–0	10–0	10–3	10–8
Weight of engine, exclusive of tender, in working order, pounds	15,000	21,500	24,000	29,000	34,000
Weight of tender in working order, pounds	12,000	12,000	20,000	20,000	20,000
Water capacity of tender-tank, gallons	500	500	800	800	800
Fuel capacity of tender { coal, pounds	2,000	2,000	3,000	3,000	3,000
{ wood, cords	3/4	3 1/4	1 1/4	1 1/4	1 1/4
Weight per yard of lightest rail advised, pounds	14	16	16	20	25
Radius of sharpest curve advised, feet	50	55	60	80	80
Radius of sharpest curve practicable, feet	32	35	40	60	60
Boiler pressure per square inch, pounds	160	160	160	160	160
Tractive force, pounds	3,330	4,680	5,435	6,350	7,680
Hauling Capacity, in tons of 2,000 pounds (exclusive of locomotive and tender), 6½ pounds per ton resistance of rolling friction:					
On absolute level	500	700	770	950	1,150
" ½ per cent grade = 26 4/10 feet per mile	185	265	290	360	435
" 1 " " = 52 8/10 " " "	110	160	175	215	260
" 2 " " = 105 6/10 " " "	55	80	90	110	135
" 3 " " = 158 4/10 " " "	35	50	60	70	85

The **Rule for Calculation** of Hauling Capacity at all rates of resistance of rolling friction and on any practicable grade is given on page 140.

For quick approximate calculation of Hauling Capacity on any practicable grade, and with resistance of rolling friction of 6½ to 40 pounds per ton, refer to **Tables of Percentages** on **pages 156 and 157**.

For quick selection of **suitable weight locomotive** for stated load, grade and resistance of rolling friction, refer to **Tables I, II, III and IV**, on **pages 162 to 169**. These tables are also useful for quick comparison of loads that can be handled by locomotives of different weights.

Six-Wheel-Connected Locomotive with Tender, Class C-T

Wide or Narrow Gauge

ILLUSTRATION No. 12, from photograph of 12 x 18 cylinders, coal-burning locomotive, 36 inches gauge of track, exported to Mexico.

TEN SIZES, each with code word, are described on the opposite page, subject to modifications to suit gauge, fuel, size of locomotive, and requirements or preferences of customers. We are prepared to build additional sizes. The rear and center driving wheels are connected by side equalizers. A cross equalizer is placed at the front driving wheels. The center driving wheels are flangeless. See page 10 for general specifications and pages 11 and 12 for choice of stacks.

For smaller sizes see preceding page.

Correspondents are Requested to Designate Locomotives by Code Word

CODE WORD	HERVOR	HERZIG	HETICO	HETMAN	HEUTIG	HEYDAY	HEZILO	HEZROM	HIABIT	HIALIN
Cylinders { diameter, inches	10	11	12	12	13	14	14	15	15	16
{ stroke, inches	16	16	16	18	18	20	24	20	24	24
Diameter of driving wheels, inches	31	33	36	36	36	40	44	40	46	46
Wheel-base of engine, feet and inches	7-8	8-1	9-0	9-0	9-10	10-6	11-3	10-6	11-9	12-0
Wheel-base of engine and tender, feet and inches	25-0	28-0	29-0	29-6	30-6	32-11	34-6	34-0	35-0	38-0
Length over all of engine and tender, feet and inches	34-6	39-2	40-0	41-0	43-0	44-0	45-0	44-6	46-0	49-6
Extreme height (head-room not limited), ft. and in.	10-6	10-10	10-10	11-2	11-6	11-9	12-0	12-10	13-2	13-6
Weight of engine, exclusive of tender, in working order, pounds	32,000	37,000	40,000	44,000	53,000	61,000	66,000	69,000	76,000	86,000
Weight of tender in working order, pounds	20,000	25,000	25,000	28,000	28,000	31,500	38,000	38,000	41,000	45,000
Water capacity of tender-tank, gallons	800	1,050	1,050	1,200	1,200	1,400	1,600	1,600	1,800	2,000
Fuel capacity of tender { coal, pounds	3,000	3,700	3,700	4,000	4,000	4,500	6,000	6,000	6,500	7,500
{ wood, cords	1¼	1⅜	1⅜	1¾	1¾	2	2½	2½	2¾	3
Weight per yard of lightest rail advised, pounds	25	30	30	30	35	40	45	50	50	55
Radius of sharpest curve advised, feet	90	100	100	125	150	170	180	170	180	200
Radius of sharpest curve practicable, feet	70	85	85	110	135	150	160	150	160	180
Boiler pressure per square inch, pounds	160	160	160	160	160	160	160	160	170	170
Tractive force, pounds	7,015	7,970	8,710	9,800	11,500	13,330	14,550	15,320	16,960	19,300

Hauling Capacity, in tons of 2,000 pounds (exclusive of locomotive and tender), 6½ pounds per ton resistance of rolling friction:

	HERVOR	HERZIG	HETICO	HETMAN	HEUTIG	HEYDAY	HEZILO	HEZROM	HIABIT	HIALIN
On absolute level	1,050	1,195	1,305	1,470	1,725	2,000	2,185	2,300	2,550	2,900
" ½ per cent grade = 26 4/10 feet per mile	395	450	490	555	655	760	825	870	970	1,100
" 1 " " = 52 8/10 " " "	235	270	295	330	390	455	495	520	580	660
" 2 " " = 105 6/10 " " "	125	140	150	175	205	240	255	275	305	350
" 3 " " = 158 4/10 " " "	80	85	95	110	130	155	165	175	195	225

The **Rule for Calculation** of Hauling Capacity at all rates of resistance of rolling friction and on any practicable grade is given on page 140.

For quick approximate calculation of Hauling Capacity on any practicable grade, and with resistance of rolling friction of 6½ to 40 pounds per ton, refer to **Tables of Percentages** on pages 156 and 157.

For quick selection of suitable weight locomotive for stated load, grade and resistance of rolling friction, refer to **Tables I, II, III and IV**, on pages 162 to 169. These tables are also useful for quick comparison of loads that can be handled by locomotives of different weights.

Eight-Wheel-Connected Locomotive with Tender, Class D-T

Wide or Narrow Gauge

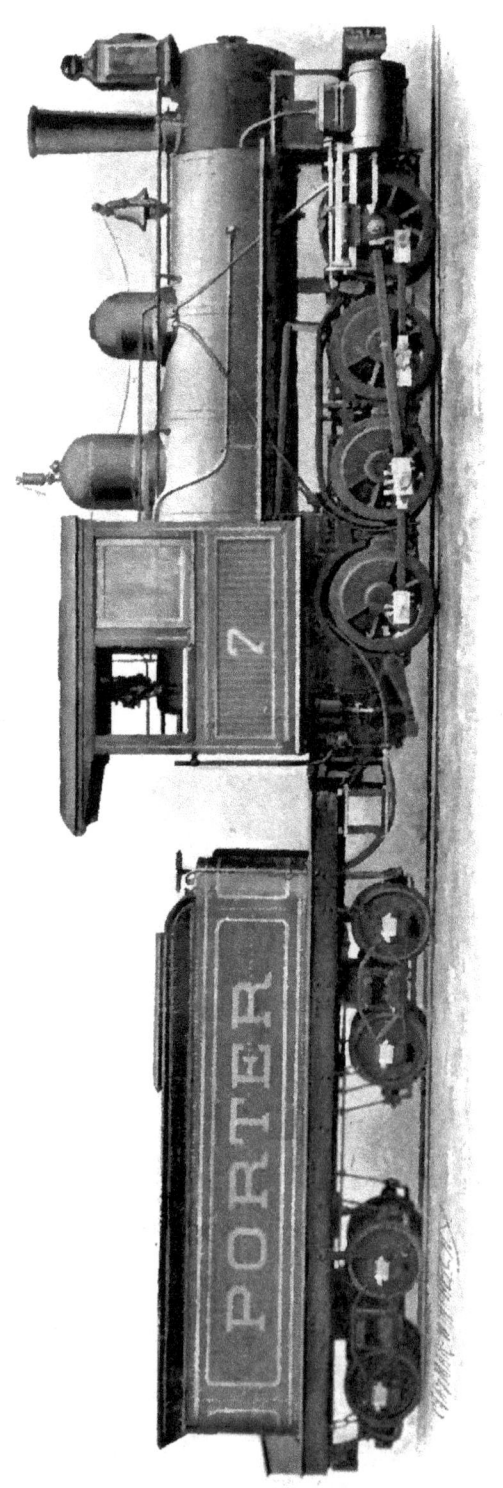

ILLUSTRATION No. 7, from photograph of 11 x 14 cylinders, coal-burning locomotive, 29½ inches gauge of track, exported to Mexico.

EIGHT SIZES, each with **code word**, are described on the opposite page, subject to modifications to suit gauge, fuel, size of locomotive, and requirements or preferences of customers. We are prepared to build additional sizes. The rear and front driving wheels are equalized with the next wheels, and the two center pairs are flangeless. The double-bar guide is seldom used for the smaller sizes. See page 10 for general specifications and pages 11 and 12 for choice of stacks.

Correspondents are Requested to Designate Locomotives by Code Word

CODE WORD	HIATER	HIBLEA	HICARD	HIDRAS	HIEDRA	HIESIG	HIEUW	HIEZU
Cylinders { diameter, inches	10	11	12	13	14	15	16	17
{ stroke, inches	14	14	16	16	18	20	20	20
Diameter of driving wheels, inches	28	28	31	33	36	40	40	42
Wheel-base of engine, feet and inches	8–0	9–0	10–0	10–6	11–3	11–10	12–2	12–8
Wheel-base of engine and tender, feet and inches	25–0	27–6	29–6	31–7	33–6	34–9	37–0	38–6
Length over all of engine and tender, feet and inches	35–0	38–6	40–6	43–0	45–0	47–0	50–0	51–6
Extreme height (head-room not limited), feet and inches	9–10	10–6	11–0	11–4	12–4	12–8	13–0	13–6
Weight of engine, exclusive of tender, in working order, lb.	31,000	37,000	46,000	54,000	64,000	76,000	85,000	92,000
Weight of tender, in working order, pounds	20,000	25,000	25,000	28,000	31,500	38,000	45,000	52,000
Water capacity of tender-tank, gallons	800	1,050	1,050	1,200	1,400	1,600	2,000	2,500
Fuel capacity of tender { coal, pounds	3,000	3,700	3,700	4,000	4,500	6,000	7,500	8,000
{ wood, cords	1¼	1⅝	1⅝	1¾	2	2½	3	3½
Weight per yard of lightest rail advised, pounds	16	20	25	30	30	35	40	45
Radius of sharpest curve advised, feet	100	125	140	160	170	175	200	220
Radius of sharpest curve practicable, feet	80	110	120	140	150	155	180	200
Boiler pressure per square inch, pounds	160	160	160	165	165	170	170	170
Tractive force, pounds	6,800	8,230	10,105	11,490	13,740	16,260	18,495	19,885
Hauling Capacity, in tons of 2,000 pounds (exclusive of locomotive and tender), 6½ pounds per ton resistance of rolling friction:								
On absolute level	1,020	1,230	1,515	1,725	2,065	2,440	2,645	2,985
" ½ per cent grade = 26 4/10 feet per mile	385	465	575	655	785	925	995	1,130
" 1 " " " = 52 8/10 " " "	230	275	345	390	470	555	595	675
" 2 " " " = 105 6/10 " " "	120	145	180	205	245	290	310	355
" 3 " " " = 158 4/10 " " "	75	90	115	130	155	185	195	225

The **Rule for Calculation** of Hauling Capacity at all rates of resistance of rolling friction and on any practicable grade is given on page 140.

For quick approximate calculation of Hauling Capacity on any practicable grade, and with resistance of rolling friction of 6½ to 40 pounds per ton, refer to **Tables of Percentages** on **pages 156 and 157**.

For **quick selection of suitable weight locomotive** for stated load, grade and resistance of rolling friction, refer to **Tables I, II, III and IV**, on pages 162 to 169. These tables are also useful for quick comparison of loads that can be handled by locomotives of different weights.

"Double-Ender" Locomotive Four Driving Wheels, Class 2-B-2-S

Wide or Narrow Gauge

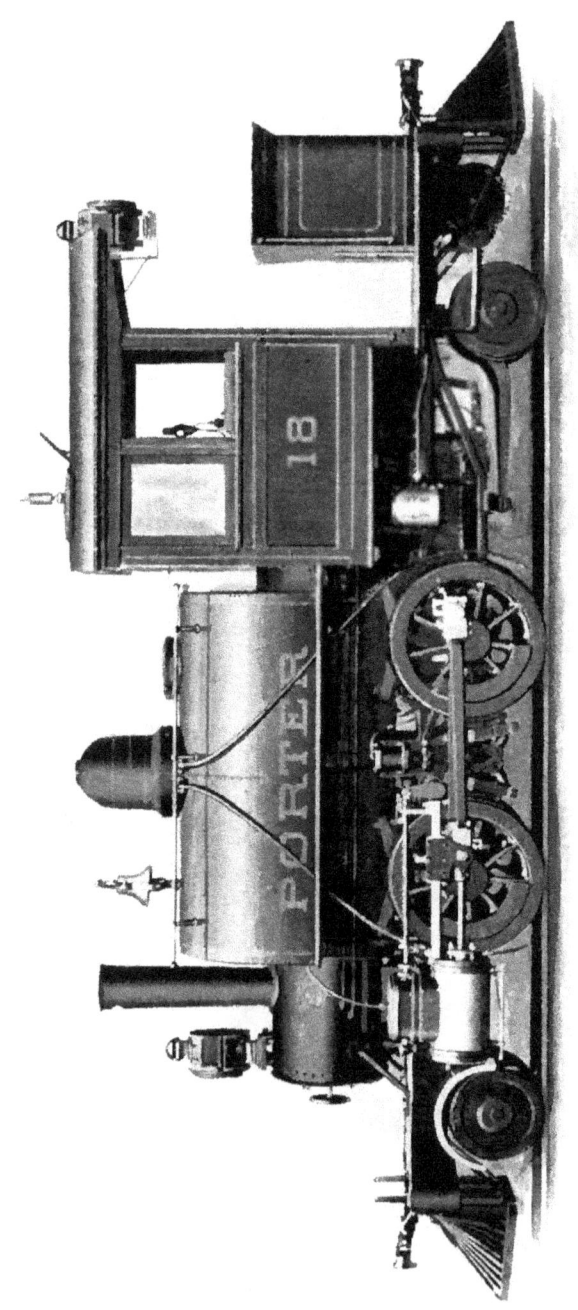

ILLUSTRATION No. 18, from photograph of 10 x 16 cylinders, coal-burning locomotive, 56½ inches gauge of track, for passenger service.

TWELVE SIZES, each with **code word**, are described on the opposite page, subject to modifications to suit gauge, fuel, size of locomotive, and requirements or preferences of customers. We are prepared to build additional sizes. The front driving wheels are equalized with the front truck and the rear driving wheels with the rear truck; when required the cab may be closed at the rear and with side doors. The trucks have pivotal, lateral and radial-bar motion. The two smaller sizes have cylinders slightly inclined. See page 10 for general specifications and pages 11 and 12 for choice of stacks.

Correspondents are Requested to Designate Locomotives by Code Word

CODE WORD	HIGADO	HIGHER	HIGHLY	HILVAN	HIMERA	HIMMEL	HIMNOS	HIMPAR	HINNOM	HIPIDO	HIPOSA	HIRONA
Cylinders { diameter, inches	7	8	9	10	10	11	12	12	13	14	14	15
{ stroke, inches	12	14	14	14	16	16	16	18	18	20	21	24
Diameter of driving wheels, inches	26	30	33	36	36	40	40	42	42	45	48	50
Diameter of truck wheels, inches	14	18	18	18	20	22	22	24	24	24	26	26
Rigid wheel-base, feet and inches	4-8	5-0	5-9	5-9	5-3	5-9	5-9	5-9	6-3	6-3	7-0	7-0
Total wheel-base, feet and inches	13-2	14-4	15-9	16-6	18-6	19-9	20-0	20-5	21-10	22-4	24-2	25-0
Length over all, feet and inches	21-3	22-10	25-0	27-0	29-6	30-0	30-6	31-6	34-0	35-0	37-0	38-6
Extreme ht. (head-room not limited), ft. and in.	9-4	9-6	10-1	10-3	10-8	11-0	11-3	11-6	12-0	12-8	13-0	13-6
Weight in working order, pounds	24,000	29,000	33,000	37,000	43,000	47,000	54,000	58,000	66,000	76,000	84,000	98,000
Weight on driving wheels, pounds	14,500	18,500	21,500	24,500	30,000	32,000	38,000	41,000	48,000	57,000	64,000	76,000
Weight on two pony trucks, pounds	9,500	10,500	11,500	12,500	13,000	15,000	16,000	17,000	18,000	19,000	20,000	22,000
Water capacity of saddle-tank, gallons	200	300	400	500	600	600	700	750	800	900	1,000	1,100
Fuel capacity { coal, pounds	400	600	700	800	1,000	1,200	1,300	1,500	1,800	2,500	3,000	3,500
{ wood, cubic feet	25	30	35	40	45	50	55	60	70	80	90	100
Weight per yard of lightest rail advised, pounds	16	20	25	25	30	30	35	35	40	45	50	65
Radius of sharpest curve advised, feet	60	65	75	80	90	100	100	110	120	130	140	150
Radius of sharpest curve practicable, feet	40	50	60	65	75	80	80	90	100	110	120	130
Boiler pressure per square inch, pounds	160	160	160	160	160	160	160	160	160	160	160	170
Tractive force, pounds	3,075	4,055	4,670	5,290	6,040	6,580	7,835	8,395	9,845	11,845	13,330	15,600
Hauling Capacity, in tons of 2,000 pounds (exclusive of locomotive), 6½ pounds per ton resistance of rolling friction:												
On absolute level	460	610	700	795	905	985	1,175	1,260	1,480	1,780	2,005	2,350
" ½ per cent grade = 26 4/10 feet per mile	170	230	270	300	345	375	445	475	565	675	765	895
" 1 " " " = 52 10/10 " " "	100	135	155	180	205	220	265	285	340	405	460	535
" 2 " " " = 105 5/16 " " "	50	70	80	90	105	115	140	150	180	215	240	285
" 3 " " " = 158 4/10 " " "	30	45	50	60	70	75	90	95	115	140	155	185

The **Rule for Calculation** of Hauling Capacity at all rates of resistance of rolling friction and on any practicable grade is given on **page 140**.
For quick approximate calculation of Hauling Capacity on any practicable grade, and with resistance of rolling friction of 6½ to 40 pounds per ton, refer to **Tables of Percentages** on pages **156 and 157**.
For quick selection of suitable weight locomotive for stated load, grade and resistance of rolling friction, refer to **Tables I, II, III and IV**, on pages **162 to 169**. These tables are also useful for quick comparison of loads that can be handled by locomotives of different weights.

"Double-Ender" Locomotive Six Driving Wheels and Saddle-Tank, Class 2-C-2-S

Wide or Narrow Gauge

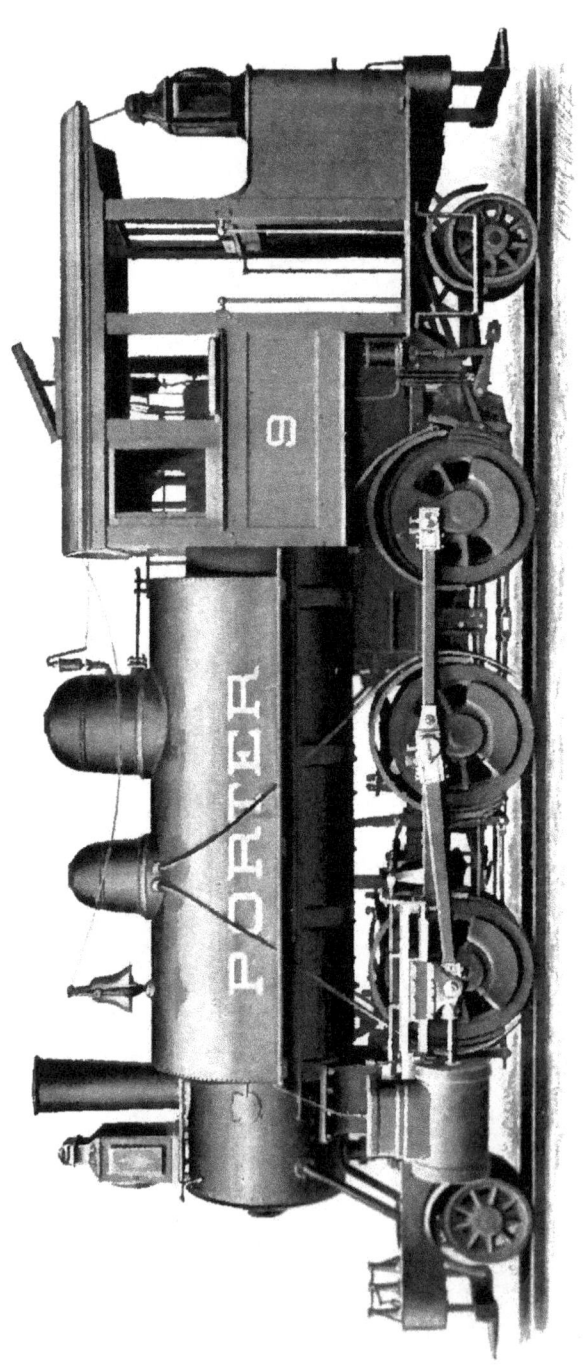

ILLUSTRATION No. 9, from photograph of **15 x 20 cylinders, coal-burning locomotive, 42 inches gauge of track, for export.**

FOURTEEN SIZES, each with **code word**, are described on the opposite page, subject to modifications to suit gauge, fuel, size of locomotive, and requirements or preferences of customers. We are prepared to build additional sizes. The center and rear driving wheels are connected by side equalizers and equalized with the rear truck. The front driving wheels are equalized with the front truck. The center driving wheels are flangeless. The trucks have pivotal, lateral, and radial-bar motion. The 8 x 14 size has cylinders slightly inclined. Double-bar guides are used only on the larger sizes. See page 10 for general specifications and pages 11 and 12 for choice of stacks.

Correspondents are Requested to Designate Locomotives by Code Word

CODE WORD	HIRTIN	HIRUDO	HISCAL	HISTON	HITIGU	HOAXES	HOBBLE	HOBNOB	HOCKEY	HOFBAU	HOFCAN	HOFFEN	HOFFIM	HOFFRAU
Cylinders { diameter, inches	8	9	10	10	11	12	12	13	14	14	15	15	16	16
{ stroke, inches	14	14	14	16	16	16	18	18	20	24	20	24	20	24
Diameter of driving wheels, in.	28	30	31	33	36	38	38	38	40	45	40	46	42	46
Diameter of truck wheels, in.	14	16	16	18	18	18	20	20	22	26	24	26	26	26
Rigid wheel-base, ft. and in.	5–6	5–10	7–3	7–8	8–1	9–0	9–0	9–10	10–6	11–0	10–6	11–0	10–6	11–0
Total wheel-base, ft. and in.	14–5	16–4	16–11	18–7	19–6	20–6	20–10	22–0	23–2	23–7	24–0	25–0	24–4	25–6
Length over all, ft. and in.	22–4	25–0	25–6	27–11	29–7	30–1	30–7	32–9	34–0	34–9	35–0	36–6	37–0	38–0
Ht. (head-room not limited), ft. and in.	9–10	10–3	10–3	10–6	10–10	11–3	11–6	12–0	13–0	12–9	13–0	13–4	13–4	13–6
Weight in working order, lb.	29,500	35,000	40,000	44,000	49,000	54,500	60,000	68,000	81,000	88,000	96,000	103,000	108,000	115,000
Weight on driving wheels, lb.	21,000	25,500	29,500	32,500	36,000	40,000	45,000	52,000	64,000	70,000	78,000	83,000	86,000	92,000
Weight on two pony trucks, lb.	8,500	9,500	10,500	11,500	13,000	14,500	15,000	16,000	17,000	18,000	18,000	20,000	22,000	23,000
Water capacity of tank, gals.	350	400	500	600	600	700	750	800	900	1,000	1,000	1,100	1,200	1,200
Fuel capacity { coal, pounds	600	700	800	1,000	1,200	1,300	1,500	1,800	2,500	3,000	3,000	3,500	4,000	4,000
{ wood, cubic ft.	30	35	40	45	50	55	60	70	80	90	90	100	110	110
Wt. per yd. of lightest rail advised, lb.	16	20	20	25	25	30	30	35	40	45	45	50	56	56
Radius of sharpest curve advised, ft.	70	75	80	85	90	110	110	135	175	175	175	175	175	190
Radius of sharpest curve practicable, ft.	55	60	65	75	80	95	95	120	145	145	145	145	145	170
Boiler pressure per sq. in., lb.	160	160	160	160	160	160	160	160	160	160	165	170	170	170
Tractive force, lb.	4,350	5,135	6,140	6,585	7,315	8,245	9,285	10,890	13,330	14,220	15,800	16,960	17,615	19,300
Hauling Capacity, in tons of 2,000 lb. (exclusive of locomotive), 6½ lb. per ton resistance of rolling friction:														
On absolute level	650	770	920	990	1,100	1,240	1,395	1,640	2,010	2,140	2,380	2,555	2,655	2,910
On ½% grade = 26 4/10 ft. per mile	245	290	350	375	415	470	530	625	765	815	905	975	1,010	1,110
On 1% grade = 52 8/10 ft. per mile	145	175	210	225	250	280	320	375	460	490	545	585	610	670
On 2% grade = 105 6/10 ft. per mile	75	90	110	115	130	145	170	200	245	260	290	310	320	355
On 3% grade = 158 4/10 ft. per mile	50	60	70	75	85	95	110	130	160	165	185	200	210	230

The **Rule for Calculation of Hauling Capacity** at all rates of resistance of rolling friction and on any practicable grade is given on **page 140**.
For quick approximate calculation of Hauling Capacity on any practicable grade, and with resistance of rolling friction of 6½ to 40 pounds per ton, refer to Tables of Percentages on **pages 156 and 157**.
For quick selection of suitable weight locomotive for stated load, grade and resistance of rolling friction, refer to **Tables I, II, III and IV**, on **pages 162 to 169**. These tables are also useful for quick comparison of loads that can be handled by locomotives of different weights.

"Forney" Locomotive, Four Driving Wheels, Class 4-B-R

Wide or Narrow Gauge

ILLUSTRATION No. 36, from photograph of 9 x 14 cylinders, coal-burning locomotive, 36 inches gauge of track, for sugar plantation in **Louisiana**.

FIFTEEN SIZES, each with code word, are described on the opposite page, subject to modifications to suit gauge, fuel, size of locomotive, and requirements or preferences of customers. We are prepared to build additional sizes. The driving wheels are connected by side equalizers. Hanging step-board may be used instead of pilot. For narrow gauge all but the smaller sizes are constructed with full-width firebox and main frames stopped off with crossbrace and tie-plate to rear frames. The truck has pivotal and lateral motion. The three smaller sizes have cylinders slightly inclined. See page 10 for general specifications and pages 11 and 12 for choice of stacks.

Correspondents are Requested to Designate Locomotives by Code Word

CODE WORD	HOOPJFS	HOORIG	HOPEAR	HOPFEN	HOPHRA	HOPMAN	HORBEL	HORELA	HORMUZ	HORNOS	HORROR	HOSTEL	HOSTAG	HOTBED	HOTELS
Cylinders { diameter, inches	6	7	8	9	10	10	11	12	12	13	14	14	15	15	16
{ stroke, inches	10	12	14	14	14	16	16	16	18	18	20	24	20	24	24
Diameter of driving wheels, in.	22	24	28	30	33	33	36	40	40	40	46	50	46	50	50
Diameter of truck wheels, inches	12	14	14	16	18	18	20	22	24	24	24	24	24	24	24
Rigid wheel-base, ft. and in.	3–6	4–0	4–0	4–6	4–6	5–3	5–3	5–9	5–9	6–3	6–3	7–0	7–0	7–0	8–0
Total wheel-base (center of front axle to center of truck), feet and inches	10–9	11–6	12–6	12–8	13–7	15–0	15–6	15–9	16–6	17–4	17–10	18–6	18–0	19–4	20–6
Length over all, feet and inches	20–6	21–2	22–10	25–0	26–0	27–0	28–0	29–0	30–2	32–2	33–8	34–8	34–2	36–0	38–0
Height (head-room not limited), feet and inches	9–6	9–8	9–10	10–0	10–3	10–6	10–10	11–3	11–6	12–0	12–6	12–9	12–6	13–2	13–6
Weight in working order, pounds	17,500	24,500	29,000	34,500	38,000	44,000	49,000	52,000	58,000	66,000	75,000	83,000	88,000	94,000	110,000
Weight on driving wheels, pounds	11,500	16,000	20,000	24,500	26,500	30,000	34,000	36,000	41,000	47,000	53,000	58,000	62,000	67,000	79,000
Weight on four-wheel truck, lb.	6,000	8,500	9,000	10,000	11,500	14,000	15,000	16,000	17,000	19,000	22,000	25,000	26,000	27,000	31,000
Water capacity of tank, gals.	300	400	450	550	650	650	700	750	750	800	900	1,000	1,000	1,200	1,400
Fuel capacity { wood, cu. ft.	750	1,000	1,200	1,600	1,800	1,800	1,800	2,000	2,000	2,400	3,000	3,500	3,500	4,000	5,000
{ coal, lb.	30	35	40	45	50	55	55	60	65	65	70	80	80	90	100
Weight per yard of lightest rail advised, pounds	12	16	20	25	25	30	30	35	35	40	45	50	56	60	65
Radius, sharpest curve advised, ft.	75	80	85	95	105	115	125	135	135	150	160	170	170	180	200
Radius of sharpest curve practicable, feet	60	65	70	75	80	90	100	115	115	125	130	140	140	150	175
Boiler pressure per square in., lb.	160	160	160	165	160	160	160	160	160	160	160	160	160	170	170
Tractive force, pounds	2,225	3,330	4,350	5,300	5,775	6,585	7,315	7,835	8,820	10,350	11,585	12,800	14,150	15,600	17,755
Hauling Capacity, in tons of 2,000 lb. (exclusive of locomotive), 6½ lb. per ton resistance of rolling friction:															
On absolute level	330	500	655	800	870	990	1,095	1,180	1,325	1,560	1,740	1,925	2,130	2,350	2,685
On ½% grade = 26 4/10 ft. per mile	125	190	245	300	330	375	415	445	505	590	665	730	810	895	1,020
On 1% grade = 52 8/10 ft. per mile	75	110	150	180	195	225	250	270	300	355	400	440	490	540	615
On 2% grade = 105 6/10 ft. per mile	35	55	75	95	105	120	130	140	155	190	230	230	260	285	325
On 3% grade = 158 4/10 ft. per mile	20	35	50	60	65	75	85	90	100	120	135	150	165	185	210

The **Rule for Calculation of Hauling Capacity** at all rates of resistance of rolling friction and on any practicable grade is given on **page 140**.
For quick approximate calculation of Hauling Capacity on any practicable grade, and with resistance of rolling friction of 6½ to 40 pounds per ton, refer to **Tables of Percentages** on **pages 156 and 157**.
For quick selection of **suitable weight locomotive** for stated load, grade and resistance of rolling friction, refer to **Tables I, II, III and IV**, on **pages 162 to 169**. These tables are also useful for quick comparison of loads that can be handled by locomotives of different weights.

"Forney" Locomotive Six Driving Wheels, Class 4-C-R

Wide or Narrow Gauge.

ILLUSTRATION No. 11, from photograph of 10 x 16 cylinders, coal-burning locomotive, 30 inches gauge of track, with stopped-off main frames and full-width firebox, exported to **Mexico**.

FOURTEEN SIZES, each with **code word**, are described on the opposite page, subject to modifications to suit gauge, fuel, size of locomotive, and requirements or preferences of customers. We are prepared to build additional sizes. Continuous frames are used for wide gauges. The truck has pivotal and lateral motion. All except the two smaller sizes have horizontal cylinders. See page 10 for general specifications and pages 11 and 12 for choice of stacks.

Correspondents are Requested to Designate Locomotives by Code Word

CODE WORD	HOUARI	HOUNAU	HOUSIA	HOWDAH	HOWQUA	HUBBUB	HUETEN	HUEVAR	HUHUEL	HUIDIG	HUIMOS	HUKBAG	HUKKOK	HULCHY
Cylinders { diameter, inches	7	8	9	10	9	11	12	12	13	14	14	15	15	16
{ stroke, inches	12	14	14	14	16	16	16	18	18	20	24	20	24	24
Diameter of driving wheels, inches	22	26	28	31	31	33	36	36	36	40	46	42	48	48
Diameter of truck wheels, inches	14	14	16	16	18	18	20	20	20	22	24	22	24	24
Rigid wheel-base, feet and inches	5-2	5-6	6-4	7-3	7-8	8-1	8-1	8-1	9-10	10-6	11-3	10-6	11-9	12-0
Total wheel-base (center of front axle to center of truck), feet and inches	10-4	10-8	11-6	12-1	12-10	13-4	14-9	15-0	15-8	17-0	18-0	18-0	18-0	19-6
Length over all, feet and inches	20-2	21-0	22-3	23-1	24-8	26-10	27-6	27-10	29-0	30-0	31-3	32-0	33-0	34-9
Extreme height (head-room not limited), feet and inches	9-8	9-10	10-0	10-3	10-6	10-10	11-6	11-6	12-0	12-6	12-9	12-6	13-2	13-6
Weight in working order, lb.	24,500	29,500	35,000	39,000	44,000	50,000	54,000	58,000	66,000	77,000	85,000	90,000	95,000	110,000
Weight on driving wheels, lb.	17,000	21,000	25,500	28,500	31,500	37,000	40,000	43,500	51,000	60,000	66,000	68,500	72,000	85,000
Weight on four-wheel truck, lb.	7,500	8,500	9,500	10,500	12,500	13,000	14,000	14,500	15,000	17,000	19,000	21,500	23,000	25,000
Water capacity of rear tank, gals.	400	500	600	700	700	750	800	800	900	1,000	1,100	1,000	1,200	1,400
Fuel capacity { coal, pounds	1,000	1,200	1,600	1,800	1,800	2,000	2,000	2,000	2,400	3,000	3,500	3,500	4,000	4,500
{ wood, cubic feet	35	40	45	50	55	60	60	60	60	70	80	80	90	100
Weight per yard of lightest rail advised, pounds	12	16	16	20	25	25	30	30	35	40	45	45	50	50
Radius of sharpest curve advised, feet	50	55	65	80	85	90	100	110	130	155	155	170	175	200
Radius of sharpest curve practicable, feet	40	50	55	60	70	80	90	95	115	135	135	140	145	175
Boiler pressure per square in., lb.	160	160	160	160	160	160	160	160	160	160	170	170	170	170
Tractive force, pounds	3,640	4,680	5,500	6,140	7,015	7,970	8,710	9,800	11,500	13,330	14,770	15,500	16,250	18,495
Hauling Capacity, in tons of 2,000 pounds (exclusive of locomotive), 6½ pounds per ton resistance of rolling friction:														
On absolute level	545	705	825	925	1,055	1,200	1,315	1,475	1,735	2,010	2,230	2,340	2,450	2,785
" ½% grade = 26 4/10 ft. per mile	205	265	315	350	400	455	500	565	660	770	850	895	935	1,065
" 1% " = 52 8/10 " " "	125	160	190	210	240	275	300	340	395	465	575	540	565	640
" 2% " = 105 6/10 " " "	65	85	100	110	125	145	160	180	210	245	275	285	300	340
" 3% " = 158 4/10 " " "	40	55	65	70	80	95	105	115	135	160	180	185	195	220

The **Rule for Calculation** of Hauling Capacity at all rates of resistance of rolling friction and on any practicable grade is given on page 140.
For **quick approximate calculation** of Hauling Capacity on any practicable grade, and with resistance of rolling friction of 6½ to 40 pounds per ton, refer to **Tables of Percentages** on pages 156 and 157.
For **quick selection of suitable weight locomotive** for stated load, grade and resistance of rolling friction, refer to **Tables I, II, III and IV**, on pages 162 to 169. These tables are also useful for quick comparison of loads that can be handled by locomotives of different weights.

"Back-'Truck" Rear-'Tank Four-Driver Locomotive, Class 2-B-R

Wide or Narrow Gauge

ILLUSTRATION No. 37, from photograph of 7 x 12 cylinders, coal-burning locomotive, 36 inches gauge, for plantation service in Louisiana.

NINE SIZES, each with **code word**, are described on the opposite page, subject to modifications to suit gauge, fuel, size of locomotive, and requirements or preferences of customers. We are prepared to build additional sizes. The driving wheels are connected by side equalizers. The truck has pivotal, lateral, and radial bar motion. For narrow gauge all except the smaller sizes have the main frames stopped off in front of full-width straight-sides firebox. Hanging step-boards and hand-holds may be used instead of pilot. All except the three smaller sizes have horizontal cylinders. See page 10 for general specifications and pages 11 and 12 for choice of stacks.

Correspondents are Requested to Designate Locomotives by Code Word

CODE WORD	HULAGU	HTLOAH	HUMAIN	HUMAVI	HUNNOS	HURANO	HUREEK	HURKEN	HURGAR
Cylinders { diameter, inches	6	7	8	9	10	10	11	12	12
{ stroke, inches	10	12	14	14	14	16	16	16	18
Diameter of driving wheels, inches	22	24	28	30	33	33	36	40	40
Diameter of truck wheels, inches	14	16	16	18	20	20	22	22	22
Rigid wheel-base, feet and inches	3–6	4–0	4–0	4–6	4–6	5–3	5–3	5–9	5–9
Total wheel-base, feet and inches	9–7	10–7	11–8	13–4	13–10	14–0	14–6	14–10	15–0
Length over all, feet and inches	16–0	17–0	18–3	20–6	22–0	22–10	23–8	24–0	24–4
Extreme height (head-room not limited), ft. and in.	9–6	9–8	9–10	10–0	10–3	10–6	10–10	11–0	11–2
Weight in working order, pounds	16,000	22,500	28,000	33,000	36,000	42,000	47,000	50,000	55,000
Weight on driving wheels, pounds	11,000	16,000	20,000	24,500	26,500	30,000	34,000	36,000	40,000
Weight on two-wheel truck, pounds	5,000	6,500	8,000	8,500	9,500	12,000	13,000	14,000	15,000
Water capacity of rear tank, gallons	250	350	400	450	550	600	650	650	750
Fuel capacity { coal, pounds	750	900	1,000	1,100	1,200	1,400	1,500	1,500	1,500
{ wood, cubic feet	18	20	25	30	35	40	45	45	50
Weight per yard of lightest rail advised, pounds	12	16	20	25	25	30	30	30	35
Radius of sharpest curve advised, feet	55	65	75	95	100	100	105	110	110
Radius of sharpest curve practicable, feet	40	45	50	65	70	70	80	85	85
Boiler pressure per square inch, pounds	160	160	160	165	160	160	160	160	160
Tractive force, pounds	2,225	3,330	4,350	5,300	5,775	6,585	7,315	7,835	8,820

Hauling Capacity, in tons of 2,000 pounds (exclusive of locomotive), 6½ pounds per ton resistance of rolling friction:

	HULAGU	HTLOAH	HUMAIN	HUMAVI	HUNNOS	HURANO	HUREEK	HURKEN	HURGAR
On absolute level	330	500	655	800	870	990	1,100	1,180	1,325
" ½ per cent grade = 26$\frac{4}{10}$ feet per mile	125	190	250	305	330	375	420	445	505
" 1 " " = 52$\frac{8}{10}$ " " "	75	110	150	180	200	225	250	270	300
" 2 " " = 105$\frac{6}{10}$ " " "	35	60	75	95	105	120	130	140	160
" 3 " " = 158$\frac{4}{10}$ " " "	25	35	50	60	65	75	85	90	100

The **Rule for Calculation of Hauling Capacity** at all rates of resistance of rolling friction and on any practicable grade is given on **page 140**.

For **quick approximate calculation** of Hauling Capacity on any practicable grade, and with resistance of rolling friction of 6½ to 40 pounds per ton, refer to **Tables of Percentages** on **pages 156 and 157**.

For **quick selection of suitable weight locomotive** for stated load, grade and resistance of rolling friction, refer to **Tables I, II, III and IV**, on **pages 162 to 169**. These tables are also useful for quick comparison of loads that can be handled by locomotives of different weights.

"Back-Truck" Rear-Tank Six-Driver Locomotive, Class 2-C-R

Wide or Narrow Gauge

ILLUSTRATION No. 48, from photograph of 9 x 14 cylinders, coal-burning locomotive, 36 inches gauge, for plantation service in Louisiana.

TWELVE SIZES, each with **code word**, are described on the opposite page, subject to modifications to suit gauge, fuel, size of locomotive, and requirements or preferences of customers. We are prepared to build additional sizes. The driving wheels are equalized. The truck has pivotal, lateral, and radial-bar motion. Hanging step-boards and hand-holds may be used instead of pilot. All except the two smaller cylinders have horizontal cylinders. See page 10 for general specifications and pages 11 and 12 for choice of stacks.

Correspondents are Requested to Designate Locomotives by Code Word

CODE WORD	HURRIX	HUTZEL	HYAPEA	HYBELA	HYCSOS	HYDAGE	HYDRIC	HYGINO	HYGRAM	HYLLOS	HYPNUM	HYSMON
Cylinders { diameter, inches	7	8	9	10	10	11	12	12	13	14	14	15
stroke, inches	12	14	14	14	16	16	16	18	18	20	21	24
Diameter of driving wheels, inches	22	26	28	31	31	33	36	36	36	40	46	48
Diameter of truck wheels, inches	16	16	16	16	18	18	20	20	20	22	24	26
Rigid wheel-base, feet and inches	5-2	5-6	6-4	7-3	7-8	8-1	8-1	9-0	9-10	10-6	11-3	11-9
Total wheel-base, feet and inches	10-4	10-11	12-2	13-5	14-0	14-4	15-2	15-5	16-0	16-10	17-6	19-0
Length over bumpers, feet and inches	17-0	17-6	19-9	20-7	21-10	23-0	23-6	24-3	25-3	26-6	27-2	29-6
Extreme ht. (head-room not limited), ft. and in.	9-8	9-10	10-0	10-3	10-6	10-10	11-4	12-0	12-0	12-6	12-9	13-2
Weight in working order, pounds	23,000	28,000	33,500	37,500	42,500	48,000	52,000	56,000	64,000	74,000	82,000	91,000
Weight on driving wheels, pounds	16,500	20,500	25,000	28,000	31,500	36,500	40,000	43,500	51,000	59,000	66,000	72,000
Weight on pony truck, pounds	6,500	7,500	8,500	9,500	11,000	11,500	12,000	12,500	13,000	15,000	16,000	19,000
Water capacity of rear tank, gallons	400	450	550	650	650	700	800	800	850	900	1,000	1,100
Fuel capacity { coal, pounds	1,000	1,200	1,600	1,700	1,700	1,800	2,000	2,000	2,100	2,100	2,200	2,400
wood, cubic feet	20	25	30	35	40	40	45	45	50	50	55	60
Weight per yard of lightest rail advised, pounds	14	15	16	20	25	25	30	30	30	35	40	50
Radius of sharpest curve advised, feet	55	65	80	90	100	110	110	120	130	155	160	175
Radius of sharpest curve practicable, feet	45	55	70	80	90	95	95	105	115	135	140	145
Boiler pressure per square inch, pounds	160	160	160	160	160	160	160	160	160	160	170	170
Tractive force, pounds	3,640	4,680	5,500	6,140	7,015	7,070	8,710	9,800	11,500	13,330	14,770	16,250
Hauling Capacity, in tons of 2,000 pounds (exclusive of locomotive), 6½ pounds per ton resistance of rolling friction:												
On absolute level	545	705	825	925	1,055	1,200	1,315	1,480	1,735	2,010	2,230	2,455
" ½ per cent grade = 26 4/10 feet per mile	205	265	315	350	400	455	500	565	665	770	850	940
" 1 " " = 52 8/10 " " "	125	160	190	220	240	275	300	340	400	465	515	565
" 2 " " = 105 6/10 " " "	65	85	100	110	130	145	160	185	210	245	275	300
" 3 " " = 158 4/10 " " "	40	55	65	70	80	95	95	115	140	160	180	195

The **Rule for Calculation** of Hauling Capacity at all rates of resistance of rolling friction and on any practicable grade is given on page 140.

For quick approximate calculation of Hauling Capacity on any practicable grade, and with resistance of rolling friction of 6½ to 40 pounds per ton, refer to **Tables of Percentages** on pages 156 and 157.

For quick selection of suitable weight locomotive for stated load, grade and resistance of rolling friction, refer to **Tables I, II, III and IV**, on pages 162 to 169. These tables are also useful for quick comparison of loads that can be handled by locomotives of different weights.

"Forney" Saddle-Tank Locomotive Four Driving Wheels, Class 4-B-S

Wide or Narrow Gauge

ILLUSTRATION No. 3, from photograph of 14 x 20 cylinders, coal-burning locomotive, 56½ inches gauge, exported to Cuba for plantation railway.

FIFTEEN SIZES, each with code word, are described on the opposite page, subject to modifications to suit gauge, fuel, size of locomotive, and requirements or preferences of customers. We are prepared to build additional sizes. The driving wheels are equalized. The truck has pivotal and lateral motion. For narrow gauges all except the smaller sizes have the main frames stopped off in front of ful'-width straight-sides firebox. Hanging stepboards and hand-holds may be used instead of pilots. All except the three smaller sizes have horizontal cylinders. See page 10 for general specifications and pages 11 and 12 for choice of stacks.

Correspondents are Requested to Designate Locomotives by Code Word

CODE WORD	KABUFF	KABYLE	KADMOS	KAFTAN	KAFZAK	KAHLER	KAIMAN	KAISER	KAJUIT	KAKOUR	KALIUM	KALMIA	KALMOD	KALMUS	KALMTE
Cylinders { diameter, inches	6	7	8	9	10	10	11	12	12	13	14	14	15	15	16
{ stroke, inches	10	12	14	14	14	16	16	16	18	18	20	24	20	24	24
Diameter of driving wheels, inches	22	24	28	30	33	33	36	38	40	40	42	46	45	50	50
Diameter of truck wheels, inches	16	16	16	16	18	18	20	22	22	24	24	24	24	24	24
Rigid wheel-base, feet and inches	3–6	4–0	4–0	4–6	4–6	5–3	5–3	5–9	5–9	6–3	6–3	7–0	7–0	7–0	8–0
Total wheel-base (center of front axle to center of truck), feet and inches	10–6	11–3	12–0	12–8	13–0	14–6	15–0	15–6	15–6	16–3	16–10	17–6	17–6	18–2	19–0
Length over all, feet and inches	19–6	20–8	21–6	23–0	24–0	25–3	20–8	27–6	28–0	29–8	31–0	32–0	28–0	33–0	35–0
Extreme height (head-room not limited), feet and inches	9–6	9–8	9–10	10–0	10–3	10–6	10–10	11–4	11–6	12–0	12–6	12–9	12–6	13–2	13–6
Weight in working order, pounds	17,000	24,000	29,000	33,500	37,000	42,500	47,000	52,000	56,000	64,000	75,500	82,000	86,000	92,000	107,000
Weight on driving wheels, pounds	12,000	16,500	21,000	25,000	28,000	33,000	37,000	41,000	44,000	51,500	62,500	67,500	70,000	76,000	89,000
Weight on four-wheel truck, lb	5,000	7,500	8,000	8,500	9,000	9,500	10,000	11,000	12,000	12,500	13,000	14,500	16,000	16,000	17,000
Water capacity, saddle-tank, gals.	200	300	350	400	500	600	650	700	750	800	900	1,000	1,000	1,100	1,200
Fuel capacity { coal, lb	600	700	800	1,000	1,200	1,500	2,000	2,000	2,500	3,000	3,500	4,500	4,500	5,500	6,000
{ wood, cu. ft.	30	35	40	45	50	60	65	65	70	80	90	100	100	110	120
Weight per yard of lightest rail advised, pounds	14	16	20	25	25	30	30	35	40	45	50	60	60	65	70
Radius, sharpest curve advised, ft.	75	80	85	95	105	115	125	125	135	150	160	170	160	180	200
Radius of sharpest curve practicable, feet	55	65	70	75	80	90	100	100	110	120	125	135	135	145	175
Boiler pressure, per square inch, pounds	160	160	160	160	160	160	160	160	160	160	160	160	170	170	170
Tractive force, pounds	2,225	3,330	4,350	5,135	5,775	6,585	7,315	8,245	8,820	10,350	12,600	13,900	14,450	15,600	17,755
Hauling Capacity, in tons of 2,000 lb. (exclusive of locomotive). 6½ lb. per ton resistance of rolling friction:															
On absolute level	330	500	650	770	870	990	1,100	1,240	1,325	1,560	1,910	2,100	2,180	2,350	2,675
" ½% grade= 26 4/10 ft. per mile	125	190	250	295	330	375	420	470	505	595	730	800	830	900	1,020
" 1% " = 52 8/10 " "	75	110	150	175	200	225	250	280	300	355	440	480	500	540	615
" 2% " = 105 6/10 " "	35	55	80	90	105	120	130	150	160	190	235	255	265	290	325
" 3% " = 158 4/10 " "	20	35	50	65	65	75	85	95	100	120	150	165	170	185	210

The **Rule for Calculation of Hauling Capacity** at all rates of resistance of rolling friction and on any practicable grade is given on **page 140**.
For quick approximate calculation of Hauling Capacity on any practicable grade, and with resistance of rolling friction of 6½ to 40 pounds per ton, refer to Tables of Percentages on **pages 156 and 157**.
For quick selection of suitable weight locomotive for stated load, grade and resistance of rolling friction, refer to **Tables I, II, III and IV**, on **pages 162 to 169**. These tables are also useful for quick comparison of loads that can be handled by locomotives of different weights.

5

"Forney" Saddle-Tank Locomotive Six Driving Wheels, Class 4-C-S

Wide or Narrow Gauge

ILLUSTRATION No. 15, from photograph of 10 x 16 cylinders, coal-burning locomotive, 30 inches gauge of track, with stopped-off frames and full-width fire box, exported to Mexico for ore railway.

FOURTEEN SIZES, each with **code word**, are described on the opposite page, subject to modifications of details to suit gauge, fuel, size of locomotive, and requirements or preferences of customers. We are prepared to build additional sizes. The driving wheels are equalized. The truck has pivotal and lateral motion. For wide gauges the frames are continuous. Pilots may be used instead of hanging step-boards. The two smaller sizes have cylinders slightly inclined. See page 10 for general specifications and pages 11 and 12 for choice of stacks.

Correspondents are Requested to Designate Locomotives by Code Word

CODE WORD	KALONG	KALVEN	KAMBLI	KAMBOU	KAMLAT	KAMWOL	KAMUIS	KANONE	KANSSU	KAPAUN	KAPMES	KAPMOT	KAPUZE	KAPTUR
Cylinders { diameter, inches	7	8	9	10	10	11	12	12	13	14	14	15	15	16
stroke, inches	12	14	14	14	16	16	16	18	18	20	24	20	24	24
Diameter of driving wheels, inches	23	28	28	30	31	33	36	36	36	40	46	42	48	48
Diameter of truck wheels, inches	14	14	16	16	18	18	18	18	18	22	24	20	24	24
Rigid wheel-base, feet and inches	5-2	5-6	5-10	7-3	7-8	8-1	8-1	8-1	9-10	10-6	11-3	10-6	11-9	12-0
Total wheel-base (center of front axle to center of truck), feet and inches	10-4	10-8	11-1	12-1	12-10	13-9	14-0	14-6	14-10	15-8	16-4	17-6	17-4	19-6
Length over all, feet and inches	20-2	20-8	21-10	22-6	24-6	25-10	26-0	27-4	28-5	29-8	30-6	31-6	32-0	33-6
Extreme height (head-room not limited), feet and inches	9-8	9-10	10-0	10-3	10-6	10-10	11-4	11-6	12-0	12-6	12-9	12-6	13-2	13-10
Weight in working order, lb	23,500	28,500	34,000	39,000	42,500	48,000	52,000	57,000	66,000	76,500	84,000	88,500	96,000	108,000
Weight on driving wheels, lb	17,500	22,000	27,000	31,500	34,500	40,000	43,000	47,000	55,000	65,000	71,000	75,000	82,000	91,000
Weight on four-wheel truck, lb	6,000	6,500	7,000	7,500	8,000	8,000	9,000	10,000	11,000	11,500	13,000	13,500	14,000	17,000
Water capacity of saddle-tank, gallons	300	350	400	500	600	650	700	750	800	900	1,000	1,000	1,100	1,200
Fuel capacity { coal, pounds	900	1,000	1,000	1,200	1,500	1,600	1,700	2,000	2,500	3,000	3,500	3,500	4,000	4,500
wood, cubic feet	20	25	30	35	40	40	45	50	60	70	80	80	90	100
Wt. per yard of lightest rail advised, lbs	14	16	20	20	25	25	30	30	35	40	45	45	50	55
Radius of sharpest curve advised, feet	50	60	65	80	90	100	110	115	135	155	155	160	175	200
Radius of sharpest curve practicable, feet	40	50	55	60	70	80	90	95	115	135	135	135	145	170
Boiler pressure per square in, lb	160	160	160	160	160	160	160	160	160	160	170	170	170	170
Tractive force, pounds	3,480	4,350	5,500	6,350	7,015	7,970	8,710	9,800	11,500	13,330	14,770	15,500	16,250	18,495
Hauling Capacity, in tons of 2,000 lb. (exclusive of locomotive), 6½ lb. per ton resistance of rolling friction:														
On absolute level	520	655	825	955	1,055	1,200	1,310	1,480	1,735	2,010	2,230	2,340	2,450	2,790
" ½% grade = 26 4/10 ft. per mile	195	245	315	365	400	455	500	565	660	770	850	895	935	1,065
" 1% " = 52 8/10 " "	120	150	190	220	240	275	300	340	400	465	515	540	565	640
" 2% " = 105 6/10 " "	60	75	100	110	130	145	160	180	210	245	275	285	300	340
" 3% " = 158 4/10 " "	40	50	65	75	80	95	105	115	140	160	180	185	195	220

The **Rule for Calculation of Hauling Capacity** at all rates of resistance of rolling friction and on any practicable grade is given on **page 140**.
For quick approximate calculation of Hauling Capacity on any practicable grade, and with resistance of rolling friction of 6½ to 40 pounds per ton, refer to **Tables of Percentages** on pages **156 and 157**.
For **quick selection of suitable weight locomotive** for stated load, grade and resistance of rolling friction, refer to **Tables I, II, III and IV**, on pages **162 to 169**. These tables are also useful for quick comparison of loads that can be handled by locomotives of different weights.

57

Light "Back-Truck" Saddle-Tank Locomotive Four Driving Wheels, Class 2-B-S

Wide or Narrow Gauge

ILLUSTRATION No. 20, from photograph of 9 x 14 cylinders, coal-burning locomotive, 37½ inches gauge of track, for phosphate mines.

FIVE SIZES, each with code word, are described on the opposite page, subject to modifications of details to suit gauge, fuel, size of locomotive, and requirements or preferences of customers. We are prepared to build additional sizes. The driving wheels are equalized. The truck has pivotal, lateral, and radial-bar motion. If narrow gauge makes it desirable, the frames are stopped off in front of full-width straight-sides firebox. The two larger sizes have horizontal cylinders. See page 10 for general specifications and pages 11 and 12 for choice of stacks.

For larger sizes see next page.

Correspondents are Requested to Designate Locomotives by Code Word

CODE WORD { with closed end cab, like Illustration No. 20. / with open end cab, without doors	KASVEL KAYACK	KATOEN KEBLAH	KATTUN KECKSY	KATZEN KEGGEN	KAUERN KEGUEM
Cylinders { diameter, inches	6	7	8	9	10
{ stroke, inches	10	12	14	14	14
Diameter of driving wheels, inches	22	24	28	30	33
Diameter of truck wheels, inches	14	16	16	18	20
Rigid wheel-base, feet and inches	3–6	4–0	4–0	4–6	4–6
Total wheel-base, feet and inches	9–7	10–7	11–8	12–2½	12 2½
Length over bumpers, feet and inches	16–0	17–0	18–3	19–6	21–0
Extreme height (head-room not limited), feet and inches	9–6	9–8	9–10	10–0	10–3
Weight in working order, pounds	15,500	21,500	27,000	32,000	35,500
Weight on driving wheels, pounds	11,500	16,500	21,000	25,000	28,000
Weight on two-wheel truck, pounds	4,000	5,000	6,000	7,000	7,500
Water capacity of saddle-tank, gallons	150	200	300	400	500
Fuel capacity { coal, pounds	300	400	600	700	800
{ wood, cubic feet	20	25	30	35	40
Weight per yard of lightest rail advised, pounds	14	16	20	25	25
Radius of sharpest curve advised, feet	60	70	80	90	90
Radius of sharpest curve practicable, feet	45	50	55	60	60
Boiler pressure per square inch, pounds	160	160	160	160	160
Tractive force, pounds	2,225	3,330	4,350	5,135	5,775
Hauling Capacity, in tons of 2,000 pounds (exclusive of locomotive), 6½ pounds per ton resistance of rolling friction:					
On absolute level	330	500	655	775	870
" ½ per cent grade = 26 4/10 feet per mile	125	190	250	295	330
" 1 " " " = 52 8/10 " " "	75	115	150	175	200
" 2 " " " = 105 6/10 " " "	40	60	80	95	105
" 3 " " " = 158 4/10 " " "	25	40	50	60	65

The **Rule for Calculation** of Hauling Capacity at all rates of resistance of rolling friction and on any practicable grade is given on page 140.

For quick approximate calculation of Hauling Capacity on any practicable grade, and with resistance of rolling friction of 6½ to 40 pounds per ton, refer to **Tables of Percentages** on pages 156 and 157.

For quick **selection of suitable weight locomotive** for stated load, grade and resistance of rolling friction, refer to **Tables I, II, III and IV,** on pages 162 to 169. These tables are also useful for quick comparison of loads that can be handled by locomotives of different weights.

"Back-Truck" Saddle-Tank Locomotive Four Driving Wheels, Class 2-B-S

Wide or Narrow Gauge

ILLUSTRATION No. 21, from photograph of 13 x 18 cylinders, coal-burning locomotive, 56½ inches gauge, with extended tank, and air brake and dump, for phosphate mines.

TEN SIZES, each with code word, are described on the opposite page, subject to modifications of details to suit gauge, fuel, size of locomotive, and requirements or preferences of customers. We are prepared to build additional sizes. The driving wheels are equalized. The truck has pivotal, lateral, and radial-bar motion. For narrow gauges the frames are stopped off in front of full-width straight-sides firebox. Pilots may be used instead of step-boards. Short tank may be used. See page 10 for general specifications and pages 11 and 12 for choice of stacks.

For smaller sizes see preceding page.

Correspondents are Requested to Designate Locomotives by Code Word

CODE WORD { With closed end cab, like Illustration No. 21 / With open end cab, without doors	KEHAYA KERNIG	KEHREN KERSEN	KEHLIG KESLOP	KEILEN KESORA	KEMIG KESSEL	KEINER KETUPA	KEMOUN KEYAGE	KEMURN KEVELL	KENATH KHALIL	KERKER KHENNA
Cylinders { diameter, inches	10	11	12	12	13	14	14	15	15	16
{ stroke, inches	16	16	16	18	18	20	24	20	24	24
Diameter of driving wheels, inches	33	36	38	40	40	42	46	45	50	50
Diameter of truck wheels, inches	22	22	22	24	24	26	26	26	26	26
Rigid wheel-base, feet and inches	5-3	5-3	5-0	5-0	5-0	6-3	7-0	7-0	7-0	8-0
Total wheel-base, feet and inches	13-4	13-9	14-0	14-0	14-10	15-0	15-0	15-0	17-0	18-6
Length over bumpers, feet and inches	21-6	22-0	22-6	22-6	23-6	25-0	26-0	26-6	27-6	30-0
Extreme height (head-room not limited), ft. and in	10-6	10-10	11-4	11-6	12-0	12-6	12-9	12-8	13-2	13-10
Weight in working order, pounds	41,000	45,000	49,000	53,000	62,000	74,000	79,000	82,000	88,000	104,000
Weight on driving wheels, pounds	33,000	36,500	40,500	44,000	52,000	63,500	67,500	70,000	76,000	91,000
Weight on two-wheel truck, pounds	8,000	8,500	8,500	9,000	10,000	10,500	11,500	12,000	12,000	13,000
Water capacity of saddle-tank, gallons	600	600	700	750	800	900	1,000	1,000	1,100	1,250
Fuel capacity { wood, cubic feet	1,000	1,200	1,300	1,500	1,800	2,600	3,000	3,000	3,500	4,000
{ coal, pounds	45	50	55	60	70	80	90	80	100	110
Weight per yard of lightest rail advised, pounds	30	35	35	40	45	55	60	60	70	75
Radius of sharpest curve advised, feet	95	95	100	100	105	110	120	120	120	135
Radius of sharpest curve practicable, feet	65	65	70	70	80	85	90	90	90	110
Boiler pressure per square inch, pounds	160	160	160	160	160	160	160	170	170	175
Tractive force, pounds	6,585	7,315	8,245	8,820	10,350	12,690	13,000	14,450	15,600	18,275
Hauling Capacity, in tons of 2,000 pounds (exclusive of locomotive), 6½ pounds per ton resistance of rolling friction:										
On absolute level	990	1,100	1,240	1,330	1,560	1,915	2,100	2,180	2,355	2,755
" ½ per cent grade = 26 4/10 feet per mile	375	420	475	505	595	730	800	835	900	1,055
" 1 " " " = 52 8/10 " "	225	250	285	305	355	440	480	500	540	635
" 2 " " " = 105 6/10 " "	120	130	150	160	190	235	255	270	290	340
" 3 " " " = 158 4/10 " "	75	85	100	105	125	155	165	175	190	220

The Rule for Calculation of Hauling Capacity at all rates of resistance of rolling friction and on any practicable grade is given on page 140.

For quick approximate calculation of Hauling Capacity on any practicable grade, and with resistance of rolling friction of 6½ to 40 pounds per ton, refer to **Tables of Percentages** on pages 156 and 157.

For quick selection of suitable weight locomotive for stated load, grade and resistance of rolling friction, refer to **Tables I, II, III and IV**, on pages 162 to 169. These tables are also useful for quick comparison of loads that can be handled by locomotives of different weights.

"Back-Truck" Saddle-Tank Locomotive Six Driving Wheels, Class 2-C-S

Wide or Narrow Gauge

ILLUSTRATION No. 49, from photograph of 8 x 14 cylinders, coal-burning locomotive, 36 inches gauge of track, for sugar plantation in Louisiana.

FOURTEEN SIZES, each with **code word**, are described on the opposite page, subject to modifications of details to suit gauge, fuel, size of locomotive, and requirements or preferences of customers. We are prepared to build additional sizes. The driving wheels are equalized. The truck has pivotal, lateral, and radial-bar motion. If narrowness of gauge demands, the frames are stopped off in front of full-width straight-sides firebox. Pilot or hanging step-board may be used. The cylinders of all except the two smaller sizes are horizontal. See page 10 for general specifications and pages 11 and 12 for choice of stacks.

Correspondents are Requested to Designate Locomotives by Code Word

CODE WORD	KIAFUR	KIBBLE	KIBLAH	KIDNAP	KIDRON	KIEVIT	KIJANG	KILDIR	KIMBOW	KINCOB	KIOSCO	KIPALL	KIPPEN	KIRBYE
Cylinders { diameter, inches	7	8	9	10	10	11	12	12	13	14	14	15	15	16
{ stroke, inches	12	14	14	14	16	16	16	18	18	20	24	20	24	24
Diameter of driving wheels, in.	23	28	28	30	31	33	36	36	36	40	46	42	48	48
Diameter of truck wheels, inches	16	16	16	16	16	18	20	20	20	22	24	22	24	24
Rigid wheel-base, feet and inches	5-2	5-6	5-10	7-3	7-8	8-1	8-1	9-0	9-10	10-6	11-3	10-6	11-9	12-0
Total wheel-base, feet and inches	9-10	10-6	11-5	12-6	13-4	13-9	14-6	15-0	15-8	16-6	17-0	17-0	18-6	20-0
Length over bumpers, ft. and in.	16-6	17-0	18-8	19-5	20-8	22-0	23-0	23-5	24-6	25-8	27-0	27-0	29-0	31-6
Extreme height (head-room not limited), feet and inches	9-8	9-10	10-0	10-3	10-6	10-10	11-3	11-6	12-0	12-6	12-9	12-7	13-2	13-8
Weight in working order, lb.	22,000	27,000	32,500	38,000	41,000	47,000	50,000	55,000	63,500	76,000	82,000	85,500	90,000	104,000
Weight on driving wheels, lb.	17,500	22,000	27,000	31,500	34,500	40,000	42,500	47,000	55,000	66,500	71,500	75,000	79,000	92,000
Weight on pony truck, lb.	4,500	5,000	5,500	6,500	6,500	7,000	7,500	8,000	8,500	9,500	10,500	10,500	11,000	12,000
Water capacity of saddle-tank, gallons	300	350	400	500	600	600	700	750	900	1,000	1,000	1,000	1,100	1,200
Fuel capacity { coal, pounds	400	600	700	800	1,000	1,200	1,300	1,500	1,800	2,500	3,000	3,000	3,500	4,000
{ wood, cubic feet	25	30	35	40	45	50	55	60	70	80	90	90	100	110
Weight per yard of lightest rail advised, pounds	14	16	20	20	25	30	30	30	35	40	45	45	50	60
Radius of sharpest curve advised, feet	50	60	70	80	85	90	90	110	130	155	160	155	175	200
Radius of sharpest curve practicable, feet	40	50	60	65	75	80	80	95	115	135	140	140	145	170
Boiler pressure per square in., lb.	160	160	160	160	160	160	160	160	160	160	170	170	170	170
Tractive force, pounds	3,480	4,350	5,500	6,350	7,015	7,970	8,710	9,800	11,500	13,330	14,770	15,500	16,250	18,495
Hauling Capacity, in tons of 2,000 lb. (exclusive of locomotive), 6½ lb. per ton resistance of rolling friction:														
On absolute level	520	655	825	955	1,055	1,200	1,315	1,475	1,735	2,010	2,230	2,340	2,450	2,790
" ½% grade = 26 1/10 ft. per mile	200	245	315	365	400	455	500	560	665	770	850	895	935	1,065
" 1% " = 52 1/10 " "	120	150	190	220	240	275	300	335	400	465	515	540	565	645
" 2% " = 105 6/10 " "	60	75	100	115	130	145	160	180	215	245	275	290	300	345
" 3% " = 158 4/10 " "	40	50	65	75	80	95	105	115	140	160	180	190	195	225

The **Rule for Calculation** of Hauling Capacity at all rates of resistance of rolling friction and on any practicable grade is given on **page 140**.
For quick approximate calculation of Hauling Capacity on any practicable grade, and with resistance of rolling friction of 6½ to 40 pounds per ton, refer to Tables of Percentages on **pages 156 and 157**.
For **quick selection of suitable weight locomotive** for stated load, grade and resistance of rolling friction, refer to Tables **I, II, III and IV**, on **pages 162 to 169**. These tables are also useful for quick comparison of loads that can be handled by locomotives of different weights.

Light Four-Wheel-Connected Saddle-Tank Locomotive, Class B-S

For Contractors' Use and other Special Service. Wide or Narrow Gauge

ILLUSTRATION No. 26, from photograph of contractors' service, coal-burning locomotive, 36 inches gauge of track, showing proportions of **8 x 14 cylinders size**.
(NOTE.—Kirwan, 36 inch gauge, is usually on hand in stock ready to ship.)

FIVE SIZES, each with **code word,** are described on the opposite page, subject to modifications of details to suit gauge, fuel, size of locomotive, and requirements or preferences of customers. We are prepared to build additional sizes. A cross equalizer is used at the front driving wheels. For extra narrow gauge the wheel-base is shortened and the frames stopped off in front of full-width straight-sides firebox. Hanging step-boards may be used front and rear. See page 10 for general specifications and pages 11 and 12 for choice of stacks.

For larger sizes see next four pages.

Correspondents are Requested to Designate Locomotives by Code Word

CODE WORD	KIRBER	KIRCHE	KIRMES	KIRWAN	KISMET
Cylinders { diameter, inches	5	5	6	7	8
{ stroke, inches	8	10	10	12	14
Diameter of driving wheels, inches	20	20	20	24	26
Wheel-base, feet and inches	3–6	4–0	4–0	4–8	5–0
Length over bumpers, feet and inches	10–6	11–0	11–6	12–9	14–0
Extreme height, (head-room not limited), feet and inches	9–4	9–4	9–6	9–8	9–10
Weight in working order, all on driving wheels, pounds	8,500	11,000	14,000	17,500	24,000
Water capacity of saddle-tank, gallons	100	125	150	200	250
Fuel capacity { coal, pounds	175	200	200	250	300
{ wood, cubic feet	15	15	18	20	20
Weight per yard of lightest rail advised, pounds	12	14	16	16	20
Radius of sharpest curve advised, feet	25	30	30	35	35
Radius of sharpest curve practicable, feet	15	15	15	16	18
Boiler pressure per square inch, pounds	160	160	160	160	160
Tractive force, pounds	1,360	1,700	2,445	3,330	4,680
Hauling Capacity, in tons of 2,000 pounds (exclusive of locomotive), 6½ pounds per ton resistance of rolling friction:					
On absolute level	200	255	365	500	705
" ½ per cent grade = 26 4/10 feet per mile	75	95	140	190	270
" 1 " " " = 52 10/10 " " "	45	55	85	115	160
" 2 " " " = 105 4/10 " " "	20	30	40	60	85
" 3 " " " = 158 4/10 " " "	14	18	25	40	55

The Rule for Calculation of Hauling Capacity at all rates of resistance of rolling friction and on any practicable grade is given on page 140.

For quick approximate calculation of Hauling Capacity on any practicable grade, and with resistance of rolling friction of 6½ to 40 pounds per ton, refer to **Tables of Percentages** on **pages 156 and 157**.

For quick selection of suitable weight locomotive for stated load, grade and resistance of rolling friction, refer to **Tables I, II, III and IV**, on **pages 162 to 169**. These tables are also useful for quick comparison of loads that can be handled by locomotives of different weights.

Four-Wheel-Connected Saddle-Tank Locomotive, Class B-S

For Contractors' Use, Shifting, and Special Services. Wide and Narrow Gauge

ILLUSTRATION No. 246, from photograph of 10 x 16 cylinders, coal-burning locomotive, 36 inches gauge of track, for contractors' service, with main frames stopped off in front of full-width straight-sides firebox with steel cross-brace and tie plate to rear frames.

KITTEL, 36 inches gauge, and KIZLOZ, 36 inches gauge and 56½ inches gauge, are favorites for contractors' service and are kept on hand in stock ready to ship.

NINE SIZES, each with code word, are described on the opposite page, subject to modifications to suit gauge, fuel, size of locomotive, and requirements or preferences of customers. We are prepared to build additional sizes. A cross equalizer is used at the front driving wheels. For wide gauges the frames are continuous. See page 10 for general specifications and pages 11 and 12 for choice of stacks.

For smaller sizes see preceding page; for larger sizes see next page.

Correspondents are Requested to Designate Locomotives by Code Word

CODE WORD	KITTEL	KITTIM	KIZLOZ	KLACHT	KLADDE	KLMST	KLASSE	KLATER	KLEBEN
Cylinders { diameter, inches	9	10	10	11	11	12	12	13	13
{ stroke, inches	14	14	16	14	16	16	18	16	18
Diameter of driving wheels, inches	27	30	30	30	31	33	36	33	36
Wheel-base, feet and inches	4–6	4–6	5–0	4–6	5–0	5–0	5–9	5–9	5–9
Length over bumpers, feet and inches	16–10	17–0	18–3	18–0	18–6	19–0	20–0	21–6	21–6
Extreme height (head-room not limited), ft. and in.	9–10	10–0	10–0	10–2	10–9	11–3	11–6	12–0	12–0
Weight in working order, all on driving wheels, lb	29,000	32,000	36,500	39,000	42,000	47,000	51,000	56,000	60,000
Water capacity of saddle-tank, gallons	400	500	600	600	600	700	750	800	900
Fuel capacity { coal, pounds	350	450	500	500	600	800	800	900	900
{ wood, cubic feet	25	25	30	30	30	35	35	40	40
Weight per yard of lightest rail advised, pounds	25	30	35	40	40	45	45	50	50
Radius of sharpest curve advised, feet	35	35	45	40	45	45	50	60	60
Radius of sharpest curve practicable, feet	18	18	25	20	25	25	30	35	35
Boiler pressure per square inch, pounds	165	160	160	160	160	160	165	165	165
Tractive force, pounds	5,890	6,350	7,250	7,680	8,480	9,495	10,110	11,490	11,850

Hauling Capacity, in tons of 2,000 pounds (exclusive of locomotive), 6½ pounds per ton resistance of rolling friction:

	KITTEL	KITTIM	KIZLOZ	KLACHT	KLADDE	KLMST	KLASSE	KLATER	KLEBEN
On absolute level	890	960	1,095	1,160	1,280	1,430	1,525	1,740	1,795
" ½ per cent grade = 26 4/10 feet per mile	340	365	420	445	490	550	585	665	685
" 1 " " = 52 8/10 " "	205	220	255	270	295	330	355	405	415
" 2 " " = 105 6/10 " "	110	115	135	145	160	180	190	215	225
" 3 " " = 158 4/10 " "	70	75	90	95	105	115	125	140	145

The **Rule for Calculation** of Hauling Capacity at all rates of resistance of rolling friction and on any practicable grade is given on page 140.

For quick approximate calculation of Hauling Capacity on any practicable grade, and with resistance of rolling friction of 6½ to 40 pounds per ton, refer to **Tables of Percentages** on pages 156 and 157.

For quick selection of suitable weight locomotive for stated load, grade and resistance of rolling friction, refer to **Tables I, II, III and IV,** on pages 162 to 169. These tables are also useful for quick comparison of loads that can be handled by locomotives of different weights.

Four-Wheel-Connected Saddle-Tank Locomotive, Class B-S

For Shifting, Contractors' Use, and Special Service. Wide or Narrow Gauge

ILLUSTRATION No. 24, from photograph of 14 x 20 cylinders, shifting locomotive, 56½ inches gauge of track, with air brake. KLINGE, 56½ inches gauge, is kept on hand in stock ready to ship.

SIX SIZES, each with code word, are described on the opposite page, subject to modifications of details to suit gauge, fuel, size of locomotive, and requirements or preferences of customers. We are prepared to build additional sizes. A cross equalizer is used at the front driving wheels. For narrow gauge the main frames are stopped off in front of full-width straight-sides firebox with steel cross-brace and tie-plate to rear frames with rear entrance to cab as shown by Illustration 246 on the preceding page. See page 10 for general specifications and pages 11 and 12 for choice of stacks.

For smaller sizes see four preceding pages.

Correspondents are Requested to Designate Locomotives by Code Word

CODE WORD	KLEPEL	KLERIC	KLERUS	KLINIC	KLINGE	KLIMOP
Cylinders { diameter, inches	14	14	14	15	15	16
{ stroke, inches	20	22	24	20	24	24
Diameter of driving wheels, inches	40	42	45	42	46	46
Wheel-base, feet and inches	6-3	6-6	7-0	6-3	7-0	8-0
Length over bumpers, feet and inches	23-0	23-10	24-6	24-0	25-6	27-6
Extreme height (head-room not limited), feet and inches	12-6	12-6	12-9	12-9	13-2	13-8
Weight in working order, all on driving wheels, pounds	69,000	71,000	74,000	78,000	84,000	100,000
Water capacity of saddle-tank, gallons	900	1,000	1,000	1,200	1,200	1,200
Fuel capacity { coal, pounds	1,400	1,500	1,600	1,500	1,800	2,200
{ wood, cubic feet	45	45	50	45	60	80
Weight per yard of lightest rail advised, pounds	55	60	60	60	70	80
Radius of sharpest curve advised, feet	60	65	70	60	70	85
Radius of sharpest curve practicable, feet	35	40	40	40	45	65
Boiler pressure per square inch, pounds	165	165	165	170	170	180
Tractive force, pounds	13,740	14,395	14,660	15,480	16,960	20,435
Hauling Capacity, in tons of 2,000 pounds (exclusive of locomotive), $6\frac{3}{4}$ pounds per ton resistance of rolling friction:						
On absolute level	2,080	2,175	2,215	2,340	2,565	3,095
" ½ per cent grade = $26\frac{4}{10}$ feet per mile	795	835	850	895	985	1,185
" 1 " " = $52\frac{8}{10}$ " " "	480	505	515	545	595	720
" 2 " " = $105\frac{6}{10}$ " " "	260	270	275	290	320	390
" 3 " " = $158\frac{4}{10}$ " " "	170	180	185	190	210	255

The **Rule for Calculation** of Hauling Capacity at all rates of resistance of rolling friction and on any practicable grade is given on page 140.

For quick approximate calculation of Hauling Capacity on any practicable grade, and with resistance of rolling friction of $6\frac{1}{2}$ to 40 pounds per ton, refer to **Tables of Percentages** on **pages 156 and 157**.

For quick selection of suitable weight locomotive for stated load, grade and resistance of rolling friction, refer to **Tables I, II, III and IV**, on pages 162 to 169. These tables are also useful for quick comparison of loads that can be handled by locomotives of different weights.

Light Six-Wheel-Connected Saddle-Tank Locomotive, Class C-S

Wide or Narrow Gauge

ILLUSTRATION No. 22, from photograph of 8 x 14 cylinders, coal-burning locomotive, 30 inches gauge of track, plantation service, exported to Japan.

SIX SIZES, each with code word, are described on the opposite page, subject to modifications of details to suit gauge, fuel, size of locomotive, and requirements or preferences of customers. We are prepared to build additional sizes. The rear and center driving wheels are connected by side equalizers. A cross equalizer is placed at the front driving wheels. The center tires are flangeless. The three larger sizes have horizontal cylinders. Hanging step-boards may be used at front and rear. Memo. The above illustration shows height slightly reduced to accommodate head-room and the bell is concealed by the stack and head-light. (See illustration, page 71.) See page 10 for general specifications and pages 11 and 12 for choice of stacks.

For larger sizes see next page.

Correspondents are Requested to Designate Locomotives by Code Word

CODE WORD	KLONAS	KLOTHO	KLUCHS	KLUWEN	KNALOE	KOBANG
Cylinders { diameter, inches	6	7	8	9	10	11
{ stroke, inches	10	12	14	14	14	14
Diameter of driving wheels, inches	18	22	24	26	28	28
Wheel-base, feet and inches	4-10	5-2	5-6	5-10	7-3	7-8
Length over bumpers, feet and inches	13-6	14-9	15-6	16-9	18-0	20-6
Extreme height (head-room not limited), feet and inches	9-4	9-6	10-0	10-0	10-3	10-8
Weight in working order, all on driving wheels, pounds	15,000	19,000	24,500	29,500	34,000	41,000
Water capacity of saddle-tank, gallons	175	250	300	400	500	600
Fuel capacity { coal, pounds	300	350	400	450	600	800
{ wood, cubic feet	25	30	32	35	40	45
Weight per yard of lightest rail advised, pounds	12	14	16	20	25	30
Radius of sharpest curve advised, feet	40	50	55	60	80	90
Radius of sharpest curve practicable, feet	25	30	35	40	60	70
Boiler pressure per square inch, pounds	160	160	160	160	160	160
Tractive force, pounds	2,715	3,640	5,070	5,925	6,800	8,230
Hauling Capacity, in tons of 2,000 pounds (exclusive of locomotive), 6½ pounds per ton resistance of rolling friction:						
On absolute level	405	550	765	895	1,025	1,245
" ½ per cent grade = $26\tfrac{4}{10}$ feet per mile	155	210	295	340	395	475
" 1 " " = $52\tfrac{8}{10}$ " " "	90	125	175	205	235	285
" 2 " " = $105\tfrac{6}{10}$ " " "	50	65	95	110	125	155
" 3 " " = $158\tfrac{4}{10}$ " " "	30	40	60	70	80	100

The **Rule for Calculation of Hauling Capacity** at all rates of resistance of rolling friction and on any practicable grade is given on page 140.

For quick approximate calculation of Hauling Capacity on any practicable grade, and with resistance of rolling friction of 6½ to 40 pounds per ton, refer to **Tables of Percentages** on pages 156 and 157.

For quick selection of suitable weight locomotive for stated load, grade and resistance of rolling friction, refer to **Tables I, II, III and IV**, on **pages 162 to 169**. These tables are also useful for quick comparison of loads that can be handled by locomotives of different weights.

Six-Wheel-Connected Saddle-Tank Locomotive, Class C-S

Wide or Narrow Gauge

ILLUSTRATION NO. 23, from photograph of 15 x 20 cylinders, coal-burning locomotive, 56½ inches gauge of track, for mine railway in California.

ELEVEN SIZES, each with code word, are described on the opposite page, subject to modification of details to suit gauge, fuel, size of locomotive, and requirements or preferences of customers. We are prepared to build additional sizes. Double guides are seldom used except for the larger sizes. The rear and center driving wheels are connected by side equalizers. A cross equalizer is placed at the front driving wheels. The center tires are flangeless. See page 10 for general specifications and pages 11 and 12 for choice of stacks.

For smaller sizes see preceding page

Correspondents are Requested to Designate Locomotives by Code Word

CODE WORD	KOATOO	KOBELL	KOBENS	KOBOLD	KODATA	KODROS	KOEDEK	KOEGES	KOETER	KOEPUS	KOEPOK
Cylinders { diameter, inches	10	11	12	12	13	14	14	15	15	16	16
{ stroke, inches	16	16	16	18	18	20	21	20	24	20	24
Diameter of driving wheels, inches	30	31	33	34	36	40	45	40	46	42	46
Wheel-base, feet and inches	7-8	8-1	8-1	9-0	9-10	10-6	11-0	10-6	11-0	11-0	11-0
Length over bumpers, feet and inches	20-6	21-0	21-6	22-0	23-6	25-0	26-6	27-6	28-6	28-0	29-0
Extreme height (head-room not limited), ft..in.	10-3	10-9	11-2	11-6	12-0	12-6	12-9	12-9	13-2	13-2	13-8
Weight in working order, all on driving wheels, pounds	38,500	43,500	49,500	55,000	61,000	71,000	78,000	83,000	87,000	94,000	106,000
Water capacity of saddle-tank, gallons	600	600	700	750	800	900	950	1,025	1,025	1,100	1,200
Fuel capacity { coal, pounds	800	1,000	1,100	1,200	1,300	1,400	1,600	1,800	1,800	2,000	2,200
{ wood, cubic feet	45	45	50	50	55	60	65	70	70	60	75
Weight per yard of lightest rail advised, lb	25	30	30	35	40	45	50	50	55	60	60
Radius of sharpest curve advised, feet	90	100	100	125	150	170	180	170	180	180	180
Radius of sharpest curve practicable, feet	70	85	85	110	135	145	160	145	160	160	160
Boiler pressure per square inch, pounds	165	165	165	165	165	165	170	175	175	180	180
Tractive force, pounds	7,480	8,750	9,790	10,090	11,850	13,740	15,445	16,735	17,400	18,650	20,435
Hauling Capacity, in tons of 2,000 pounds (exclusive of locomotive), 6½ pounds per ton resistance of rolling friction:											
On absolute level	1,130	1,320	1,480	1,615	1,790	2,085	2,345	2,530	2,640	2,820	3,000
" ½ per cent grade = 26 4/10 feet per mile	430	505	570	620	685	800	900	970	1,015	1,080	1,185
" 1 " " = 52 8/10 " " "	260	305	340	375	415	485	545	585	615	655	720
" 2 " " = 105 6/10 " " "	140	165	185	200	225	260	290	315	330	350	385
" 3 " " = 158 4/10 " " "	90	105	120	130	145	170	190	210	215	230	255

The **Rule for Calculation of Hauling Capacity** at all rates of resistance of rolling friction and on any practicable grade is given on page 140.

For quick approximate calculation of Hauling Capacity on any practicable grade, and with resistance of rolling friction of 6½ to 40 pounds per ton, refer to **Tables of Percentages** on pages 156 and 157.

For quick selection of **suitable weight locomotive** for stated load, grade and resistance of rolling friction, refer to **Tables I, II, III and IV**, on pages 162 to 169. These tables are also useful for quick comparison of loads that can be handled by locomotives of different weights.

Eight-Wheel-Connected Saddle-Tank Locomotive, Class D-S
Wide or Narrow Gauge

ILLUSTRATION No. 60, from photograph of 10 x 14 cylinders, coal-burning locomotive, meter gauge, for plantation service, exported to the **West Indies**.

NINE SIZES, each with **code word**, are described on the opposite page, subject to modifications of details to suit gauge, fuel, size of locomotive, and requirements or preferences of customers. We are prepared to build additional sizes. The driving wheels are equalized. The two center pairs are flangeless. The cylinders of all the sizes described are usually placed horizontal. Larger sizes have bell on tank instead of left side of stack. See page 10 for general specifications and pages 11 and 12 for choice of stacks.

Correspondents are Requested to Designate Locomotives by Code Word

CODE WORD	KOOOOO	KOOMAN	KOOLEE	KOOZEN	KOPJES	KOPTEN	KORKUD	KORNIS	KORNHOF
Cylinders { diameter, inches	9	10	11	12	13	14	15	16	17
{ stroke, inches	14	14	14	14	16	18	18	20	20
Diameter of driving wheels, inches	25	26	27	29	31	34	36	42	42
Wheel-base, feet and inches	7-6	8-0	8-6	9-0	9-8	10-6	11-3	11-10	13-0
Length over bumpers, feet and inches	18-6	19-0	21-0	22-6	24-0	25-6	27-0	28-6	32-0
Extreme height (head-room not limited), ft. and in.	9-6	9-10	10-6	11-0	11-6	12-0	12-6	13-0	13-6
Weight in working order, all on driving wheels, lb	31,000	36,000	46,000	50,000	65,000	78,000	87,000	96,000	106,000
Water capacity of saddle-tank, gallons	400	500	600	700	800	900	1,050	1,200	1,300
Fuel capacity { coal, pounds	800	1,000	1,200	1,500	1,800	2,000	2,500	3,500	4,000
{ wood, cubic feet	25	30	35	40	45	50	60	80	90
Weight per yard of lightest rail advised, pounds	16	16	20	25	30	35	40	45	50
Radius of sharpest curve advised, feet	90	100	110	125	140	160	170	175	200
Radius of sharpest curve practicable, feet	70	80	90	110	120	140	150	155	180
Boiler pressure per square inch, pounds	160	160	170	170	175	175	180	180	180
Tractive force, pounds	6,170	7,330	9,065	10,045	12,975	15,435	17,210	18,650	21,055
Hauling Capacity, in tons of 2,000 pounds (exclusive of locomotive), 6½ pounds per ton resistance of rolling friction:									
On absolute level	930	1,110	1,370	1,515	1,960	2,335	2,600	2,820	3,185
" ½ per cent grade = 26 4/10 feet per mile	355	425	525	580	750	895	995	1,080	1,220
" 1 " " " = 52 8/10 " "	215	255	315	350	455	540	605	655	740
" 2 " " " = 105 6/10 " "	115	135	170	190	245	290	325	350	400
" 3 " " " = 158 4/10 " "	75	90	110	125	160	190	215	230	260

The **Rule for Calculation of Hauling Capacity** at all rates of resistance of rolling friction and on any practicable grade is given on page 140.

For quick approximate calculation of Hauling Capacity on any practicable grade, and with resistance of rolling friction of 6½ to 40 pounds per ton, refer to **Tables of Percentages** on pages 156 and 157.

For **quick selection of suitable weight locomotive** for stated load, grade and resistance of rolling friction, refer to **Tables I, II, III and IV**, on pages 162 to 169. These tables are also useful for quick comparison of loads that can be handled by locomotives of different weights.

Light Four-Wheel-Connected Saddle-Tank Open-Canopy Locomotive, Class B-S-K

Wide or Narrow Gauge

ILLUSTRATION No. 38, from photograph of 7 x 12 cylinders, coal-burning locomotive, 30 inches gauge, for plantation service, exported to Porto Rico.

EIGHT SIZES, each with code word, are described on the opposite page, subject to modifications of details to suit gauge, fuel, size of locomotive, and requirements or preferences of customers. We are prepared to build additional sizes. A cross equalizer is placed at the front driving wheels. The cylinders of the two larger sizes are placed horizontal, and saddle-tank extended forward surrounding the stack and the dome forward coming through the tank. The bumper hand-holds as shown are unusual style. See page 10 for general specifications and pages 11 and 12 for choice of stacks.

Correspondents are Requested to Designate Locomotives by Code Word

CODE WORD	KORREL	KORRIN	KORTAF	KORTOM	KORZEC	KOSEST	KOSMAS	KOTHIG
Cylinders { diameter, inches	5	5½	5	6	7	8	9	10
{ stroke, inches	8	8	10	10	12	14	14	14
Diameter of driving wheels, inches	20	20	20	20	24	26	27	30
Wheel-base, feet and inches	3-6	3-6	4-0	4-0	4-8	5-0	4-6	4-6
Length over bumpers, feet and inches	10-6	10-6	11-0	11-6	12-9	14-0	16-10	17-0
Height (head-room not limited), feet and inches	9-0	9-0	9-4	9-6	9-8	9-10	9-10	10-0
Weight in working order all on driving wheels, pounds	8,500	9,500	11,000	14,000	17,500	23,500	28,500	32,000
Water capacity of saddle-tank, gallons	100	100	125	150	200	250	400	500
Fuel capacity { coal, pounds	175	175	200	200	250	300	350	450
{ wood, cubic feet	15	15	15	18	20	20	25	25
Weight per yard of lightest rail advised, pounds	12	12	14	16	16	20	25	30
Radius of sharpest curve advised, feet	25	25	30	30	35	35	40	40
Radius of sharpest curve practicable, feet	15	15	15	15	16	18	20	18
Boiler pressure per square inch, pounds	160	160	160	160	160	160	165	160
Tractive force, pounds	1,360	1,645	1,700	2,445	3,330	4,680	5,890	6,350
Hauling Capacity, in tons of 2,000 pounds (exclusive of locomotive), 6½ pounds per ton resistance of rolling friction:								
On absolute level	200	245	255	365	500	705	890	960
" ½ per cent grade = 26 4/10 feet per mile	75	90	95	140	190	270	340	365
" 1 " " = 52 8/10 " " "	45	50	55	85	115	165	205	220
" 2 " " = 105 6/10 " " "	20	25	30	40	60	85	110	115
" 3 " " = 158 4/10 " " "	14	16	18	25	40	55	70	75

The **Rule for Calculation** of Hauling Capacity at all rates of resistance of rolling friction and on any practicable grade is given on page 140.

For quick approximate calculation of Hauling Capacity on any practicable grade, and with resistance of rolling friction of 6½ to 40 pounds per ton, refer to **Tables of Percentages** on pages **156 and 157**.

For quick selection of **suitable weight locomotive** for stated load, grade and resistance of rolling friction, refer to **Tables I II, III and IV**, on pages **162 to 169**. These tables are also useful for quick comparison of loads that can be handled by locomotives of different weights.

Four-Wheel-Connected Locomotive with Saddle-Tank (or Rear Tanks) without Cab, Class B-S-O or B-RR-O

For Mill or Industrial Service. Wide or Narrow Gauge

ILLUSTRATION No. 40, from photograph of 6 x 10 cylinders coal-burning, saddle-tank locomotive, 36 inches gauge, for light work in steel mill.

EIGHT SIZES, each with code word, are described on the opposite page, subject to modifications of details to suit gauge, fuel, size of locomotive, clearances, and requirements or preferences of customers. We are prepared to build additional sizes. A cross equalizer is placed at the front driving wheels. The cylinders of the two larger sizes may be placed horizontal. For limited head-room the stack, dome, etc., may be made flush with the tank like Class B-Mine, pages 106 and 107. For extra narrow gauges the wheel-base is shortened and the frames stopped off in front of full-width straight-sides firebox. The two larger sizes usually have the tank extended forward surrounding the stack and the dome placed forward coming up through the tank. Two rear tanks, one each side, may be used, but are not suitable for extreme narrow gauges. See page 10 for general specifications and pages 11 and 12 for choice of stacks.

Correspondents are Requested to Designate Locomotives by Code Word

CODE WORD { with saddle-tank, like Illustration No. 40...... { with rear side-tanks, like Illustration No. 34, page 86.	KOULER KRIPPE	KOUMIS KRISMO	KOUSSO KRITIK	KRABAT KRODDE	KRABBE KROKUS	KRAWAR KRONIA	KREITS KRONOS	KRESSE KROTON
Cylinders { diameter, inches............	5	5½	5	6	7	8	9	10
{ stroke, inches...............	8	8	10	10	12	14	14	14
Diameter of driving wheels, inches...........	20	20	20	20	24	26	27	30
Wheel-base, feet and inches............	3–6	3–6	4–0	4–0	4–8	5–0	4–6	4–6
Length over bumpers, feet and inches............	9–8	9–8	10–0	11–0	12–0	13–6	16–10	17–0
Height (head-room not limited), feet and inches......	8–0	8–0	8–2	8–4	8–8	9–0	9–0	9–6
Weight in working order on driving wheels, pounds......	8,500	9,500	11,000	13,500	17,000	23,000	28,000	31,500
Water capacity of saddle-tank, gallons...........	100	100	125	150	200	250	400	500
Coal-bunker capacity, pounds............	150	175	150	150	200	250	350	450
Weight per yard of lightest rail advised, pounds......	12	12	12	14	16	20	25	30
Radius of sharpest curve advised, feet............	20	25	30	30	35	35	40	35
Radius of sharpest curve practicable, feet...........	15	15	15	15	16	18	20	16
Boiler pressure per square inch, pounds...........	160	160	160	160	160	160	165	160
Tractive force, pounds............	1,360	1,645	1,700	2,445	3,330	4,680	5,890	6,350
Hauling Capacity, in tons of 2000 pounds (exclusive of locomotive) 6½ pounds per ton resistance of rolling friction:								
On absolute level............	200	245	255	365	500	705	890	960
" ½ per cent grade = 26 4/10 feet per mile	75	90	95	140	190	270	340	365
" 1 " " = 52 8/10 " " "	45	50	55	85	115	165	205	220
" 2 " " = 105 6/10 " " "	20	25	30	40	60	85	110	115
" 3 " " = 158 4/10 " " "	14	16	18	25	40	55	70	75

The **Rule for Calculation** of Hauling Capacity at all rates of resistance of rolling friction and on any practicable grade is given on page 140.

For quick approximate calculation of Hauling Capacity on any practicable grade, and with resistance of rolling friction of 6½ to 40 pounds per ton, refer to **Tables of Percentages** on pages **156 and 157**.

For quick selection of suitable weight locomotive for stated load, grade and resistance of rolling friction, refer to **Tables I, II, III and IV**, on pages **162 to 169**. These tables are also useful for quick comparison of loads that can be handled by locomotives of different weights.

Coke-Oven Locomotive Four-Wheel-Connected, Class B-S-I

Usually for Wide Gauge

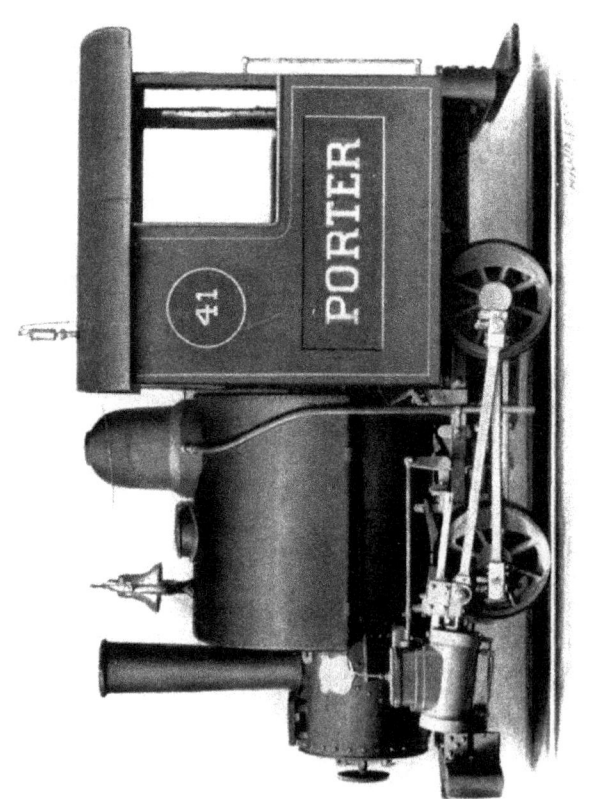

ILLUSTRATION No. 41, from photograph of 7 x 12 cylinders, 56½ inches gauge locomotive, for coke-oven service.

FIVE SIZES, each with **code word**, are described on the opposite page, subject to modifications of details to suit gauge, size of locomotive, clearances, and requirements or preferences of customers. We are prepared to build larger or smaller sizes. A cross equalizer is placed at the front driving wheels. The cylinders of the two larger sizes are horizontal. The cab is of steel, partly closed at sides, with rear entrance, and small windows front and rear. The height may be reduced for limited head-room. See page 10 for general specifications.

Correspondents are Requested to Designate Locomotives by Code Word

CODE WORD	KRYPTE	KUBBEN	KUBIEK	KUCHEN	KUECHE
Cylinders { diameter, inches	6	7	8	9	10
{ stroke, inches	10	12	14	14	14
Diameter of driving wheels, inches	20	24	26	27	28
Wheel-base, feet and inches	4–0	4–8	5–0	4–6	4–6
Length over bumpers, feet and inches	11–6	12–9	14–0	16–10	17–0
Height (head-room not limited), feet and inches	9–6	9–8	9–10	9–10	10–0
Weight in working order, all on driving wheels, pounds	15,000	18,000	24,000	29,000	33,000
Water capacity of saddle-tank, gallons	150	200	250	400	500
Coal-bunker capacity, pounds	200	250	250	350	450
Weight per yard of lightest rail advised, pounds	16	20	25	25	30
Radius of sharpest curve advised, feet	30	35	40	50	35
Radius of sharpest curve practicable, feet	16	18	22	25	18
Boiler pressure per square inch, pounds	160	160	160	165	160
Tractive force, pounds	2,445	3,330	4,680	5,890	6,800
Hauling Capacity, in tons of 2,000 pounds (exclusive of locomotive), 6½ pounds per ton resistance of rolling friction:					
On absolute level	365	500	705	890	1,025
" ½ per cent grade = 26$\frac{4}{11}$ feet per mile	140	190	270	340	395
" 1 " " = 52$\frac{7}{10}$ " " "	80	115	165	205	235
" 2 " " = 105$\frac{6}{10}$ " " "	40	60	85	110	125
" 3 " " = 158$\frac{4}{10}$ " " "	25	40	55	70	85

The **Rule for Calculation** of Hauling Capacity at all rates of resistance of rolling friction and on any practicable grade is given on page 140.

For **quick approximate calculation** of Hauling Capacity on any practicable grade, and with resistance of rolling friction of 6½ to 40 pounds per ton, refer to **Tables of Percentages** on **pages 156 and 157**.

For **quick selection of suitable weight locomotive** for stated load, grade and resistance of rolling friction, refer to **Tables I, II, III and IV**, on **pages 162 to 169**. These tables are also useful for quick comparison of loads that can be handled by locomotives of different weights.

Light Steel-Works Four-Wheel-Connected Saddle-Tank Locomotive, Class B-S-1

Wide or Narrow Gauge

ILLUSTRATION No. 67, from photograph of 10 x 14 cylinders, steel-works locomotive, full height, 30 inches gauge of track, with stopped-off main frames and cross-brace tie-plate connection to rear frames, and full-width straight-sides firebox.

SEVEN SIZES each with code word are described on the opposite page, subject to modifications of details to suit gauge, clearances, size of locomotive, and requirements or preferences of customers. We are prepared to build additional sizes. A cross equalizer is placed at the front driving wheels. The cylinders of the four smaller sizes are slightly inclined. The cab is of steel and practically no wood is used in construction. The three larger sizes are constructed with tank extended forward and with dome, coming up through tank. For limited side-room the cylinder flanges are flattened. For limited head-room the stack, dome, and other parts are made flush with the tank and the height may be like Class B-Mine, pages 106 and 107 (see also page 84). For wide gauges the frames are continuous. Guide-shields or side-aprons may be used if desired. See page 110 for general specifications.

For larger sizes see next page.

PITTSBURGH PA

Correspondents are Requested to Designate Locomotives by Code Word

CODE WORD	KUENDEN	KUERBIS	KUGEL	KUHLAUS	KUHMIST	KUIFHEN	KUKANG
Cylinders { diameter, inches	5	6	7	8	9	10	11
{ stroke, inches	10	10	12	14	14	14	14
Diameter of driving wheels, inches	20	20	24	26	27	28	30
Wheel-base, feet and inches	4-0	4-0	4-8	5-0	4-6	4-6	4-6
Length over bumpers, feet and inches	11-0	11-6	12-0	14-0	16-10	17-0	18-0
Extreme height above rail (head-room not limited), feet and inches	9-4	9-6	9-8	9-10	9-10	10-0	10-2
Extreme height, with cab, stack, etc., flush with top of tank, feet and inches	5-3	5-6	6-3	6-8½	6-9	7-3½	7-7
Weight in working order, all on driving wheels, pounds	11,000	14,000	17,500	24,000	29,000	32,500	39,000
Water capacity of saddle-tank, gallons	125	150	200	250	400	500	600
Coal-bunker capacity, pounds	200	200	250	250	350	450	500
Weight of lightest rail advised, pounds	16	16	20	25	25	30	35
Radius of sharpest curve advised, feet	25	30	35	40	50	35	40
Radius of sharpest curve practicable, feet	16	16	18	22	25	18	20
Boiler pressure per square inch, pounds	160	160	160	160	165	160	160
Tractive force, pounds	1,700	2,445	3,330	4,680	5,890	6,800	7,680

Hauling Capacity, in tons of 2,000 pounds (exclusive of locomotive).
6½ pounds per ton resistance of rolling friction:

	KUENDEN	KUERBIS	KUGEL	KUHLAUS	KUHMIST	KUIFHEN	KUKANG
On absolute level	255	365	500	705	890	1,025	1,160
½ per cent grade = 26 4/10 feet per mile	95	140	190	270	340	395	445
1 " " = 52 8/10 " "	55	80	115	165	205	235	270
2 " " = 105 6/10 " "	30	40	60	85	110	125	145
3 " " = 158 10/10 " "	19	25	40	55	70	85	95

The **Rule for Calculation of Hauling Capacity** at all rates of resistance of rolling friction and on any practicable grade is given on page 140.
For **quick approximate calculation of Hauling Capacity** on any practicable grade, and with resistance of rolling friction of 6½ to 40 pounds per ton, refer to **Tables of Percentages** on pages 156 and 157.
For **quick selection of suitable weight locomotive** for stated load, grade and resistance of rolling friction, refer to **Tables I, II, III and IV**, on pages 162 to 169. These tables are also useful for quick comparison of loads that can be handled by locomotives of different weights.

Heavy Steel-Works Four-Wheel-Connected Saddle-Tank Locomotive, Class B-S-1

Wide or Narrow Gauge

ILLUSTRATION No. 68, from photograph of 16 x 20 cylinders, steel-works locomotive, 10 ft. 10 in. height, 36 inches gauge of track, with stopped-off main frames and cross-brace tie-plate connection to rear frames, and full-width straight-sides firebox.

ELEVEN SIZES, each with **code word**, are described on the opposite page, subject to modifications of details to suit gauge, clearances, size of locomotive, and requirements or preferences of customers. We are prepared to build larger sizes. A cross equalizer is placed at the front driving wheels. The cab is of steel and practically no wood is used in construction. The tank is extended forward surrounding the stack and the dome comes up through the tank. For limited side-room the cylinder flanges are flattened. For limited head-room the stack, dome, and other parts are made flush with the tank. For unlimited head room the general appearance is like Illustration No. 67, page 82. Single-bar guides are used for the smaller sizes. For wide gauges the frames are continuous. Side-aprons covering the machinery below the tank may be used. See page 10 for general specifications.

For smaller sizes see preceding page.

Correspondents are Requested to Designate Locomotives by Code Word

CODE WORD	KUISCH	KUKUPA	KULPIS	KUMBUK	KUMTIC	KUNBIT	KUNKEL	KUNST	KUNVIM	KUNWIX	KUPDRA
Cylinders { diameter, inches	10	11	12	12	13	14	14	15	15	16	16
{ stroke, inches	16	16	16	18	16	18	20	20	24	20	24
Diameter of driving wheels, inches	30	31	33	36	33	36	38	42	46	42	46
Wheel-base, feet and inches	5–0	5–0	5–0	5–9	5–0	5–9	6–3	6–3	7–0	6–3	7–0
Length over bumpers, feet and inches	18–3	18–6	19–0	19–6	21–0	21–0	21–9	24–0	25–2	24–2	27–6
Extreme height above rail (head-room not limited), feet and inches	10–0	10–9	11–3	11–3	11–6	12–0	12–0	12–9	13–2	13–2	13–8
Extreme height, with cab, stack, etc., flush with top of saddle-tank, feet and inches	7–4½	8–2	8–8	8–8½	8–10½						
Weight in working order, all on driving wheels, pounds	36,500	42,500	48,000	52,000	57,000	70,000	72,000	80,000	85,000	96,000	101,000
Water capacity of tank, gallons	600	600	700	750	800	1,000	1,000	1,200	1,200	1,200	1,200
Coal-bunker capacity, pounds	500	600	800	750	750	850	850	1,000	1,000	1,000	1,000
Weight per yard of lightest rail advised, lb	35	40	45	45	50	50	56	60	70	80	80
Radius of sharpest curve advised, feet	40	40	40	50	45	50	55	60	70	60	85
Radius of sharpest curve practicable, feet	20	20	20	25	25	30	35	40	45	40	65
Boiler pressure per square inch, pounds	160	160	160	165	165	170	170	170	170	180	180
Tractive force, pounds	7,250	8,480	9,495	10,110	11,490	14,170	14,905	15,480	16,960	18,650	20,435
Hauling Capacity, in tons of 2,000 pounds (exclusive of locomotive). 6½ pounds per ton resistance of rolling friction:											
On absolute level	1,095	1,280	1,435	1,525	1,740	2,145	2,255	2,340	2,565	2,820	3,000
" ½ per cent grade = 26 4/10 feet per mile	420	490	550	585	665	820	865	895	985	1,080	1,185
" 1 " " = 52 8/10 " "	255	295	330	355	405	495	525	540	595	655	720
" 2 " " = 105 6/10 " "	135	160	180	190	215	265	280	290	320	350	390
" 3 " " = 158 4/10 " "	90	105	120	125	145	175	185	190	210	230	255

The **Rule for Calculation of Hauling Capacity** at all rates of resistance of rolling friction and on any practicable grade is given on page 140.

For quick approximate calculation of Hauling Capacity on any practicable grade, and with resistance of rolling friction of 6½ to 40 pounds per ton, refer to **Tables of Percentages** on pages 156 and 157.

For quick selection of suitable weight locomotive for stated load, grade and resistance of rolling friction, refer to **Tables I, II, III and IV**, on pages 162 to 169. These tables are also useful for quick comparison of loads that can be handled by locomotives of different weights.

Light Plantation and Industrial Locomotive Four-Wheel-Connected with Rear Tanks and Canopy, Class B-RR-K

Wide or Narrow Gauge

ILLUSTRATION No. 34, from photograph of 7 x 12 cylinders, wood-burning locomotive, 36 inches gauge of track, for industrial tramway, exported to Mexico.

EIGHT SIZES, each with **code word**, are described on the opposite page, subject to modifications to suit gauge, fuel, size of locomotive, and requirements or preferences of customers. We are prepared to build additional sizes. A cross equalizer is placed at the front driving wheels. The canopy is of steel. The water is carried in two tanks, one each side, at the rear. The engineer's seat is on the right and the fuel bunker on the left. The cylinders of the two larger sizes are horizontal. For extreme narrow gauges involving shorter wheel-base and stopped-off frames the tanks are placed farther forward. See page 10 for general specifications and pages 11 and 12 for choice of stacks.

Correspondents are Requested to Designate Locomotives by Code Word

CODE WORD	KUPFER	KUPLOT	KUPPEL	KURDEN	KURHUT	KURIOS	KURSIV	KURZAB
Cylinders { diameter, inches	5	5½	5	6	7	8	9	10
{ stroke, inches	8	8	10	10	12	14	14	14
Diameter of driving wheels, inches	20	20	20	20	24	26	27	30
Wheel-base, feet and inches	3-6	3-6	4-0	4-0	4-8	5-0	4-6	4-6
Length over bumpers, feet and inches	9-8	9-8	10-6	11-4	12-7	13-10	16-10	17-0
Extreme height (head-room not limited), feet and inches	8-0	8-0	9-4	9-6	9-8	9-10	9-10	10-0
Weight in working order on driving wheels, pounds	8,500	9,500	11,000	13,500	17,000	23,000	28,500	31,500
Water capacity of rear tanks, gallons	75	100	100	125	150	200	250	300
Fuel capacity { coal, pounds	120	175	125	150	150	200	250	300
{ wood, cubic feet	7	12	10	10	12	15	18	20
Weight per yard of lightest rail advised, pounds	12	12	12	14	16	20	25	30
Radius of sharpest curve advised, feet	25	25	30	30	35	40	50	40
Radius of sharpest curve practicable, feet	15	15	16	16	18	22	25	20
Boiler pressure per square inch, pounds	160	160	160	160	160	160	165	160
Tractive force, pounds	1,360	1,645	1,700	2,445	3,330	4,680	5,890	6,350
Hauling Capacity, in tons of 2,000 pounds (exclusive of locomotive), 6½ pounds per ton resistance of rolling friction:								
On absolute level	200	245	255	365	500	705	890	960
½ per cent grade = 26 4/10 feet per mile	75	90	95	140	190	270	340	365
1 " " " = 52 8/10 " " "	45	50	55	85	115	165	205	220
2 " " " = 105 6/10 " " "	20	25	30	40	60	85	110	115
3 " " " = 158 4/10 " " "	14	16	19	25	40	55	70	75

The **Rule for Calculation** of Hauling Capacity at all rates of resistance of rolling friction and on any practicable grade is given on page 140.

For quick approximate calculation of Hauling Capacity on any practicable grade, and with resistance of rolling friction of 6½ to 40 pounds per ton, refer to **Tables of Percentages** on pages 156 and 157.

For quick selection of suitable weight locomotive for stated load, grade and resistance of rolling friction, refer to **Tables I, II, III and IV**, on pages 162 to 169. These tables are also useful for quick comparison of loads that can be handled by locomotives of different weights.

Plantation and Industrial Saddle-Tank Locomotive Six-Wheel-Connected with Canopy, Class C-S-K

Wide or Narrow Gauge

ILLUSTRATION No. 72, from photograph of 8 x 14 cylinders, coal-burning locomotive, 30 inches gauge of track, for ore tramway.

NINE SIZES, each with code word, are described on the opposite page, subject to modifications to suit gauge, fuel, size of locomotive, and requirements or preferences of customers. We are prepared to build additional sizes. The rear and center driving wheels are connected by side equalizers A cross equalizer is placed at the front drivers. The center driving wheels are flangeless. Hanging step-boards and hand-holds may be used at both front and rear. The canopy cab is of steel. See page 10 for general specifications and pages 11 and 12 for choice of stacks. The cylinders of all except the three smaller sizes are horizontal.

Correspondents are Requested to Designate Locomotives by Code Word

CODE WORD	PABILO	PACATO	PACCAN	PACHAO	PACIFY	PACTYE	PADRAO	PAEANS	PAEDOR
Cylinders { diameter, inches	6	7	8	9	10	10	11	11	12
{ stroke, inches	10	12	14	14	14	16	14	16	16
Diameter of driving wheels, inches	18	22	24	26	28	30	28	31	33
Wheel-base, feet and inches	4-10	5-2	5-6	5-10	7-3	7-8	7-8	8-1	8-1
Length over bumpers, feet and inches	13-6	14-9	16-0	16-9	18-0	20-4	20-6	21-0	21-0
Extreme height (head-room not limited), ft. and in.	9-4	9-6	10-0	10-0	10-3	10-3	10-9	10-9	11-2
Weight in working order on driving wheels, pounds	15,000	19,000	24,500	29,500	34,000	38,500	41,000	43,500	49,500
Water capacity of saddle-tank, gallons	175	250	300	400	500	600	600	600	700
Fuel capacity { coal, pounds	300	350	400	450	600	800	800	1,000	1,100
{ wood, cubic feet	25	30	32	35	40	45	45	45	50
Weight per yard of lightest rail advised, pounds	12	14	16	20	25	25	30	30	30
Radius of sharpest curve advised, feet	40	50	55	60	80	90	85	100	100
Radius of sharpest curve practicable, feet	25	30	35	40	60	70	60	85	85
Boiler pressure per square inch, pounds	160	160	160	160	160	165	160	165	165
Tractive force, pounds	2,715	3,640	5,070	5,925	6,800	7,480	8,230	8,750	9,790
Hauling Capacity, in tons of 2,000 pounds (exclusive of locomotive), 6½ pounds per ton resistance of rolling friction:									
On absolute level	405	550	765	895	1,025	1,130	1,245	1,320	1,480
" ½ per cent grade = 26 4/10 feet per mile	155	210	295	340	395	430	475	505	570
" 1 " " = 52 8/10 " " "	90	125	175	205	235	260	285	305	340
" 2 " " = 105 6/10 " " "	50	65	95	110	125	140	155	165	185
" 3 " " = 158 4/10 " " "	30	40	60	70	80	90	100	105	120

The **Rule for Calculation** of Hauling Capacity at all rates of resistance of rolling friction and on any practicable grade is given on page 140.

For quick approximate calculation of Hauling Capacity on any practicable grade and with resistance of rolling friction of 6½ to 40 pounds per ton, refer to **Tables of Percentages** on pages 156 and 157.

For quick selection of **suitable weight locomotive** for stated load, grade and resistance of rolling friction, refer to **Tables I, II, III and IV**, on pages 162 to 169. These tables are also useful for quick comparison of loads that can be handled by locomotives of different weights.

Plantation and Industrial Locomotive Four Driving Wheels Back-Truck Rear Tank, Class 2-B-R-K

Wide or Narrow Gauge

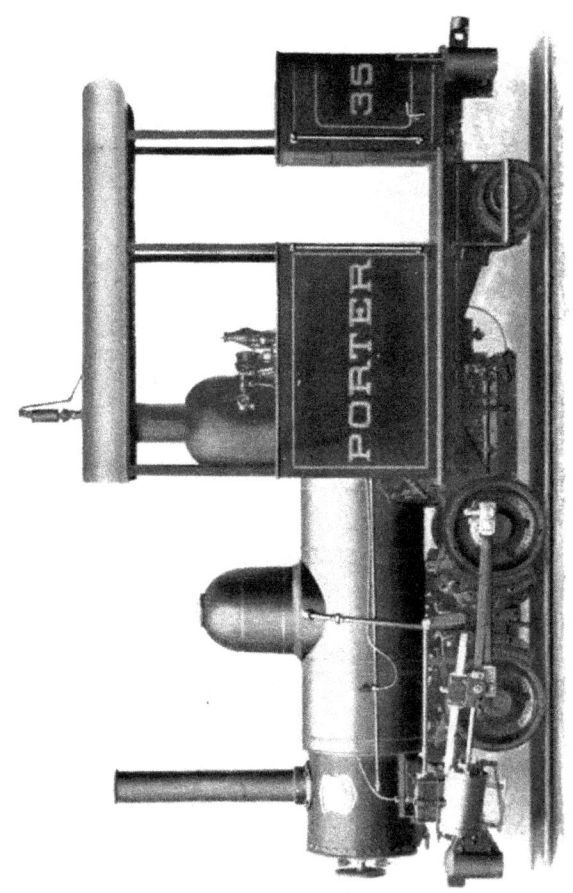

ILLUSTRATION No. 35, from photograph of 5 x 8 cylinders, coal-burning locomotive, 30 inches gauge of track, for plantation, exported to Central America.

ELEVEN SIZES, each with **code word,** are described on the opposite page, subject to modifications to suit gauge, fuel, size of locomotive, and requirements or preferences of customers. We are prepared to build additional sizes. The truck has pivotal, lateral, and radial-bar motion. The driving wheels are connected by side equalizers. The canopy cab is of steel. Cylinders 9 x 14 and larger are horizontal. Hanging step-board and hand-hold front and rear may be used. If narrowness of gauge requires, the frames are stopped off in front of full-width straight-sides firebox. See page 10 for general specifications and pages 11 and 12 for choice of stacks.

Correspondents are Requested to Designate Locomotives by Code Word

CODE WORD	PAENIT	PAEON	PAELEX	PAFLON	PAGLIA	PAIRAR	PAIXAO	PAJARA	PAJOSA	PAKJES	PALAGE
Cylinders { diameter, inches	5	5	6	7	8	9	10	10	11	12	12
{ stroke, inches	8	10	10	12	14	14	14	16	16	16	18
Diameter driving wheels, inches	20	20	22	24	28	30	33	33	36	40	40
Diameter of truck wheels, inches	14	14	14	16	16	18	18	18	22	22	22
Rigid wheel-base, feet and inches	3-0	3-0	3-6	4-0	4-0	4-6	4-6	5-3	5-3	5-9	5-9
Total wheel-base, feet and inches	8-8	9-0	9-7	10-7	11-8	13-4	13-10	14-0	14-6	14-10	15-0
Length over bumpers, feet and inches	14-3	15-3	16-0	17-0	18-3	20-6	22-0	22-10	23-8	24-0	24-4
Height (head-room not limited), feet and inches	9-0	9-2	9-6	9-8	9-10	10-0	10-3	10-6	10-10	11-0	11-2
Weight in working order, pounds	11,500	13,000	16,000	22,500	28,000	33,000	36,000	42,000	47,000	50,000	55,000
Weight on driving wheels, pounds	8,000	9,000	11,000	16,000	20,000	24,500	26,500	30,000	34,000	36,000	40,000
Weight on two-wheel truck, pounds	3,500	4,000	5,000	6,500	8,000	8,500	9,500	12,000	13,000	14,000	15,000
Water capacity of rear tank, gallons	150	200	250	350	400	450	550	600	650	650	750
Fuel capacity { coal, pounds	300	400	750	900	1,000	1,100	1,200	1,400	1,500	1,500	1,500
{ wood, cubic feet	12	14	18	20	25	30	35	40	45	45	50
Weight per yard of lightest rail advised, pounds	10	12	14	16	20	20	25	25	30	30	35
Radius of sharpest curve advised, feet	40	45	55	65	75	95	100	100	105	110	110
Radius of sharpest curve practicable, feet	30	35	40	45	50	65	70	70	80	85	85
Boiler pressure per square inch, pounds	160	160	160	160	160	165	160	160	160	160	160
Tractive force, pounds	1,360	1,700	2,225	3,330	4,350	5,300	5,775	6,585	7,315	7,835	8,820
Hauling Capacity, in tons of 2,000 pounds (exclusive of locomotive). 6½ pounds per ton resistance of rolling friction:											
On absolute level	200	250	330	500	655	800	870	990	1,100	1,180	1,325
" ½ per cent grade = 26 4/10 feet per mile	75	95	125	190	250	305	330	375	420	445	505
" 1 " " = 52 8/10 " " "	45	55	75	110	150	180	200	225	250	270	300
" 2 " " = 105 6/10 " " "	20	30	35	60	75	95	105	120	130	140	160
" 3 " " = 158 4/10 " " "	14	18	25	35	50	60	65	75	85	90	100

The **Rule for Calculation** of Hauling Capacity at all rates of resistance of rolling friction and on any practicable grade is given on page 140.

For **quick approximate calculation** of Hauling Capacity on any practicable grade, and with resistance of rolling friction of 6½ to 40 pounds per ton, refer to **Tables of Percentages** on pages 156 and 157.

For **quick selection of suitable weight locomotive** for stated load, grade and resistance of rolling friction, refer to **Tables I, II, III and IV,** on pages 162 to 169. These tables are also useful for quick comparison of loads that can be handled by locomotives of different weights.

Tramway and Plantation "Forney" Locomotive Four Driving Wheels with Canopy, Class 4-B-R-K

Wide or Narrow Gauge

ILLUSTRATION No. 76, from photograph of 10 x 14 cylinders, coal-burning locomotive, 23⅝ inches gauge, for sugar plantation, exported to West Indies.

NINE SIZES, each with code word, are described on the opposite page, subject to modifications to suit gauge, fuel, size of locomotive, and requirements or preferences of customers. We are prepared to build additional sizes. The driving wheels are connected by side equalizers. The truck has pivotal and lateral motion. The canopy cab is of steel. Hanging step-boards and hand-holds, or pilots, may be used at front and rear. Cylinders 9 x 14 and larger are usually horizontal. If required by narrowness of gauge the frames are stopped off in front of full-width straight-sides firebox as shown by Illustration No. 76. See page 10 for general specifications and pages 11 and 12 for choice of stacks.

Correspondents are Requested to Designate Locomotives by Code Word

CODE WORD	PALCHI	PALMED	PALMON	PALTOS	PANDUR	PANDYA	PANIZO	PANJIL	PANNUM
Cylinders { diameter, inches	6	7	8	9	10	10	11	12	12
{ stroke, inches	10	12	14	14	14	16	16	16	18
Diameter of driving wheels, inches	22	24	28	30	33	33	36	40	40
Diameter of truck wheels, inches	12	14	14	16	18	18	20	22	22
Rigid wheel-base, feet and inches	3–6	4–0	4–0	4–6	4–6	5–3	5–3	5–9	5–9
Total wheel-base (center of front axle to center of truck), feet and inches	10–6	11–6	12–6	13–6	14–0	15–0	15–6	15–9	16–6
Length over bumpers, feet and inches	17–6	18–8	20–0	21–6	22–6	24–2	25–4	29–0	27–0
Extreme height (head-room not limited), ft. and in.	9–6	9–8	9–10	10–0	10–3	10–6	10–10	11–3	11–6
Weight in working order, pounds	17,500	24,500	29,000	34,500	38,000	44,000	49,000	52,000	58,000
Weight on driving wheels, pounds	11,500	16,000	20,000	24,500	26,500	30,000	34,000	36,000	41,000
Weight on four-wheel truck, pounds	6,000	8,500	9,000	10,000	11,500	14,000	15,000	16,000	17,000
Water capacity of rear tank, gallons	300	400	450	550	650	650	700	750	750
Fuel capacity { coal, pounds	750	1,000	1,200	1,600	1,800	1,800	1,800	2,000	2,000
{ wood, cubic feet	20	25	30	35	40	45	50	55	55
Weight per yard of lightest rail advised, pounds	14	16	20	35	25	25	30	30	35
Radius of sharpest curve advised, feet	75	80	85	95	105	115	125	135	135
Radius of sharpest curve practicable, feet	55	65	70	75	80	90	100	115	115
Boiler pressure per square inch, pounds	160	160	160	165	160	160	160	160	160
Tractive force, pounds	2,225	3,330	4,350	5,300	5,775	6,585	7,315	7,835	8,820
Hauling Capacity, in tons of 2,000 pounds (exclusive of locomotive), 6½ pounds per ton resistance of rolling friction:									
On absolute level	330	500	655	800	870	990	1,095	1,180	1,325
" ½ per cent grade = 26 4/10 feet per mile	125	190	245	300	330	375	415	445	505
" 1 " " " = 52 8/10 " " "	75	110	130	180	195	225	250	270	300
" 2 " " " = 105 6/10 " " "	35	55	75	95	105	120	130	140	155
" 3 " " " = 158 4/10 " " "	20	35	50	60	65	75	85	90	100

The **Rule for Calculation** of Hauling Capacity at all rates of resistance of rolling friction and on any practicable grade is given on page 140.

For quick approximate calculation of Hauling Capacity on any practicable grade, and with resistance of rolling friction of 6½ to 40 pounds per ton, refer to **Tables of Percentages** on pages 156 and 157.

For quick selection of **suitable weight locomotive** for stated load, grade and resistance of rolling friction, refer to **Tables I, II, III and IV**, on pages 162 to 169. These tables are also useful for quick comparison of loads that can be handled by locomotives of different weights.

Tramway and Plantation Rear Tank Locomotive Six Driving Wheels Back-Truck with Canopy, Class 2-C-R-K

Wide or Narrow Gauge

ILLUSTRATION No. 78, from photograph of 9 x 14 cylinders, coal-burning locomotive, 36 inches gauge, for sugar plantation.

EIGHT SIZES, each with code word, are described on the opposite page, subject to modifications to suit gauge, fuel, size of locomotive, and requirements or preferences of customers. We are prepared to build additional sizes. The rear and center driving wheels are connected by side equalizers. A cross equalizer is placed at the front driving wheels. The truck has pivotal, lateral and radial-bar motion. The canopy cab is of steel. All except the two smaller sizes have horizontal cylinders. Hanging step-boards with hand-holds may be used at front and rear. See page 10 for general specifications and pages 11 and 12 for choice of stacks.

Correspondents are Requested to Designate Locomotives by Code Word

CODE WORD	PANXIT	PAPION	PAPYRO	PARAMO	PARDON	PARFUM	PARGER	PARRAL
Cylinders } diameter, inches	7	8	9	10	10	11	12	12
Cylinders } stroke, inches	12	14	14	14	16	16	16	18
Diameter of driving wheels, inches	22	26	28	31	31	33	36	36
Diameter of truck wheels, inches	14	16	16	16	18	18	20	20
Rigid wheel-base, feet and inches	5-2	5-6	6-4	7-3	7-8	8-1	8-1	8-1
Total wheel-base, feet and inches	10-4	10-10	12-2	13-5	14-0	14-4	15-2	14-10
Length over bumpers, feet and inches	17-0	17-6	19-9	20-7	21-10	23-0	23-6	23-10
Extreme height (head-room not limited), feet and inches	9-8	9-10	10-0	10-3	10-6	10-10	11-3	11-3
Weight in working order, pounds	23,000	28,000	33,500	37,500	42,500	48,000	52,000	56,000
Weight on driving wheels, pounds	16,500	20,500	25,000	28,000	31,500	36,500	40,000	43,500
Weight on pony truck, pounds	6,500	7,500	8,500	9,500	11,000	11,500	12,000	12,500
Water capacity of rear tank, gallons	400	450	550	650	650	700	800	800
Fuel capacity } coal, pounds	1,000	1,200	1,600	1,700	1,700	1,800	2,000	2,000
Fuel capacity } wood, cubic feet	20	25	30	35	40	40	45	45
Weight per yard of lightest rail advised, pounds	14	16	16	20	20	25	25	30
Radius of sharpest curve advised, feet	55	65	80	90	100	110	110	115
Radius of sharpest curve practicable, feet	45	55	70	80	90	95	95	100
Boiler pressure per square inch, pounds	160	160	160	160	160	160	160	160
Tractive force, pounds	3,640	4,680	5,500	6,140	7,015	7,970	8,710	9,800

Hauling Capacity, in tons of 2,000 pounds (exclusive of locomotive), 6½ pounds per ton resistance of rolling friction:

	PANXIT	PAPION	PAPYRO	PARAMO	PARDON	PARFUM	PARGER	PARRAL
On absolute level	545	705	825	925	1,055	1,200	1,315	1,480
½ per cent grade = 26 4/10 feet per mile	205	265	315	350	400	455	500	565
1 " " " = 52 8/10 " "	125	160	190	210	240	275	300	340
2 " " " = 105 6/10 " "	65	85	100	110	130	145	160	185
3 " " " = 158 4/10 " "	40	55	65	70	80	95	105	115

The **Rule for Calculation of Hauling Capacity** at all rates of resistance of rolling friction and on any practicable grade is given on page 140.

For quick approximate calculation of Hauling Capacity on any practicable grade, and with resistance of rolling friction of 6½ to 40 pounds per ton, refer to **Tables of Percentages** on **pages 156 and 157.**

For quick selection of suitable weight locomotive for stated load, grade and resistance of rolling friction, refer to **Tables I, II, III and IV,** on pages 162 to 169. These tables are also useful for quick comparison of loads that can be handled by locomotives of different weights.

Plantation Logging and Industrial Saddle-Tank Locomotive Four Driving Wheels
Back-Truck with Canopy, Class 2-B-S-K

Wide or Narrow Gauge

ILLUSTRATION No. 39, from photograph of 6 x 10 cylinders, coal-burning locomotive, 30 inches gauge of track, for sugar plantation in Central America.

NINE SIZES, each with code word, are described on the opposite page, subject to modifications to suit gauge, fuel, size of locomotive, and requirements or preferences of customers. We are prepared to build additional sizes. The driving wheels are connected by side equalizers. The truck has pivotal, lateral, and radial-bar motion. The canopy cab is of steel. Cylinders 9 x 14 and larger are horizontal. Hanging step-boards with hand-holds may be used at front and rear. If required by narrowness of gauge the main frames are stopped off in front of full-width straight-sides firebox. See page 10 for general specifications and pages 11 and 12 for choice of stacks.

Correspondents are Requested to Designate Locomotives by Code Word

CODE WORD	PARSOS	PARTEZ	PARTIJ	PARURE	PARVAS	PASACH	PASEAN	PASEOS	PASIVO
Cylinders { diameter, inches	6	7	8	9	10	10	11	12	12
{ stroke, inches	10	12	14	14	14	16	16	16	18
Diameter of driving wheels, inches	22	24	28	30	33	33	36	38	40
Diameter of truck wheels, inches	14	16	16	18	20	20	20	22	22
Rigid wheel-base, feet and inches	3–6	4–0	4–0	4–6	4–6	5–3	5–3	5–9	5–9
Total wheel-base, feet and inches	9–7	10–8	11–8	12–2½	12–2½	13–4	13–9	14–0	14–0
Length over bumpers, feet and inches	16–6	17–0	18–3	19–6	21–0	21–6	22–0	22–6	22–6
Height (head-room not limited), feet and inches	9–6	9–8	9–10	10–0	10–3	10–6	10–10	11–4	11–4
Weight in working order, pounds	15,500	21,500	27,000	32,000	35,500	41,000	45,000	49,000	53,000
Weight on driving wheels, pounds	11,500	16,500	21,000	25,000	28,000	33,000	36,500	40,500	44,000
Weight on two-wheel truck, pounds	4,000	5,000	6,000	7,000	7,500	8,000	8,500	8,500	9,000
Water capacity of saddle-tank, gallons	150	200	250	400	500	600	600	700	750
Fuel capacity { coal, pounds	500	600	700	800	900	1,000	1,200	1,400	1,500
{ wood, cubic feet	25	30	35	40	45	50	55	60	65
Weight per yard of lightest rail advised, pounds	14	16	20	25	25	30	30	35	40
Radius of sharpest curve advised, feet	60	70	80	90	90	95	100	100	100
Radius of sharpest curve practicable, feet	45	50	55	60	60	65	70	70	70
Boiler pressure per square inch, pounds	160	160	160	160	160	160	160	160	160
Tractive force, pounds	2,225	3,330	4,350	5,135	5,775	6,585	7,315	8,245	8,820
Hauling Capacity, in tons of 2,000 pounds (exclusive of locomotive), 6½ pounds per ton resistance of rolling friction:									
On absolute level	330	500	655	775	870	990	1,100	1,240	1,330
" ½ per cent grade = 26.4 feet per mile	125	190	250	295	330	375	420	475	505
" 1 " " = 52.8 " " "	75	115	150	175	200	225	250	285	305
" 2 " " = 105.6 " " "	40	60	80	95	105	120	130	150	160
" 3 " " = 158.4 " " "	25	40	50	60	65	75	85	100	105

The **Rule for Calculation** of Hauling Capacity at all rates of resistance of rolling friction and on any practicable grade is given on page 140.

For quick approximate calculation of Hauling Capacity on any practicable grade, and with resistance of rolling friction of 6½ to 40 pounds per ton, refer to **Tables of Percentages** on pages 156 and 157.

For quick selection of suitable weight locomotive for stated load, grade and resistance of rolling friction, refer to **Tables I, II, III and IV**, on pages 162 to 169. These tables are also useful for quick comparison of loads that can be handled by locomotives of different weights.

Tramway Plantation and Logging Saddle-Tank Locomotive Four Driving Wheels Four-Wheel Back-Truck with Canopy, Class 4-B-S-K

Wide or Narrow Gauge

ILLUSTRATION No. 50, from photograph of 7 x 12 cylinders, wood-burning locomotive, 23¾ inches gauge of track, for phosphate mine tramway.

NINE SIZES, each with **code word**, are described on the opposite page, subject to modifications to suit gauge, fuel, size of locomotive, and requirements or preferences of customers. We are prepared to build additional sizes. The driving wheels are connected by side equalizers. The truck has pivotal and lateral motion. The canopy cab is of steel. Cylinders 9 x 14 and larger are horizontal. If required by narrowness of gauge the main frames are stopped off in front of full-width straight-sides firebox. Hanging step-boards and hand-holds may be used at both front and rear. See page 10 for general specifications and pages 11 and 12 for choice of stacks.

Correspondents are Requested to Designate Locomotives by Code Word

CODE WORD	PATRON	PATUDO	PAUCOS	PAUVRE	PAVANA	PAVEAM	PAWNOR	PAWPAW	PAYANT
Cylinders { diameter, inches	6	7	8	9	10	10	11	12	12
{ stroke, inches	10	12	14	14	14	16	16	16	18
Diameter of driving wheels, inches	22	24	28	30	33	33	36	38	40
Diameter of truck wheels, inches	14	14	14	16	18	18	20	22	22
Rigid wheel-base, feet and inches	3–6	4–0	4–0	4–6	4–6	5–3	5–3	5–9	5–9
Total wheel-base (center of front axle to center of truck), feet and inches	10–6	11–3	12–0	12–8	13–0	14–6	15–0	15–6	15–6
Length over bumpers, feet and inches	17–6	18–8	19–4	20–8	21–6	22–6	23–10	24–6	25–0
Height (head-room not limited), ft. and in.	9–6	9–8	9–10	10–0	10–3	10–6	10–10	11–4	11–6
Weight in working order, pounds	17,000	24,000	29,000	33,500	37,000	42,500	47,000	52,000	56,000
Weight on driving wheels, pounds	12,000	16,500	21,000	25,000	28,000	33,000	37,000	41,000	44,000
Weight on four-wheel truck, pounds	5,000	7,500	8,000	8,500	9,000	9,500	10,000	11,000	12,000
Water capacity of saddle tank, gallons	200	300	350	400	500	600	650	700	750
Fuel capacity { coal, pounds	600	700	800	1,000	1,200	1,500	2,000	2,000	2,500
{ wood, cubic feet	30	35	40	45	50	60	65	65	70
Weight per yard of lightest rail advised, pounds	14	16	20	25	25	30	30	35	40
Radius of sharpest curve advised, feet	75	80	85	95	105	115	125	125	135
Radius of sharpest curve practicable, feet	55	65	70	75	80	90	100	100	110
Boiler pressure per square inch, pounds	160	160	160	160	160	160	160	160	170
Tractive force, pounds	2,225	3,330	4,350	5,135	5,775	6,585	7,315	8,245	8,820
Hauling Capacity, in tons of 2,000 pounds (exclusive of locomotive), 6½ pounds per ton resistance of rolling friction:									
On absolute level	330	500	650	770	870	990	1,100	1,240	1,325
" ½ per cent grade = 26 4/10 feet per mile	125	190	250	295	330	375	420	470	505
" 1 " " = 52 8/10 " " "	75	110	150	175	200	225	250	280	300
" 2 " " = 105 6/10 " " "	35	55	80	90	105	120	130	150	160
" 3 " " = 158 4/10 " " "	20	35	50	60	65	75	85	95	100

The **Rule for Calculation** of Hauling Capacity at all rates of resistance of rolling friction and on any practicable grade is given on page 140.

For quick approximate calculation of Hauling Capacity on any practicable grade, and with resistance of rolling friction of 6½ to 40 pounds per ton, refer to **Tables of Percentages** on pages 156 and 157.

For quick selection of suitable weight locomotive for stated load, grade and resistance of rolling friction, refer to **Tables I, II, III and IV**, on pages 162 to 169. These tables are also useful for quick comparison of loads that can be handled by locomotives of different weights.

Tramway Logging and Plantation Saddle-Tank Locomotive Six Driving Wheels Back-Truck with Canopy, Class 2-C-S-K

Wide or Narrow Gauge

ILLUSTRATION No. 84, from photograph of 8 x 14 cylinders, coal-burning locomotive, 36 inches gauge of track, for sugar plantation in Louisiana.

SEVEN SIZES, each with code word, are described on the opposite page, subject to modifications to suit gauge, fuel, size of locomotive, and requirements or preferences of customers. We are prepared to build additional sizes. The rear and center driving wheels are connected by side equalizers. A cross equalizer is placed at the front driving wheels. The truck has pivotal, lateral, and radial-bar motion. The canopy cab is of steel. Hanging step-boards and hand-holds may be used at front and rear. Cylinders 9 x 14 and larger are horizontal. See page 10 for general specifications and pages 11 and 12 for choice of stacks.

Correspondents are Requested to Designate Locomotives by Code Word

CODE WORD	PAYASO	PAYENS	PAYEUR	PAYNIM	PAZADA	PEAHEN	PEATON
Cylinders { diameter, inches	7	8	9	10	10	11	12
{ stroke, inches	12	14	14	14	16	16	16
Diameter of driving wheels, inches	23	28	28	30	31	33	36
Diameter of truck wheels, inches	16	16	16	16	16	18	20
Rigid wheel-base, feet and inches	5-2	5-5	5-10	7-3	7-8	8-1	8-1
Total wheel-base, feet and inches	9-10	10-6	11-5	12-6	13-4	13-9	13-9
Length over bumpers, feet and inches	16-6	17-0	18-8	19-5	20-8	22-0	22-8
Extreme height (head-room not limited), feet and inches	9-8	9-10	10-0	10-3	10-6	10-10	11-3
Weight in working order, pounds	22,000	27,000	32,500	38,000	41,000	47,000	50,000
Weight on driving wheels, pounds	17,500	22,000	27,000	31,500	34,500	40,000	42,500
Weight on pony truck, pounds	4,500	5,000	5,500	6,500	6,500	7,000	7,500
Water capacity of saddle-tank, gallons	300	350	400	500	600	600	700
Fuel capacity { coal, pounds	400	600	700	800	1,000	1,200	1,300
{ wood, cubic feet	25	30	35	40	45	50	55
Weight per yard of lightest rail advised, pounds	14	16	20	20	25	25	30
Radius of sharpest curve advised, feet	50	55	65	80	85	90	90
Radius of sharpest curve practicable, feet	45	50	55	65	75	80	80
Boiler pressure per square inch, pounds	160	160	160	160	160	160	160
Tractive force, pounds	3,480	4,350	5,500	6,350	7,015	7,970	8,710
Hauling Capacity, in tons of 2,000 pounds (exclusive of locomotive), 6½ pounds per ton resistance of rolling friction:							
On absolute level	520	655	830	955	1,055	1,200	1,315
" ½ per cent grade = 26.4 feet per mile	200	245	315	365	400	455	500
" 1 " " = 52.8 " " "	120	150	190	220	240	275	300
" 2 " " = 105.6 " " "	60	75	100	115	130	145	160
" 3 " " = 158.4 " " "	40	50	65	75	80	95	105

The **Rule for Calculation** of Hauling Capacity at all rates of resistance of rolling friction and on any practicable grade is given on page 140.
For quick approximate calculation of Hauling Capacity on any practicable grade, and with resistance of rolling friction of 6½ to 40 pounds per ton, refer to **Tables of Percentages** on **pages 156 and 157**.
For quick selection of suitable weight locomotive for stated load, grade and resistance of rolling friction, refer to **Tables I, II, III and IV**, on **pages 162 to 169**. These tables are also useful for quick comparison of loads that can be handled by locomotives of different weights.

Four-Wheel-Connected Noiseless Steam Street Motor, Class B-R-M

Wide or Narrow Gauge

ILLUSTRATION No. 32, from photograph of 9 x 14 cylinders motor, 56½ inches gauge of track.

NINE SIZES, each with code word, are described on the opposite page, subject to modifications to suit gauge, size of motor, and requirements or preferences of customers. We are prepared to build additional sizes. These motors are not constructed to carry passengers, but to haul cars. The fuel is anthracite coal or coke, to avoid smoke; and the motor is equipped with muffled exhaust. The side flaps may be omitted. The cab has windows to let down and the engineer has good outlook in all directions and easy control of all valves and levers. See page 10 for general specifications.

Correspondents are Requested to Designate Locomotives by Code Word

CODE WORD	PELEON	PELLAO	PELTES	PELVIS	PELZEN	PEPIGI	PERADA	PEREZA	PERIGO
Cylinders { diameter, inches	6	7	8	9	10	11	12	14	15
{ stroke, inches	10	12	14	14	14	16	18	20	24
Diameter of driving wheels, inches	20	24	26	27	30	31	36	40	46
Wheel-base, feet and inches	4–0	4–8	5–0	5–3	4–6	5–3	5–9	6–3	7–0
Length over bumpers, feet and inches	12–0	13–0	14–0	15–6	17–6	18–8	20–0	23–0	25–0
Extreme height above rail, feet and inches	10–2	10–2	10–6	10–9	10–11	11–6	11–10	12–2	12–9
Weight in working order, all on driving wheels, lb	15,000	18,000	24,000	29,000	33,000	42,000	52,000	70,000	85,000
Water capacity of rear tank, gallons	125	200	250	325	400	600	750	900	1,000
Fuel capacity, pounds	200	250	300	350	450	650	850	1,000	1,200
Radius of sharpest curve advised, feet	25	30	30	35	35	40	45	55	65
Boiler pressure per square inch, pounds	160	160	160	165	160	160	165	165	170
Tractive force, pounds	2,445	3,330	4,680	5,890	6,350	8,480	10,110	13,740	16,960
Hauling Capacity, in tons of 2,000 pounds (exclusive of locomotive), 6½ pounds per ton resistance of rolling friction:									
On absolute level	365	500	705	890	960	1,280	1,525	2,080	2,565
" ½ per cent grade = 26 4/10 feet per mile	140	190	270	340	365	490	585	795	985
" 1 " " " = 52 8/10 " " "	85	115	160	205	220	295	355	480	595
" 2 " " " = 105 6/10 " " "	40	60	85	110	115	160	190	260	320
" 3 " " " = 158 4/10 " " "	25	40	55	70	75	105	125	170	210

The **Rule for Calculation of Hauling Capacity** at all rates of resistance of rolling friction and on any practicable grade is given on page 140.

For quick approximate calculation of Hauling Capacity on any practicable grade, and with resistance of rolling friction of 6½ to 40 pounds per ton, refer to **Tables of Percentages** on pages 156 and 157.

For quick selection of suitable weight locomotive for stated load, grade and resistance of rolling friction, refer to **Tables I, II, III and IV**, on pages 162 to 169. These tables are also useful for quick comparison of loads that can be handled by locomotives of different weights.

Back-Truck Four-Driver Noiseless Steam Street Motor, Class 2-B-R-M

Wide or Narrow Gauge

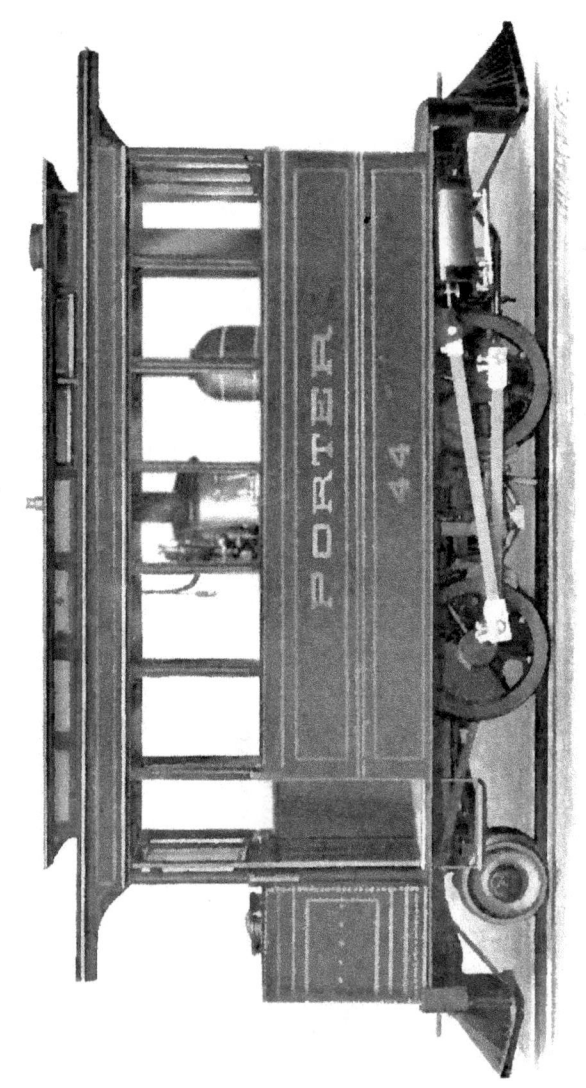

ILLUSTRATION No. 44, from photograph of 10 x 14 cylinders motor, 56½ inches gauge of track.

EIGHT SIZES, each with code word, are described on the opposite page, subject to modifications to suit gauge, size of motor, and requirements or preferences of customers. We are prepared to build additional sizes. These motors are not constructed to carry passengers, but to haul cars. The fuel is anthracite coal or coke, to avoid smoke; and the motor is equipped with muffled exhaust. Side flaps may be used to conceal the machinery. The cab has windows to let down and the engineer has good outlook in all directions and easy control of all valves and levers. See page 10 for general specifications.

Correspondents are Requested to Designate Locomotives by Code Word

CODE WORD	PESONS	PETALE	PETEUS	PETRIR	PEWITS	PEZUNA	PIAFAR	PICAZA
Cylinders } diameter, inches	7	8	9	10	11	12	14	15
stroke, inches	12	14	14	14	16	18	20	24
Diameter of driving wheels, inches	24	30	30	33	36	40	46	50
Diameter of truck wheels, inches	14	18	18	20	22	22	26	26
Rigid wheel-base, feet and inches	4–0	4–0	4–6	4–6	5–3	5–9	6–3	7–0
Total wheel-base, feet and inches	9–0	9–8	10–11	10–11	12–6	14–0	15–0	17–0
Length over bumpers, feet and inches	14–4	16–6	18–0	19–3	22–0	23–6	26–6	29–0
Extreme height above rail, feet and inches	10–4	10–8	10–10	11–0	11–6	12–0	12–4	13–0
Weight in working order, pounds	23,000	28,500	33,500	36,500	48,000	56,000	71,000	90,000
Weight on drivers (rear-tank design), pounds	16,000	20,000	24,500	26,500	34,500	40,500	54,000	72,000
Weight on pony truck (rear-tank design), pounds	7,000	8,500	9,000	10,000	13,500	15,500	17,000	18,000
Water capacity of rear tank, gallons	200	300	325	400	600	750	900	1,000
Fuel capacity, pounds	250	300	350	450	600	750	900	1,000
Radius of sharpest curve advised, feet	35	40	45	50	55	60	75	90
Boiler pressure per square inch, pounds	160	160	160	160	160	160	165	170
Tractive force, pounds	3,330	4,055	5,135	5,775	7,315	8,820	11,950	15,600
Hauling Capacity, in tons of 2,000 pounds (exclusive of locomotive), 6½ pounds per ton resistance of rolling friction:								
On absolute level	500	610	770	870	1,100	1,325	1,800	2,355
½ per cent grade = 26 4⁄10 feet per mile	190	230	290	330	420	505	685	900
1 " " " = 52 8⁄10 " " "	110	140	175	200	250	300	415	540
2 " " " = 105 6⁄10 " " "	60	70	90	105	130	160	220	290
3 " " " = 158 4⁄10 " " "	35	45	60	65	85	100	140	190

The **Rule for Calculation** of Hauling Capacity at all rates of resistance of rolling friction and on any practicable grade is given on page 140.

For quick approximate calculation of Hauling Capacity on any practicable grade, and with resistance of rolling friction of 6½ to 40 pounds per ton, refer to **Tables of Percentages** on pages 156 and 157.

For **quick selection of suitable weight locomotive** for stated load, grade and resistance of rolling friction, refer to **Tables I, II, III** and **IV**, on pages 162 to 169. These tables are also useful for quick comparison of loads that can be handled by locomotives of different weights.

Four-Wheel-Connected Steam Mine Locomotive, Class B-Mine
Wide or Narrow Gauge

ILLUSTRATION No. 30, from photograph of 10 x 14 cylinders locomotive, 44 inches gauge of track, 5 ft. 6 in. height.

THIRTEEN SIZES, each with code word, are described on the opposite page, subject to modifications to suit gauge, clearances, size of locomotive, and requirements or preferences of customers. We are prepared to build additional sizes. A cross equalizer is placed at the front driving wheels. The cab is of steel and of shape to suit clearances. For extra limited side room the cylinder flanges are flattened or the width may be further decreased by modification in construction. For sake of dry steam, draft of stack, and engineer's comfort the locomotive should not be lower height than the entry compels. Two inches clearance to the mine roof is sufficient. For extreme narrow gauges the main frames are stopped off in front of full-width straight-sides firebox. By special modification of designs we can construct to heights less than given on the opposite page. The 9 x 14 cylinders may be horizontal or slightly inclined; larger cylinders than 9 x 14 are horizontal. See page 10 for general specifications.

NOTE.—FOR COMPRESSED-AIR MINE LOCOMOTIVES see our Catalogue of **COMPRESSED-AIR HAULAGE.**

Correspondents are Requested to Designate Locomotives by Code Word

CODE WORD	PICHOT	PICNIC	PIDAIS	PIENSO	PIESMA	PIEZIS	PIGARO	PIGUIT	PIJROK	PILADO	PILORI	PIMARD	PIMARIC
Cylinders { diameter, inches	5	5	6	7	8	9	10	10	11	11	12	13	14
{ stroke, inches	8	10	10	12	14	14	14	16	14	16	16	16	18
Diameter of driving wheels, inches	18	20	20	23	26	28	30	30	30	31	33	33	36
Wheel-base, feet and inches	3-0	3-6	4-0	4-0	4-0	4-6	4-6	5-3	4-6	5-3	5-9	6-3	6-3
Length over bumpers, feet and inches	10-0	10-10	11-7	14-4	14-9	16-6	16-9	18-0	17-9	18-4	19-6	21-6	22-0
Excess of width at cylinders over gauge of track, feet and inches	1-11¼	2-1½	2-1½	2-3⅜	2-5¼	2-7⅜	2-9⅞	2-11¼	3-0	3-0⅜	3-1⅞	3-6¼	3-8⅛
Height above rail least desirable, ft. and in	4-10	5-0	5-2	5-4	5-7	5-9	5-11	6-1	6-3	6-4	6-6	7-0	8-6
Height above rail least practicable, without change of patterns, feet and inches	4-4	4-6	4-7	4-9	5-0	5-3	5-5	5-6	5-8½	5-9	6-0	6-6	7-9
Weight in working order, pounds	8,500	11,000	14,000	17,500	24,000	27,500	32,000	36,000	39,000	42,000	47,000	56,000	66,000
Capacity of saddle-tank, gallons	80	100	125	200	250	300	400	500	500	500	600	700	800
Weight per yard of lightest rail advised, lb	12	14	16	20	20	25	30	35	35	40	45	50	60
Radius of sharpest curve advised, feet	20	22	25	25	25	30	30	35	30	35	45	50	60
Radius of sharpest curve practicable, feet	12	12	15	15	15	16	16	20	16	20	25	30	50
Boiler pressure per square inch, pounds	160	160	160	160	160	160	160	160	160	160	160	160	160
Tractive force, pounds	1,510	1,700	2,445	3,480	4,680	5,500	6,350	7,250	7,680	8,480	9,495	11,150	13,330
Hauling Capacity, in tons of 2,000 pounds (exclusive of locomotive), 6½ pounds per ton resistance of rolling friction:													
On absolute level	225	255	365	525	705	830	960	1,095	1,160	1,280	1,435	1,685	2,015
" ½ per cent grade = 26 4/10 ft. per mile	85	95	140	200	270	315	365	420	445	490	550	645	775
" 1 " " = 52 8/10 " "	50	55	85	120	165	190	220	255	265	295	330	390	470
" 2 " " = 105 6/10 " "	25	30	45	65	85	100	115	135	145	160	175	210	250
" 3 " " = 158 4/10 " "	15	19	30	40	55	65	75	90	95	105	115	135	165

The **Rule** for Calculation of Hauling Capacity at all rates of resistance of rolling friction and on any practicable grade is given on **page 140**.

For **quick approximate** calculation of Hauling Capacity on any practicable grade, and with resistance of rolling friction of 6½ to 40 pounds per ton, refer to **Tables of Percentages** on **pages 156 and 157**.

For **quick selection of suitable weight** locomotive for stated load, grade and resistance of rolling friction, refer to **Tables I, II, III and IV**, on **pages 162 to 169**. These tables are also useful for quick comparison of loads that can be handled by locomotives of different weights.

Six-Wheel-Connected Steam Mine Locomotive, Class C-Mine

Wide or Narrow Gauge

ILLUSTRATION No. 28, from photograph of 10 x 16 cylinders locomotive, 36 inches gauge of track, 6 ft. height.

NINE SIZES, each with code word, are described on the opposite page, subject to modifications to suit gauge, clearances, size of locomotive, and requirements or preferences of customers. We are prepared to build additional sizes. The rear and center driving wheels are connected by side equalizers. A cross equalizer is placed at the front driving wheels. The cab is of steel and of shape to suit clearances. For extra limited side room the cylinder flanges are flattened. For sake of dry steam, draft of stack, and engineer's comfort the locomotive should not be lower height than the entry compels. Two inches clearance to the mine roof is sufficient. For extreme narrow gauges the main frames are stopped off in front of full-width straight-sides firebox. By special modification of designs we can construct to heights less than given on the opposite page. See page 10 for general specifications.

NOTE.— FOR COMPRESSED-AIR MINE LOCOMOTIVES see our Catalogue of COMPRESSED-AIR HAULAGE.

Correspondents are Requested to Designate Locomotives by Code Word

CODE WORD	PIMPAO	PINCHO	PINHAO	PINNES	PINOLE	PINSON	PIOPPO	PIORNO	PIPAGE
Cylinders { diameter, inches	6	7	8	9	10	11	12	13	14
{ stroke, inches	10	12	14	14	14	14	16	16	18
Diameter of driving wheels, inches	18	22	24	26	28	28	33	33	36
Wheel-base, feet and inches	4-8	4-8	5-0	5-0	5-6	6-3	7-0	7-6	8-6
Length over bumpers, feet and inches	12-6	13-1	14-7	17-0	18-0	19-0	21-0	21-10	24-0
Excess of width at cylinders over gauge of track, feet and inches	2-1½	2-3⅜	2-5¼	2-7⅜	2-9⅞	3-0⅜	3-1⅞	3-6¼	3-8⅛
Height above rail least desirable, feet and inches	5-0	5-4	5-9	6-0	6-3	6-7	6-8	7-0	8-0
Height above rail least practicable, feet and inches	4-6	5-0	5-4	5-7	5-9	5-11	6-0	6-3	6-10
Weight in working order, pounds	15,000	19,000	24,500	29,000	34,000	42,000	49,000	57,000	68,000
Capacity of saddle-tank, gallons	175	200	275	325	400	500	600	750	900
Weight per yard of lightest rail advised, pounds	12	16	16	20	25	25	30	35	45
Radius of sharpest curve advised, feet	30	30	45	45	50	55	65	75	100
Radius of sharpest curve practicable, feet	20	20	25	30	35	40	50	55	75
Boiler pressure per square inch, pounds	160	160	160	160	160	160	165	165	165
Tractive force, pounds	2,715	3,640	5,070	5,925	6,800	8,230	9,790	11,490	13,740
Hauling Capacity, in tons of 2,000 pounds (exclusive of locomotive). 6½ pounds per ton resistance of rolling friction:									
On absolute level	405	550	765	895	1,025	1,245	1,480	1,740	2,075
" ½ per cent grade = 26 4/10 feet per mile	155	210	295	335	395	475	565	665	795
" 1 " " = 52 8/10 " " "	90	125	175	205	235	285	340	405	480
" 2 " " = 105 6/10 " " "	50	65	95	110	125	155	185	215	260
" 3 " " = 158 4/10 " " "	30	40	60	70	85	100	120	145	170

The **Rule for Calculation** of Hauling Capacity at all rates of resistance of rolling friction and on any practicable grade is given on page 140.

For quick approximate calculation of Hauling Capacity on any practicable grade, and with resistance of rolling friction of 6½ to 40 pounds per ton, refer to **Tables of Percentages** on pages **156 and 157**.

For quick selection of suitable weight locomotive for stated load, grade and resistance of rolling friction, refer to **Tables I, II, III and IV**, on pages 162 to 169. These tables are also useful for quick comparison of loads that can be handled by locomotives of different weights.

Light Plantation and Industrial Four-Wheel-Connected Locomotive with Side Tanks, Class B-SS

Wide or Narrow Gauge

ILLUSTRATION No. 59, from photograph of 10 x 16 cylinders coal-burning locomotive, 30 inches gauge of track, with main frames stopped off and full-width straight-sides firebox, for coal-mine tramway.

EIGHT SIZES, each with **code word**, are described on the opposite page, subject to modifications to suit gauge, fuel, size of locomotive, and requirements or preferences of customers. We are prepared to build additional sizes. A cross equalizer is placed at the front driving wheels. The side tanks have connecting pipe. All except the two larger sizes have cylinders slightly inclined. Unless required by narrowness of gauge the frames are continuous. See page 10 for general specifications and pages 11 and 12 for choice of stacks.

For larger sizes see next page.

Correspondents are Requested to Designate Locomotives by Code Word

CODE WORD	PULQUE	PULROD	PTLSOS	PULVER	PUNCTA	PUNDIT	PUNGIR	PUNIAN
Cylinders { diameter, inches	5	5½	5	6	7	8	9	10
{ stroke, inches	8	8	10	10	12	14	14	14
Diameter of driving wheels, inches	20	20	20	20	24	20	27	30
Wheel-base, feet and inches	3-6	3-6	4-0	4-0	4-0	4-6	4-6	4-6
Length over bumpers, feet and inches	10-6	10-6	11-0	11-6	12-0	14-0	16-10	17-0
Extreme height (head-room not limited), feet and inches	9-0	9-0	9-4	9-6	9-8	9-10	9-10	10-0
Weight in working order, all on driving wheels, pounds	8,500	9,500	11,000	14,000	17,500	24,000	29,000	32,000
Water capacity of side tanks, gallons	100	100	125	150	200	250	400	500
Fuel capacity { coal, pounds	175	175	200	200	250	250	300	350
{ wood, cubic feet	25	25	30	30	35	35	40	40
Weight per yard of lightest rail advised, pounds	12	12	14	16	16	20	25	30
Radius of sharpest curve advised, feet	25	25	30	30	35	35	35	35
Radius of sharpest curve practicable, feet	15	15	15	15	16	18	18	18
Boiler pressure per square inch, pounds	160	160	160	160	160	160	165	160
Tractive force, pounds	1,360	1,645	1,700	2,445	3,330	4,680	5,890	6,350
Hauling Capacity, in tons of 2,000 pounds (exclusive of locomotive), 6½ pounds per ton resistance of rolling friction:								
On absolute level	200	245	255	365	500	705	890	960
" ½ per cent grade = 26 4/10 feet per mile	75	90	95	140	190	270	340	365
" 1 " " " = 52 8/10 " " "	45	50	55	85	115	165	205	220
" 2 " " " = 105 6/10 " " "	20	25	30	40	60	85	110	115
" 3 " " " = 158 4/10 " " "	14	16	19	25	40	55	70	75

The **Rule for Calculation** of Hauling Capacity at all rates of resistance of rolling friction and on any practicable grade is given on page 140.

For quick approximate calculation of Hauling Capacity on any practicable grade, and with resistance of rolling friction of 6½ to 40 pounds per ton, refer to **Tables of Percentages** on **pages 156 and 157**.

For quick selection of suitable weight locomotive for stated load, grade and resistance of rolling friction, refer to **Tables I, II, III and IV**, on pages 162 to 169. These tables are also useful for quick comparison of loads that can be handled by locomotives of different weights.

Plantation and Industrial Four-Wheel-Connected Locomotive with Side Tanks, Class B-SS

Wide or Narrow Gauge

ILLUSTRATION No. 59, from photograph of 10 x 16˝ cylinders, coal-burning locomotive, 30 inches gauge of track, with main frames stopped off and full-width straight-sides firebox, for coal-mine tramway.

NINE SIZES, each with code word, are described on the opposite page, subject to modifications to suit gauge, fuel, size of locomotive, and requirements or preferences of customers. We are prepared to build additional sizes. A cross equalizer is placed at the front driving wheels. The side tanks have connecting pipe. For wide gauges the frames are continuous. See page 10 for general specifications and pages 11 and 12 for choice of stacks.

For smaller sizes see preceding page.

Correspondents are Requested to Designate Locomotives by Code Word

CODE WORD	PURFLE	PURELY	PURGOR	PURIFY	PURSUE	PURSANE	PUSCAE	PUTABO	PUTLOG
Cylinders { diameter, inches	10	11	11	12	12	13	14	14	15
{ stroke, inches	16	14	16	16	18	18	20	24	24
Diameter of driving wheels, inches	30	30	31	33	36	36	40	45	46
Wheel-base, feet and inches	5–0	4–6	5–0	5–0	5–9	5–9	6–3	7–0	7–0
Length over bumpers, feet and inches	18–3	18–0	18–6	19–0	20–0	21–6	23–0	24–6	25–6
Height, (head-room, not limited), ft. and in.	10–0	10–0	10–9	11–3	11–6	12–0	12–6	12–9	13–2
Weight in working order, all on driving wheels, lb.	36,500	39,000	42,000	47,000	51,000	60,000	69,000	74,000	84,000
Water capacity of side tanks, gallons	600	600	600	700	750	850	900	1,000	1,200
Fuel capacity { coal, pounds	500	500	600	800	800	900	900	900	900
{ wood, cubic feet	30	30	30	35	35	40	40	40	40
Weight per yard of lightest rail advised, pounds	35	40	40	45	45	50	55	60	70
Radius of sharpest curve advised, feet	45	40	45	45	50	60	60	70	70
Radius of sharpest curve practicable, feet	25	20	25	25	30	35	35	40	45
Boiler pressure per square inch, pounds	160	160	160	160	165	165	165	165	170
Tractive force, pounds	7,250	7,680	8,480	9,495	10,110	11,850	13,740	14,660	16,960
Hauling Capacity, in tons of 2,000 pounds (exclusive of locomotive), 6½ pounds per ton resistance of rolling friction:									
On absolute level	1,095	1,160	1,280	1,435	1,525	1,790	2,080	2,215	2,565
" ½ per cent grade = 26 4/10 feet per mile	420	445	490	550	585	685	795	850	985
" 1 " " = 52 8/10 " " "	255	270	295	330	355	415	480	515	595
" 2 " " = 105 10/16 " " "	135	145	160	180	190	225	260	275	320
" 3 " " = 158 4/16 " " "	90	95	105	115	125	145	170	180	210

The **Rule for Calculation** of Hauling Capacity at all rates of resistance of rolling friction and on any practicable grade is given on page 140.

For quick approximate calculation of Hauling Capacity on any practicable grade, and with resistance of rolling friction of 6½ to 40 pounds per ton, refer to **Tables of Percentages** on **pages 156 and 157**.

For quick selection of suitable weight locomotive for stated load, grade and resistance of rolling friction, refer to **Tables I, II, III and IV**, on pages 162 to 169. These tables are also useful for quick comparison of loads that can be handled by locomotives of different weights.

Light Plantation and Industrial Four-Wheel-Connected Locomotive with Side Tanks and Canopy, Class B-SS-K

ILLUSTRATION No. 29, from photograph of 8 x 14 cylinders, coal-burning locomotive, 24 inches gauge of track, with main frames stopped off and full-width straight-sides firebox, for export.

EIGHT SIZES, each with code word, are described on the opposite page, subject to modifications of gauge, fuel, size of locomotive, and requirements or preferences of customers. We are prepared to build additional sizes. A cross equalizer is placed at the front driving wheels. The side tanks have connecting pipe. The canopy cab is of steel. All except the two larger sizes have cylinders slightly inclined. Unless required by narrowness of gauge the frames are continuous. See page 10 for general specifications and pages 11 and 12 for choice of stacks.

For larger sizes see next page.

Correspondents are Requested to Designate Locomotives by Code Word

CODE WORD	PSORIS	PUBAST	PUBERE	PUBLIO	PUCARO	PUCHAR	PUDUER	PUGILO
Cylinders { diameter, inches	5	5½	5	6	7	8	9	10
{ stroke, inches	8	8	10	10	12	14	14	14
Diameter of driving wheels, inches	20	20	20	20	24	26	27	30
Wheel-base, feet and inches	3-6	3-6	4-0	4-0	4-0	4-6	4-6	4-6
Length over bumpers, feet and inches	10-6	10-6	11-0	11-6	12-9	14-0	16-10	17-0
Extreme height (head-room not limited), feet and inches	9-0	9-0	9-4	9-6	9-8	9-10	9-10	10-0
Weight in working order, all on driving wheels, pounds	8,500	9,500	11,000	14,000	17,500	24,000	29,000	32,000
Water capacity of side tanks, gallons	100	100	125	150	200	250	400	500
Fuel capacity { coal, pounds	175	175	200	200	250	250	300	350
{ wood, cubic feet	25	25	30	30	35	35	40	40
Weight per yard of lightest rail advised, pounds	12	12	14	16	16	20	25	30
Radius of sharpest curve advised, feet	25	25	30	30	35	35	35	35
Radius of sharpest curve practicable, feet	15	15	15	15	16	18	18	18
Boiler pressure per square inch, pounds	160	160	160	160	160	160	165	160
Tractive force, pounds	1,360	1,645	1,700	2,445	3,330	4,680	5,890	6,350
Hauling Capacity, in tons of 2,000 pounds (exclusive of locomotive), 6½ pounds per ton resistance of rolling friction:								
On absolute level	200	245	255	365	500	705	890	960
" ½ per cent grade = 26 4/10 feet per mile	75	90	95	140	190	270	340	365
" 1 " " " = 52 8/10 " " "	45	50	55	85	115	165	205	220
" 2 " " " = 105 6/10 " " "	20	25	30	40	60	85	110	115
" 3 " " " = 158 4/10 " " "	14	16	19	25	40	55	70	75

The **Rule for Calculation** of Hauling Capacity at all rates of resistance of rolling friction and on any practicable grade is given on page 140.

For quick approximate calculation of Hauling Capacity on any practicable grade, and with resistance of rolling friction of 6½ to 40 pounds per ton, refer to **Tables of Percentages** on pages 156 and 157.

For quick selection of suitable weight locomotive for stated load, grade and resistance of rolling friction, refer to **Tables I, II, III and IV**, on pages 162 to 169. These tables are also useful for quick comparison of loads that can be handled by locomotives of different weights.

Plantation and Industrial Four-Wheel-Connected Locomotive with Side Tanks and Canopy, Class B-SS-K

ILLUSTRATION No. 29, from photograph of 8 x 14 cylinders, coal-burning locomotive, 24 inches gauge of track, with main frames stopped off and full-width straight-sides firebox, for export.

NINE SIZES, each with **code word**, are described on the opposite page, subject to modifications to suit gauge, fuel, size of locomotive, and requirements or preferences of customers. We are prepared to build additional sizes. A cross equalizer is placed at the front driving wheels. The side tanks have connecting pipe. The cylinders are horizontal instead of inclined. The canopy cab is of steel. For wide gauges the frames are continuous. See page 10 for general specifications and pages 11 and 12 for choice of stacks.

For smaller sizes see preceding page.

Correspondents are Requested to Designate Locomotives by Code Word

CODE WORD	PUNJUM	PUNTAL	PUPIUM	PUPOSA	PUPPET	PIUPUGI	PURAVA	PURCAS	PURCON
Cylinders { diameter, inches	10	11	11	12	12	13	14	14	15
{ stroke, inches	16	14	16	16	18	18	20	24	24
Diameter of driving wheels, inches	30	30	31	33	36	36	40	45	46
Wheel-base, feet and inches	5-0	4-6	5-0	5-0	5-9	5-9	6-3	7-0	7-0
Length over bumpers, feet and inches	18-3	18-0	18-6	19-0	20-0	21-0	23-0	24-6	25-6
Height (head-room not limited), ft. and in.	10-0	10-3	10-9	11-3	11-6	12-0	12-6	12-9	13-2
Weight in working order, all on driving wheels, lb.	36,500	39,000	42,000	47,000	51,000	60,000	69,000	74,000	84,000
Water capacity of side tanks, gallons	600	600	600	700	750	850	900	950	1,025
Fuel capacity { coal, pounds	800	800	1,000	1,100	1,200	1,300	1,400	1,600	1,800
{ wood, cubic feet	30	30	30	35	35	40	45	50	60
Weight per yard of lightest rail advised, pounds	35	35	40	40	45	50	55	60	70
Radius of sharpest curve advised, feet	45	40	45	45	50	60	60	70	70
Radius of sharpest curve practicable, feet	25	20	25	25	30	35	35	40	45
Boiler pressure per square inch, pounds	160	160	160	160	165	165	165	165	170
Tractive force, pounds	7,250	7,680	8,480	9,495	10,110	11,850	13,740	14,660	16,960
Hauling Capacity, in tons of 2,000 pounds (exclusive of locomotive), 6½ pounds per ton resistance of rolling friction:									
On absolute level	1,095	1,160	1,280	1,435	1,525	1,790	2,080	2,215	2,565
" ½ per cent grade = 26 4/10 feet per mile	420	445	490	550	585	685	795	850	985
" 1 " " = 52 8/10 " " "	255	270	295	330	355	415	480	515	595
" 2 " " = 105 6/10 " " "	135	145	160	180	190	225	260	275	320
" 3 " " = 158 4/10 " " "	90	95	105	115	125	145	170	180	210

The **Rule for Calculation of Hauling Capacity** at all rates of resistance of rolling friction and on any practicable grade is given on page 140.

For quick approximate calculation of Hauling Capacity on any practicable grade, and with resistance of rolling friction of 6½ to 40 pounds per ton, refer to **Tables of Percentages** on pages 156 and 157.

For quick selection of suitable weight locomotive for stated load, grade and resistance of rolling friction, refer to **Tables I, II, III and IV**, on pages 162 to 169. These tables are also useful for quick comparison of loads that can be handled by locomotives of different weights.

Light Six-Wheel-Connected Side-Tanks Locomotive, Class C-SS

Wide or Narrow Gauge

ILLUSTRATION No. 56, from photograph of 9 x 14 cylinders, coal-burning locomotive, 29½ inches gauge of track, exported to Russia.

SIX SIZES, each with **code word**, are described on the opposite page, subject to modifications to suit gauge, fuel, size of locomotive, and requirements or preferences of customers. We are prepared to build additional sizes. The rear and center driving wheels are connected by side equalizers. A cross equalizer is placed at the front driving wheels. The center driving wheels are flangeless. The side tanks have connecting pipe. Cylinders 9 x 14 and larger are horizontal. See page 10 for general specifications and pages 11 and 12 for choice of stacks.

For larger sizes see next page.

Correspondents are Requested to Designate Locomotives by Code Word

	PUTPUT PYJAMA	PUTUIT RABATO	PUXADO RABETA	PYCTAM RABIZA	PYGELA RABMAG	PYGMEN RABOTE
Cylinders { diameter, inches	6	7	8	9	10	11
{ stroke, inches	10	12	14	14	14	14
Diameter of driving wheels, inches	18	22	24	26	28	28
Wheel-base, feet and inches	4–10	5–2	5–6	5–10	7–3	7–3
Length over bumpers, feet and inches	13–6	14–9	15–6	16–9	18–9	20–6
Extreme height (head-room not limited), feet and inches	9–4	9–6	10–0	10–0	10–3	10–8
Weight in working order, all on driving wheels, pounds	15,000	19,000	24,500	29,500	34,000	41,000
Water capacity of side tanks, gallons	175	250	300	400	500	600
Fuel capacity { coal, pounds	300	350	400	450	600	800
{ wood, cubic feet	25	30	32	35	40	45
Weight per yard of lightest rail advised, pounds	12	14	16	20	25	30
Radius of sharpest curve advised, feet	40	50	55	60	80	80
Radius of sharpest curve practicable, feet	25	30	35	40	60	60
Boiler pressure per square inch, pounds	160	160	160	160	160	160
Tractive force, pounds	2,715	3,640	5,070	5,925	6,800	8,230
Hauling Capacity, in tons of 2,000 pounds (exclusive of locomotive), 6½ pounds per ton resistance of rolling friction:						
On absolute level	405	550	765	895	1,025	1,245
" ½ per cent grade = 26 4/10 feet per mile	155	210	295	340	395	475
" 1 " " = 52 8/10 " " "	90	125	175	205	235	285
" 2 " " = 105 6/10 " " "	50	65	95	110	125	155
" 3 " " = 158 4/10 " " "	30	40	55	70	80	100

CODE WORD { with cab like Illustration No. 56
{ with open canopy like Illustration No. 29, p. 116

The **Rule for Calculation** of Hauling Capacity at all rates of resistance of rolling friction and on any practicable grade is given on page 140.

For quick approximate calculation of Hauling Capacity on any practicable grade, and with resistance of rolling friction of 6½ to 40 pounds per ton, refer to **Tables of Percentages** on **pages 156 and 157**.

For quick selection of suitable weight locomotive for stated load, grade and resistance of rolling friction, refer to **Tables I, II, III and IV,** on **pages 162 to 169.** These tables are also useful for quick comparison of loads that can be handled by locomotives of different weights.

Six-Wheel-Connected Side-Tanks Locomotive Class C-SS

Wide or Narrow Gauge

ILLUSTRATION No. 56, from photograph of 9 x 14 cylinders, coal-burning locomotive, 29½ inches gauge of track, exported to Russia.

NINE SIZES, each with **code word**, are described on the opposite page, subject to modifications to suit gauge, fuel, size of locomotive, and requirements or preferences of customers. We are prepared to build additional sizes. The rear and center driving wheels are connected by side equalizers. A cross equalizer is placed at the front driving wheels. The center driving wheels are flangeless. The side tanks have connecting pipe. The cylinders are horizontal instead of inclined. See page 10 for general specifications and pages 11 and 12 for choice of stacks.

For smaller sizes see preceding page.

Correspondents are Requested to Designate Locomotives by Code Word

CODE WORD { with cab like Illustration No. 56...... { with open canopy like Illustration No. 29, page 116	RACILY RADIJS	RACIMO RADOUB	RACLON RADREG	RACOMA RADUNT	ADARM AEDAM	RADBOD RAENKE	RADDIA RAERSE	RADCOL RAETAR	RADIER RAETOS
Cylinders { diameter, inches..................	10	11	12	12	13	14	14	15	15
{ stroke, inches.....................	16	16	16	18	18	20	24	20	24
Diameter of driving wheels, inches.............	30	31	33	34	36	40	45	40	46
Wheel-base, feet and inches...................	7-8	8-1	8-1	9-0	9-10	10-6	11-0	10-6	11-0
Length over bumpers, feet and inches...........	20-6	21-0	21-6	22-0	23-6	25-0	26-6	27-6	28-0
Extreme height (head-room not limited), ft. and in.	10-3	10-9	11-6	11-6	12-0	12-6	12-9	12-9	13-2
Weight in working order, all on driving wheels, pounds	38,500	43,500	49,500	55,000	61,000	71,000	78,000	83,000	87,000
Water capacity of side tanks, gallons...........	600	600	700	750	800	900	950	1,025	1,025
Fuel capacity { coal, pounds..................	800	1,000	1,100	1,200	1,300	1,400	1,600	1,800	1,800
{ wood, cubic feet..............	45	45	50	50	55	60	65	70	70
Weight per yard of lightest rail advised, pounds...	25	30	30	35	40	45	50	50	55
Radius of sharpest curve advised, feet..........	90	100	100	125	150	170	180	170	180
Radius of sharpest curve practicable, feet.......	70	85	85	110	135	145	160	145	160
Boiler pressure per square inch, pounds.........	165	165	165	165	165	165	175	175	175
Tractive force, pounds.........................	7,480	8,750	9,790	10,690	11,850	13,740	15,445	16,735	17,460
Hauling Capacity, in tons of 2,000 pounds (exclusive of locomotive), 6½ pounds per ton resistance of rolling friction:									
On absolute level...........................	1,130	1,320	1,480	1,615	1,790	2,075	2,345	2,535	2,640
" ½ per cent grade = 26 4/10 feet per mile	430	505	570	620	685	795	900	970	1,015
" 1 " " = 52 8/10 " " "	260	305	340	375	415	480	545	590	615
" 2 " " = 105 6/10 " " "	140	165	185	200	225	260	290	315	330
" 3 " " = 158 4/10 " " "	90	105	120	130	145	170	190	210	215

The Rule for Calculation of Hauling Capacity at all rates of resistance of rolling friction and on any practicable grade is given on page 140.

For quick approximate calculation of Hauling Capacity on any practicable grade, and with resistance of rolling friction of 6½ to 40 pounds per ton, refer to **Tables of Percentages** on pages 156 and 157.

For quick selection of suitable weight locomotive for stated load, grade and resistance of rolling friction, refer to **Tables I, II, III and IV**, on pages 162 to 169. These tables are also useful for quick comparison of loads that can be handled by locomotives of different weights.

Eight-Wheel-Connected Side-Tanks Locomotive, Class D-SS

Wide or Narrow Gauge

ILLUSTRATION No. 66, from photograph of 14 x 18 cylinders, coal-burning locomotive, 42 inches gauge of track, exported to Japan.

NINE SIZES, each with code word, are described on the opposite page, subject to modifications to suit gauge, fuel, size of locomotive, and requirements or preferences of customers. We are prepared to build additional sizes. The two center pairs are flangeless. The side tanks have connecting pipe. The driving wheels are equalized. See page 10 for general specifications and pages 11 and 12 for choice of stacks.

Correspondents are Requested to Designate Locomotives by Code Word

CODE WORD	RAETOT	RAETRO	RAETUM	RAETWO	RAETZA	RAEVAM	RAEVEL	RAEVOR	RAEVUS
Cylinders { diameter, inches	9	10	11	12	13	14	15	16	17
Cylinders { stroke, inches	14	14	14	14	16	18	18	20	20
Diameter of driving wheels, inches	25	26	27	29	31	34	36	42	42
Wheel-base, feet and inches	7-6	8-0	8-6	9-0	9-8	10-6	11-3	11-10	13-0
Length over bumpers, feet and inches	18-6	19-6	21-0	22-6	24-0	25-6	27-0	28-6	32-0
Height (head-room not limited), ft. and in.	9-6	9-10	10-6	11-0	11-6	12-0	12-6	13-0	13-6
Weight in working order, all on driving wheels, lbs.	31,000	36,000	46,000	50,000	65,000	78,000	87,000	96,000	106,000
Water capacity of side tanks, gallons	400	500	600	700	800	900	1,050	1,200	1,300
Fuel capacity { coal, pounds	800	1,000	1,200	1,500	1,800	2,000	2,500	3,500	4,000
Fuel capacity { wood, cubic feet	25	30	35	40	45	50	60	80	90
Weight per yard of lightest rail advised, pounds	16	16	20	25	30	35	40	45	50
Radius of sharpest curve advised, feet	90	100	110	125	140	160	170	175	200
Radius of sharpest curve practicable, feet	70	80	90	110	120	140	150	155	180
Boiler pressure per square inch, pounds	160	160	170	170	175	175	180	180	180
Tractive force, pounds	6,170	7,330	9,065	10,045	12,975	15,435	17,210	18,650	21,055
Hauling Capacity, in tons of 2,000 pounds (exclusive of locomotive), 6½ pounds per ton resistance of rolling friction:									
On absolute level	930	1,110	1,370	1,515	1,960	2,335	2,600	2,820	3,185
½ per cent grade = 26 4/10 feet per mile	355	425	525	580	750	895	995	1,080	1,220
1 " " = 52 8/10 " "	215	255	315	350	455	540	605	655	740
2 " " = 105 6/10 " "	115	135	170	190	245	290	325	350	400
3 " " = 158 4/10 " "	75	90	110	125	160	190	215	230	260

The **Rule for Calculation** of Hauling Capacity at all rates of resistance of rolling friction and on any practicable grade is given on page 140.

For quick approximate calculation of Hauling Capacity on any practicable grade, and with resistance of rolling friction of 6½ to 40 pounds per ton, refer to **Tables of Percentages** on pages 156 and 157.

For quick selection of suitable weight locomotive for stated load, grade and resistance of rolling friction, refer to **Tables I, II, III and IV**, on pages 162 to 169. These tables are also useful for quick comparison of loads that can be handled by locomotives of different weights.

Light "Back-Truck" Four-Driving-Wheels Side-Tanks Locomotive, Class 2-B-SS

Wide or Narrow Gauge

ILLUSTRATION No. 81, from photograph of 8 x 14 cylinders, coal-burning locomotive, 36 inches gauge of track, exported to Mexico.

SEVEN SIZES, each with code word, are described on the opposite page, subject to modifications to suit gauge, fuel, size of locomotive, and requirements or preferences of customers. We are prepared to build additional sizes. The driving wheels are connected by side equalizers. The truck has pivotal, lateral, and radial-bar motion. The side tanks have connecting pipe. Cylinders 9 x 14 and larger are horizontal. If required by narrowness of gauge the main frames are stopped off in front of full-width straight-sides firebox. See page 10 for general specifications and pages 11 and 12 for choice of stacks.

For larger sizes see next page.

Correspondents are Requested to Designate Locomotives by Code Word

CODE WORD	RAFAEL	RAGOUT	RAGUET	RAIDIR	RAIGAS	RAIVAR	RAJPUT
Cylinders { diameter, inches	5	5	6	7	8	9	10
{ stroke, inches	8	10	10	12	14	14	14
Diameter of driving wheels, inches	20	20	22	24	28	30	33
Diameter of truck wheels, inches	14	14	14	16	16	18	18
Rigid wheel-base, feet and inches	3-0	3-0	3-6	4-0	4-0	4-6	4-6
Total wheel-base, feet and inches	8-8	9-0	9-7	10-7	11-8	12-2½	12-2½
Length over bumpers, feet and inches	13-6	14-3	16-0	17-0	18-3	19-6	21-0
Extreme height (head-room not limited), feet and inches	9-0	9-2	9-6	9-8	9-10	10-0	10-3
Weight in working order, pounds	11,000	13,000	15,500	21,500	27,000	32,000	35,500
Weight on driving wheels, pounds	8,000	9,500	11,500	16,500	21,000	25,000	28,000
Weight on two-wheel truck, pounds	3,000	3,500	4,000	5,000	6,000	7,000	7,500
Water capacity of side tanks, gallons	75	100	150	200	250	400	500
Fuel capacity { coal, pounds	300	400	600	700	800	900	1,000
{ wood, cubic feet	10	15	25	30	35	40	45
Weight per yard of lightest rail advised, pounds	12	12	14	16	20	25	25
Radius of sharpest curve advised, feet	55	55	60	70	80	90	90
Radius of sharpest curve practicable, feet	40	40	45	50	55	60	60
Boiler pressure per square inch, pounds	160	160	160	160	160	160	160
Tractive force, pounds	1,360	1,700	2,225	3,330	4,350	5,135	5,775
Hauling Capacity, in tons of 2,000 pounds (exclusive of locomotive), 6½ pounds per ton resistance of rolling friction:							
On absolute level	200	255	330	500	655	775	870
" ½ per cent grade = 26 4/10 feet per mile	75	95	125	190	250	295	330
" 1 " " = 52 8/10 " " "	45	55	75	115	150	175	200
" 2 " " = 105 6/10 " " "	20	30	40	60	80	95	105
" 3 " " = 158 4/10 " " "	14	19	25	40	50	60	65

The **Rule for Calculation of Hauling Capacity** at all rates of resistance of rolling friction and on any practicable grade is given on page 140.

For quick approximate calculation of Hauling Capacity on any practicable grade, and with resistance of rolling friction of 6½ to 40 pounds per ton, refer to **Tables of Percentages** on pages 156 and 157.

For quick selection of suitable weight locomotive for stated load, grade and resistance of rolling friction, refer to **Tables I, II, III and IV**, on pages 162 to 169. These tables are also useful for quick comparison of loads that can be handled by locomotives of different weights.

"Back-Truck" Four-Driving-Wheels Side-Tanks Locomotive, Class 2-B-SS

Wide or Narrow Gauge

ILLUSTRATION No. 83, from photograph of 12 x 18 cylinders, wood-burning locomotive, 36 inches gauge of track, with main frames stopped off and with full-width straight-sides firebox, for sugar plantation in Mexico.

EIGHT SIZES, each with code word, are described on the opposite page, subject to modifications to suit gauge, fuel, size of locomotive, and requirements or preferences of customers. We are prepared to build additional sizes. The driving wheels are connected by side equalizers. The truck has pivotal, lateral, and radial-bar motion. The side tanks have connecting pipe. For wide gauges the frames are continuous. Double-bar guides are seldom used except for the larger sizes. See page 10 for general specifications and pages 11 and 12 for choice of stacks.

For smaller sizes see preceding page.

Correspondents are Requested to Designate Locomotives by Code Word

CODE WORD	RAMNER	RAMROD	RAMTIL	RANCAR	RANGUE	RANKIG	RAPACE	RAPEUX
Cylinders { diameter, inches	10	11	12	12	13	14	14	15
Cylinders { stroke, inches	16	16	16	18	18	20	24	24
Diameter of driving wheels, inches	33	36	38	40	40	42	46	50
Diameter of truck wheels, inches	20	20	22	22	24	26	26	26
Rigid wheel-base, feet and inches	5–0	5–3	5–9	5–9	5–9	6–3	7–0	7–0
Total wheel-base, feet and inches	13–4	13–6	14–0	14–0	14–10	15–6	15–9	17–0
Length over bumpers, feet and inches	21–6	22–0	22–6	22–6	23–0	25–0	26–0	27–6
Extreme height (head-room not limited), ft. and in.	10–6	10–10	11–4	11–6	12–0	12–6	12–9	13–2
Weight in working order, pounds	41,000	45,000	49,000	53,000	62,000	74,000	79,000	88,000
Weight on driving wheels, pounds	33,000	36,500	40,500	44,000	52,000	63,500	67,500	76,000
Weight on two-wheel truck, pounds	8,000	8,500	8,500	9,000	10,000	10,500	11,500	12,000
Water capacity of side tanks, gallons	600	600	700	750	800	900	1,000	1,100
Fuel capacity { coal, pounds	1,000	1,200	1,300	1,500	1,800	2,500	3,000	3,500
Fuel capacity { wood, cubic feet	45	50	55	60	70	80	90	100
Weight per yard of lightest rail advised, pounds	30	30	35	40	45	50	60	70
Radius of sharpest curve advised, feet	95	100	100	100	105	110	120	120
Radius of sharpest curve practicable, feet	65	70	70	70	80	85	90	90
Boiler pressure per square inch, pounds	160	160	160	160	160	160	160	160
Tractive force, pounds	6,585	7,315	8,245	8,820	10,350	12,690	13,900	15,600
Hauling Capacity, in tons of 2,000 pounds (exclusive of locomotive), 6½ pounds per ton resistance of rolling friction:								
On absolute level	990	1,100	1,240	1,330	1,560	1,915	2,100	2,355
" ½ per cent grade = 26.4 feet per mile	375	420	475	505	595	730	800	900
" 1 " " " = 52.8 " " "	225	250	285	305	355	440	480	540
" 2 " " " = 105.6 " " "	120	130	150	160	190	235	255	290
" 3 " " " = 158.4 " " "	75	85	100	105	125	155	165	190

The **Rule for Calculation** of Hauling Capacity at all rates of resistance of rolling friction and on any practicable grade is given on page 140.

For quick approximate calculation of Hauling Capacity on any practicable grade, and with resistance of rolling friction of 6½ to 40 pounds per ton, refer to **Tables of Percentages** on pages 156 and 157.

For quick selection of suitable weight locomotive for stated load, grade and resistance of rolling friction, refer to **Tables I, II, III and IV**, on pages 162 to 169. These tables are also useful for quick comparison of loads that can be handled by locomotives of different weights.

Light "Back-Truck" Four-Driving-Wheels Side-Tanks Locomotive with Canopy, Class 2-B-SS-K

Wide or Narrow Gauge

ILLUSTRATION No. 82, from photograph of 7 x 12 cylinders, coal-burning locomotive, meter gauge of track, for sugar plantation in the West Indies.

SEVEN SIZES, each with code word, are described on the opposite page, subject to modifications to suit gauge, fuel, size of locomotive, and requirements or preferences of customers. We are prepared to build additional sizes. The driving wheels are connected by side equalizers. The truck has pivotal, lateral, and radial-bar motion. The side tanks have connecting pipe. If required by narrowness of gauge the main frames are stopped off with full-width straight-sides firebox. Cylinders 8 x 14 and smaller are slightly inclined. The canopy cab is of steel. See page 10 for general specifications and pages 11 and 12 for choice of stacks.

For larger sizes see next page.

Correspondents are Requested to Designate Locomotives by Code Word

CODE WORD	RALHOS	RAMBEH	RAMEAL	RAMIAH	RAMIFY	RAMIRO	RAMIST
Cylinders { diameter, inches	5	5	6	7	8	9	10
{ stroke, inches	8	10	10	12	14	14	14
Diameter of driving wheels, inches	20	20	22	24	28	30	33
Diameter of truck wheels, inches	14	14	16	16	16	18	18
Rigid wheel-base, feet and inches	3-0	3-0	3-6	4-0	4-0	4-0	4-6
Total wheel-base, feet and inches	8-8	9-0	9-7	10-7	11-8	12-2½	12-2½
Length over bumpers, feet and inches	13-6	14-3	16-0	17-0	18-3	19-6	21-0
Extreme height (head-room not limited), feet and inches	9-0	9-2	9-6	9-8	9-10	10-0	10-3
Weight in working order, pounds	11,000	13,000	15,500	21,500	27,000	32,000	35,500
Weight on driving wheels, pounds	8,000	9,500	11,500	16,500	21,000	25,000	28,000
Weight on two-wheel truck, pounds	3,000	3,500	4,000	5,000	6,000	7,000	7,500
Water capacity of side tanks, gallons	75	100	150	200	250	400	500
Fuel capacity { coal, pounds	300	400	600	700	800	900	1,000
{ wood, cubic feet	10	15	25	30	35	40	45
Weight per yard of lightest rail advised, pounds	12	12	14	16	20	25	25
Radius of sharpest curve advised, feet	55	55	60	70	80	90	90
Radius of sharpest curve practicable, feet	40	40	45	50	55	60	60
Boiler pressure per square inch, pounds	160	160	160	160	160	160	160
Tractive force, pounds	1,360	1,700	2,225	3,330	4,350	5,135	5,775
Hauling Capacity, in tons of 2,000 pounds (exclusive of locomotive) 6½ pounds per ton resistance of rolling friction:							
On absolute level	200	255	330	500	655	775	870
" ½ per cent grade = 26 4/10 feet per mile	75	95	125	190	250	295	330
" 1 " " " = 52 8/10 " " "	45	55	75	115	150	175	195
" 2 " " " = 105 6/10 " " "	20	30	40	60	80	95	105
" 3 " " " = 158 4/10 " " "	14	19	25	40	50	60	65

The **Rule for Calculation of Hauling Capacity** at all rates of resistance of rolling friction and on any practicable grade is given on page 140.

For **quick approximate calculation** of Hauling Capacity on any practicable grade, and with resistance of rolling friction of 6½ to 40 pounds per ton, refer to **Tables of Percentages** on pages 156 and 157.

For **quick selection of suitable weight locomotive** for stated load, grade and resistance of rolling friction, refer to **Tables I, II, III and IV**, on pages 162 to 169. These tables are also useful for quick comparison of loads that can be handled by locomotives of different weights.

"Back-Truck" Four-Driving-Wheels Side-Tanks Locomotive With Canopy, Class 2-B-SS-K

Wide or Narrow Gauge

ILLUSTRATION No. 82, from photograph of 7 x 12 cylinders, coal-burning locomotive, meter gauge of track, for sugar plantation in the West Indies.

EIGHT SIZES, each with code word, are described on the opposite page, subject to modifications to suit gauge, fuel, size of locomotive, and requirements or preferences of customers. We are prepared to build additional sizes. The driving wheels are connected by side equalizers. The truck has pivotal, lateral, and radial-bar motion. The side tanks have connecting pipe. If required by narrowness of gauge the frames are stopped off with full-width straight-sides firebox. The canopy cab is of steel. See page 10 for general specifications and pages 11 and 12 for choice of stacks.

For smaller sizes see preceding page.

Correspondents are Requested to Designate Locomotives by Code Word

CODE WORD	RAPHUN	RAPTOR	RAPTUS	RAQUET	RAREFY	RARITY	RASCOA	RASGAR
Cylinders { diameter, inches	10	11	12	12	13	14	14	15
{ stroke, inches	16	16	16	18	18	20	24	24
Diameter of driving wheels, inches	33	36	40	40	40	42	46	50
Diameter of truck wheels, inches	20	20	22	22	24	26	26	26
Rigid wheel-base, feet and inches	5–0	5–3	5–9	5–9	5–9	6–3	7–0	7–0
Total wheel-base, feet and inches	13–4	13–6	14–0	14–0	14–10	15–6	15–9	17–0
Length over bumpers, feet and inches	21–6	22–0	22–6	22–6	23–6	25–0	26–0	27–0
Extreme height (head-room not limited), feet and inches	10–6	10–10	11–4	11–6	12–6	12–6	12–9	13–2
Weight in working order, pounds	41,000	45,000	49,000	53,000	62,000	72,000	79,000	88,000
Weight on driving wheels, pounds	33,000	36,500	40,500	44,000	52,000	61,500	67,500	76,000
Weight on two-wheel truck, pounds	8,000	8,500	8,500	9,000	10,000	10,500	11,500	12,000
Water capacity of side tanks, gallons	600	600	700	750	800	900	1,000	1,100
Fuel capacity { coal, pounds	1,000	1,200	1,300	1,500	1,800	2,500	3,000	3,500
{ wood, cubic feet	45	50	55	60	70	80	90	100
Weight per yard of lightest rail advised, pounds	30	30	35	40	45	50	60	70
Radius of sharpest curve advised, feet	95	100	100	100	105	110	120	120
Radius of sharpest curve practicable, feet	65	70	70	70	80	85	90	90
Boiler pressure per square inch, pounds	160	160	160	160	160	160	160	160
Tractive force, pounds	6,585	7,315	8,245	8,820	10,350	12,690	13,900	15,600
Hauling Capacity, in tons of 2,000 pounds (exclusive of locomotive), 6½ pounds per ton resistance of rolling friction:								
On absolute level	990	1,100	1,240	1,330	1,560	1,915	2,100	2,355
" ½ per cent grade = 26 4⁄10 feet per mile	375	420	475	505	595	730	800	900
" 1 " " = 52 8⁄10 " "	225	250	285	305	355	440	480	540
" 2 " " = 105 6⁄10 " "	120	130	150	160	190	235	255	290
" 3 " " = 158 4⁄10 " "	75	85	100	105	125	155	165	190

The **Rule for Calculation** of Hauling Capacity at all rates of resistance of rolling friction and on any practicable grade is given on page 140.

For quick approximate calculation of Hauling Capacity on any practicable grade, and with resistance of rolling friction of 6½ to 40 pounds per ton, refer to **Tables of Percentages** on **pages 156 and 157.**

For **quick selection of suitable weight locomotive** for stated load, grade and resistance of rolling friction, refer to **Tables I, II, III and IV**, on pages 162 to 169. These tables are also useful for quick comparison of loads that can be handled by locomotives of different weights.

Light "Back-Truck" Six-Driving-Wheels Side-Tanks Locomotive, Class 2-C-SS

Wide or Narrow Gauge

ILLUSTRATION No. 97, from photograph of 9 x 14 cylinders, coal-burning locomotive, 36 inches gauge of track, for plantation in the West Indies.

SIX SIZES, each with code word, are described on the opposite page, subject to modifications to suit gauge, fuel, size of locomotive, and requirements or preferences of customers. We are prepared to build additional sizes. The driving wheels are equalized. The truck has pivotal, lateral, and radial-bar motion. The center driving wheels are flangeless. The side tanks have connecting pipe. Cylinders 9 x 14 and larger are horizontal. See page 10 for general specifications and pages 11 and 12 for choice of stacks.

For larger sizes see next page.

Correspondents are Requested to Designate Locomotives by Code Word

CODE (with closed cab like Illustration No. 97) / WORD (with open canopy like canopy of Illustration No. 82, page 128)	RASION RAUPIG	RASOIR RAUQUE	RATJES RAUSEO	RATOON RAVAGE	RAUFEN RAWISH	RAULIM RAYONS
Cylinders { diameter, inches	6	7	8	9	10	11
{ stroke, inches	10	12	14	14	14	14
Diameter of driving wheels, inches	20	23	28	28	30	30
Diameter of truck wheels, inches	14	16	16	16	16	18
Rigid wheel-base, feet and inches	4-10	5-2	5-5	5-10	7-3	7-8
Total wheel-base, feet and inches	9-4	9-10	10-6	11-5	12-6	13-0
Length over bumpers, feet and inches	15-5	16-6	17-0	18-8	19-5	20-6
Extreme height (head-room not limited), feet and inches	9-6	9-8	9-10	10-0	10-3	10-4
Weight in working order, pounds	16,000	22,000	27,000	32,500	38,000	47,000
Weight on driving wheels, pounds	12,500	17,500	22,000	27,000	31,500	40,500
Weight on two-wheel truck, pounds	3,500	4,500	5,000	5,500	6,500	6,500
Water capacity of side tanks, gallons	200	300	350	400	500	600
Fuel capacity { coal, pounds	400	600	700	800	900	900
{ wood, cubic feet	20	30	35	40	45	45
Weight per yard of lightest rail advised, pounds	12	15	16	16	20	20
Radius of sharpest curve advised, feet	50	50	55	65	80	80
Radius of sharpest curve practicable, feet	40	40	50	60	65	65
Boiler pressure per square inch, pounds	160	160	160	160	160	160
Tractive force, pounds	2,445	3,480	4,350	5,500	6,350	7,680
Hauling Capacity, in tons of 2,000 pounds (exclusive of locomotive), 6½ pounds per ton resistance of rolling friction:						
On absolute level	365	520	655	830	955	1,155
" ½ per cent grade = 26 4/10 feet per mile	140	200	245	315	365	440
" 1 " " " = 52 8/10 " " "	80	120	150	195	220	265
" 2 " " " = 105 6/10 " " "	40	60	75	100	115	140
" 3 " " " = 158 4/10 " " "	25	40	50	65	75	90

The **Rule for Calculation** of Hauling Capacity at all rates of resistance of rolling friction and on any practicable grade is given on **page 140**.

For quick approximate calculation of Hauling Capacity on any practicable grade, and with resistance of rolling friction of 6½ to 40 pounds per ton, refer to **Tables of Percentages** on **pages 156 and 157**.

For **quick selection of suitable weight locomotive** for stated load, grade and resistance of rolling friction, refer to **Tables I, II, III and IV**, on **pages 162 to 169**. These tables are also useful for quick comparison of loads that can be handled by locomotives of different weights.

"Back-Truck" Six-Driving-Wheels Side-Tanks Locomotive, Class 2-C-SS

ILLUSTRATION No. 107, from photograph of 14 x 20 cylinders, coal-burning locomotive, 42 inches gauge of track, with stopped-off main frames and with full-width straight-sides firebox, for freight service, exported to Russia.

NINE SIZES, each with code word, are described on the opposite page, subject to modifications to suit gauge, fuel, size of locomotive, and requirements or preferences of customers. We are prepared to build additional sizes. The driving wheels are equalized. The truck has pivotal, lateral, and radial-bar motion. The center driving wheels are flangeless. The side tanks have connecting pipe. Pilots or hanging step-boards may be used. For wide gauges the frames are continuous. Double-bar guides are seldom used except for the larger sizes. See page 10 for general specifications and pages 11 and 12 for choice of stacks.

For smaller sizes see preceding page.

Correspondents are Requested to Designate Locomotives by Code Word

CODE WORD { with closed cab like Illustration No. 107. with open canopy like canopy of Illustration No. 82, page 130.	RAYOSO REBECA	RAZAGO REBILI	RAZEIL REBORA	RAZZIA REBOZO	REACTI REBUFF	REAIAH RECADO	REALCO RECAIR	REALLY RECALL	REAPER RECENT
Cylinders { diameter, inches	10	11	12	1	13	14	14	15	15
{ stroke, inches	16	16	16	18	18	20	24	20	24
Diameter of driving wheels, inches	31	33	36	36	36	40	46	42	48
Diameter of truck wheels, inches	16	18	20	20	20	22	24	24	24
Rigid wheel-base, feet and inches	7-8	8-1	8-1	9-0	9-10	10-6	11-3	10-6	11-9
Total wheel-base, feet and inches	13-4	13-9	13-9	15-0	15-8	16-0	17-0	17-0	18-6
Length over bumpers, feet and inches	20-8	22-0	22-8	23-5	24-6	25-8	27-0	27-0	29-0
Extreme height (head-room not limited), ft. and in.	10-6	10-10	11-3	11-6	12-0	12-6	12-9	12-7	13-2
Weight in working order, pounds	41,000	47,000	50,000	55,000	63,500	76,000	82,000	85,500	93,000
Weight on driving wheels, pounds	34,500	40,000	42,500	47,000	55,000	66,500	71,500	75,000	82,000
Weight on two-wheel truck, pounds	6,500	7,000	7,500	8,000	8,500	9,500	10,500	10,500	11,000
Water capacity of side tanks, gallons	600	600	700	750	900	1,000	1,000	1,000	1,100
Fuel capacity { coal, pounds	1,000	1,200	1,300	1,500	1,800	2,500	3,000	3,500	3,500
{ wood, cubic feet	45	50	55	60	70	80	90	90	100
Weight per yard of lightest rail advised, pounds	25	25	30	30	40	40	45	50	50
Radius of sharpest curve advised, feet	85	90	90	110	130	155	160	155	175
Radius of sharpest curve practicable, feet	75	80	80	95	115	135	140	140	145
Boiler pressure per square inch, pounds	160	160	160	160	160	160	170	170	170
Tractive force, pounds	7,015	7,970	8,710	9,800	11,500	13,330	14,770	15,500	16,250
Hauling Capacity, in tons of 2,000 pounds (exclusive of locomotive), 6½ pounds per ton resistance of rolling friction:									
On absolute level	1,055	1,200	1,315	1,475	1,735	2,010	2,230	2,340	2,450
" ½ per cent grade = 26 4/10 feet per mile	400	455	500	500	665	770	850	895	935
" 1 " " " = 52 8/10 " " "	240	275	300	335	400	465	515	540	565
" 2 " " " = 105 6/10 " " "	130	145	160	180	215	245	275	290	300
" 3 " " " = 158 4/10 " " "	80	95	105	115	140	160	180	190	195

The **Rule for Calculation** of Hauling Capacity at all rates of resistance of rolling friction and on any practicable grade is given on page 140.

For **quick approximate calculation** of Hauling Capacity on any practicable grade, and with resistance of rolling friction of 6½ to 40 pounds per ton, refer to **Tables of Percentages** on pages **156 and 157.**

For **quick selection of suitable weight locomotive** for stated load, grade and resistance of rolling friction, refer to **Tables I, II, III and IV,** on pages **162 to 169.** These tables are also useful for quick comparison of loads that can be handled by locomotives of different weights.

"Double-Ender" Four-Driving-Wheels Side-Tanks Locomotive, Class 2-B-2-SS

Wide or Narrow Gauge

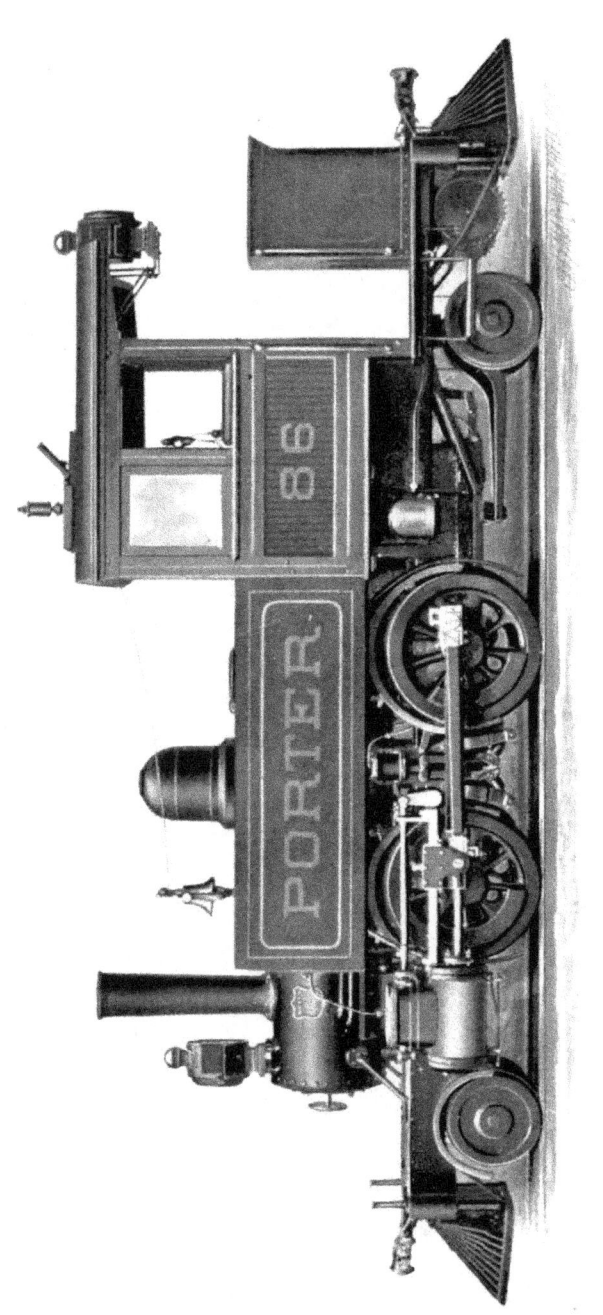

ILLUSTRATION No. 86, from photograph of 10 x 16 cylinders, coal-burning locomotive, 56½ inches gauge of track.

THIRTEEN SIZES, each with code word, are described on the opposite page, subject to modifications to suit gauge, fuel, size of locomotive, and requirements or preferences of customers. We are prepared to build additional sizes. Each pair of driving wheels is equalized with the next truck, or the four driving wheels may be equalized with the front truck. The trucks have pivotal, lateral, and radial-bar motion. The side tanks have connecting pipe Cylinders 8 x 14 and smaller are slightly inclined. See page 10 for general specifications and pages 11 and 12 for choice of stacks.

Correspondents are Requested to Designate Locomotives by Code Word

CODE WORD { with closed cab like Illustration No. 86 / with open canopy like canopy of Illustration No. 29, page 114	RECKON RECUIT	RECOAR REDADA	RECOIL REDBUD	RECOVA REDNER	RECRAN REDOMA	REDOJO REFUTO	REDWAN REGALO	REFAJO REGAIO	REFILL REGILO	REFIND REGLES	REFLET REGRAL	REFLEX REGRET	REFONT REGSAM
Cylinders { diameter, inches	6	7	8	9	10	10	11	12	12	13	14	14	15
stroke, inches	10	12	14	14	14	16	16	16	18	18	20	24	24
Diameter of driving wheels, inches	24	26	30	33	36	36	40	40	42	42	45	48	50
Diameter of truck wheels, inches	14	14	18	18	20	20	22	22	24	24	24	26	26
Rigid wheel-base, feet and inches	4-0	4-8	5-0	5-9	5-9	5-3	5-9	5-9	5-0	6-3	6-3	7-0	7-0
Total wheel-base, feet and inches	12-0	13-2	14-4	15-9	16-6	18-6	19-9	20-0	20-5	21-10	22-4	24-2	25-0
Length over bumpers, feet and inches	16-6	21-3	22-10	25-0	27-0	29-6	30-6	30-6	31-6	34-0	35-0	37-0	38-6
Height (room not limited) ft. and in	9-4	9-8	9-10	10-1	10-3	10-8	11-0	11-3	11-6	12-0	12-8	13-0	13-6
Weight in working order, pounds	17,000	24,000	29,000	33,000	37,000	43,000	47,000	54,000	58,000	66,000	76,000	84,000	98,000
Weight on driving wheels, pounds	10,500	14,500	18,500	21,500	24,500	30,000	32,000	38,000	41,000	48,000	57,000	64,000	76,000
Weight on two two-wheel trucks, pounds	6,500	9,500	10,500	11,500	12,500	13,000	15,000	16,000	17,000	18,000	19,000	20,000	22,000
Water capacity of side tanks, gallons	150	200	300	400	500	600	600	700	750	800	900	1,000	1,100
Fuel capacity { coal, pounds	400	500	600	700	800	1,000	1,200	1,300	1,500	1,800	2,500	3,000	3,500
wood, cubic feet	20	25	30	35	40	45	50	55	60	70	80	90	100
Weight per yard of lightest rail advised, lb.	14	16	20	20	25	30	30	35	40	45	50	55	65
Radius of sharpest curve advised, feet	50	50	50	65	80	90	100	100	110	120	130	140	150
Radius of sharpest curve practicable, feet	40	40	40	60	65	75	80	80	90	100	110	120	130
Boiler pressure per square inch, pounds	160	160	160	160	160	160	160	160	160	160	160	160	170
Tractive force, pounds	2,035	3,075	4,055	4,670	5,290	6,040	6,580	7,835	8,395	9,845	11,845	13,330	15,000
Hauling Capacity, in tons of 2,000 pounds (exclusive of locomotive), 6½ pounds per ton resistance of rolling friction:													
On absolute level	300	460	610	700	795	905	985	1,175	1,260	1,480	1,780	2,005	2,350
" ½ per cent grade = 26 4/10 ft. per mile	110	170	230	270	300	345	375	445	475	565	675	765	895
" 1 " " = 52 8/10 " " "	65	100	135	155	180	205	220	265	285	340	405	460	535
" 2 " " = 105 6/10 " " "	30	50	70	80	90	105	115	140	150	180	215	245	285
" 3 " " = 158 4/10 " " "	20	30	45	50	60	70	75	90	95	115	140	155	185

The **Rule for Calculation of Hauling Capacity** at all rates of resistance of rolling friction and on any practicable grade is given on page 140.

For quick approximate calculation of Hauling Capacity on any practicable grade, and with resistance of rolling friction of 6½ to 40 pounds per ton, refer to **Tables of Percentages** on pages 156 and 157.

For **quick selection of suitable weight locomotive** for stated load, grade and resistance of rolling friction, refer to **Tables I, II, III and IV**, on pages 162 to 169. These tables are also useful for quick comparison of loads that can be handled by locomotives of different weights.

"Double-Ender" Six-Driving-Wheels Side-Tanks Locomotive, Class 2-C-2-SS

Wide or Narrow Gauge

ILLUSTRATION No. 55, from photograph of 15 x 20 cylinders, coal-burning locomotive, 42 inches gauge of track, exported to South Africa.

FOURTEEN SIZES, each with **code word**, are described on the opposite page, subject to modifications to suit gauge, fuel, size of locomotive, and requirements or preferences of customers. We are prepared to build additional sizes. The front driving wheels are equalized with the front truck. The center and rear driving wheels are equalized with the rear truck. The center driving wheels are flangeless. The trucks have pivotal, lateral, and radial-bar motion. The side tanks have connecting pipe. Single-bar guides are seldom used except for the larger sizes. Cylinders 8 x 14 and smaller are slightly inclined. See page 10 for general specifications and pages 11 and 12 for choice of stacks.

Correspondents are Requested to Designate Locomotives by Code Word

CODE WORD { with closed cab like Illustration No. 55 / with open canopy instead of closed cab	REGYRO REINOL	REHASH REINST	REHELM REISJE	REHAAR REJERO	REHOGO REKRUT	RELBUN REMOJE	RELEGO RENARD	RELEJE RENCOR	RELIED RENEBO	RELOAD RENGOS	RELVAR RENHIR	REMAID RENOVO	REMATE RENQUE	REMAVI RENTON
Cylinders { diameter, inches	6	7	8	9	10	10	11	12	12	13	14	15	15	16
{ stroke, inches	10	12	14	14	14	16	16	16	18	18	20	20	24	20
Diameter of driving wheels, in	22	23	28	30	31	33	36	38	38	38	40	40	46	42
Diameter of truck wheels, in	14	14	14	16	16	18	18	18	18	18	22	24	22	26
Rigid wheel-base, feet and inches	4–10	5–2	5–6	5–10	7–3	7–8	8–1	9–0	9–0	9–10	10–6	10–6	11–0	10–6
Total wheel-base, feet and inches	13–0	14–3	14–5	16–4	16–11	18–7	19–6	20–6	20–10	22–0	23–2	24–0	25–0	24–4
Length over bumpers, ft. and in	17–6	22–2	22–4	25–0	25–6	27–11	29–7	30–1	30–7	32–9	34–0	35–0	36–6	37–0
Height (head-room not limited), feet and inches	9–4	9–8	9–10	10–0	10–3	10–6	10–10	11–3	11–6	12–0	12–6	13–0	13–2	13–4
Weight in working order, lb	18,000	24,500	29,500	35,000	40,000	44,000	49,000	54,500	60,000	68,000	81,000	96,000	103,000	108,000
Weight on driving wheels, lb	11,500	17,000	21,000	25,500	29,500	32,500	36,000	40,000	45,000	52,000	64,000	78,000	83,000	86,000
Weight on two two-wheel trucks, pounds	6,500	7,500	8,500	9,500	10,500	11,500	13,000	14,500	15,000	16,000	17,000	18,000	20,000	22,000
Water capacity of side-tanks, gal	200	300	350	400	500	600	600	700	750	800	900	1,000	1,100	1,200
Fuel capacity { coal, pounds	400	500	600	700	800	1,000	1,200	1,300	1,500	1,800	2,500	3,000	3,500	4,000
{ wood, cubic feet	20	25	30	35	40	45	50	55	60	70	80	90	100	110
Weight per yard of lightest rail advised, pounds	12	14	16	16	20	25	25	30	30	35	40	45	50	56
Radius of sharpest curve advised, feet	60	65	70	75	80	85	90	110	110	135	175	175	175	175
Radius of sharpest curve practicable, feet	30	50	55	60	65	75	80	95	95	120	145	145	145	145
Boiler pressure per sq. in., lb	160	160	160	160	160	160	160	160	160	160	160	165	170	170
Tractive force, pounds	2,225	3,480	4,350	5,135	5,140	6,585	7,315	8,245	9,285	10,890	13,330	15,800	16,960	17,615
Hauling Capacity, in tons of 2,000 lbs. (exclusive of locomotive), 6½ lb. per ton resistance of rolling friction:														
On absolute level	330	520	650	770	920	990	1,100	1,240	1,395	1,640	2,010	2,380	2,555	2,655
" ½% grade = 26 4/10 ft. per mile	125	195	245	290	350	375	415	470	530	625	765	905	975	1,010
" 1% " = 52 2/10 " "	75	120	145	175	210	225	250	280	320	375	460	545	585	610
" 2% " = 105 6/10 " "	35	60	75	90	110	115	130	145	170	200	245	290	310	320
" 3% " = 158 4/10 " "	20	40	50	60	70	75	85	95	110	130	160	185	200	210

The **Rule for Calculation** of Hauling Capacity at all rates of resistance of rolling friction and on any practicable grade is given on **page 140**.
For quick approximate calculation of Hauling Capacity on any practicable grade, and with resistance of rolling friction of 6½ to 40 pounds per ton, refer to Tables of Percentages on pages **156 and 157**.
For quick selection of suitable weight locomotive for stated load, grade and resistance of rolling friction, refer to **Tables I, II, III and IV**, on pages **162 to 169**. These tables are also useful for quick comparison of loads that can be handled by locomotives of different weights.

Tractive Force

The tractive force stated for each locomotive in this catalogue is calculated by the following formula:

$$T = \frac{D^2 \times L \times .85\,p}{d}$$

T represents the Tractive force.
D " " Diameter of the cylinders in inches.
L " " Length of the stroke of the cylinders in inches.
.85 p " 85 Per cent of the boiler pressure in pounds per square inch, which is assumed [on the basis of tests made] to be the effective pressure of the steam in the cylinders with the locomotive working at full stroke and slow speed.
d " the Diameter of the driving wheels in inches.

The above formula may be stated more fully as follows: The tractive force of a locomotive is computed by multiplying the square of the diameter of the cylinders in inches by the stroke in inches; multiplying again by 85 per cent of the boiler pressure in pounds per square inch; and then dividing by the diameter of the driving wheels in inches.

Example. The tractive force of a locomotive with cylinders 5 inches diameter by 10 inches stroke, 150 lb. boiler pressure, and driving wheels 20 inches diameter:

$$\frac{5^2 \times 10 \times .85 \times 150}{20} = 1,594 \text{ pounds.}$$

Memorandum: The above formula is arrived at as follows: The tractive force of a locomotive is due to the pressure of steam on the pistons as delivered through one revolution of the driving wheels. The tractive force increases in direct proportion to area of pistons, length of stroke, and steam pressure in the cylinders; it decreases in direct proportion to diameter of driving wheels.

To calculate the tractive force:

Ascertain the area in square inches of the two pistons. [The area of each piston is the square of one-half its diameter multiplied by 3.1416+.]

Multiply by the mean effective cylinders steam pressure in pounds per square inch [generally assumed as 85 per cent of the boiler pressure].

Multiply by the motion in inches of the two pistons during one revolution of the driving wheels—*i. e.*, two times the stroke.

Divide by the circumference of the driving wheel in inches [the circumference is equivalent to the diameter multiplied by 3.1416+].

The above is expressed by formula as follows:

$$T = \frac{2 \times \frac{D}{2} \times \frac{D}{2} \times 3.1416+ \times .85\,p \times 2 \times L}{d \times 3.1416+}$$

which by cancellation gives the formula $T = \dfrac{D^2 \times .85\,p \times L}{d}$

The **Tractive Force** and the "Draw-bar Pull" of a locomotive are usually taken to mean the same thing, but the tractive force includes the power needed to run the locomotive [and tender, if any] as well as pull the train. The "draw-bar pull" is properly applied only to the power available for pulling the train attached to the locomotive.

Tables of Tractive Force

The tractive force of each locomotive described and illustrated in this catalogue is given in the descriptive text, pages 19 to 139. In each case the tractive force may be increased or diminished, as desired, to a considerable extent by modifying the boiler pressure and the size of the driving wheels. The following tables state the tractive force for each size of locomotive as modified by different sizes of driving wheels and by different pressures of steam. The sizes of locomotives covered by these tables range from cylinders 4 inches diameter by 8 inches stroke to 17 inches diameter by 24 inches stroke, the sizes of driving wheels from 18 to 56 inches, and the boiler pressures from 120 to 200 pounds per square inch.

A separate table is given for each size of locomotive, the size being designated by the diameter and stroke of the cylinders in inches as noted in the upper left-hand corner of each table.

Boiler pressures are noted in the left-hand column, in pounds per square inch.

Diameters of driving wheels in inches are noted in the upper line of each table.

The tractive force for the desired boiler pressure and size of driving wheels is found at the intersection of the proper horizontal and perpendicular lines.

EXAMPLE.—The tractive force of a locomotive, 5 x 10 cylinders, 24-inch driving wheels, and 140 pounds boiler pressure, is found (in the third table below) under the figure 24 and on a line with the figure 140—viz., 1,240 pounds.

NOTE.—In every case the tractive force is computed by the formula on page 140, and for sake of even figures any figures in excess of multiples of 5 are disregarded.

NOTE.—The tractive force and the weight on the driving wheels of a locomotive must be properly proportioned to secure satisfactory results. If the weight is too small, the locomotive is over-cylindered, and will slip the driving wheels too easily. If the weight is too great, the engine is under-cylindered, and cannot slip its driving wheels. In adjusting the best proportion of tractive force and weight on driving wheels due regard must be paid to the character of service for which the engine is intended. For passenger service the weight on the driving wheels may be as little as four times the tractive force. For freight service a driving weight of about four and one-quarter times the tractive force is usual. For contractors', steel works and mine locomotives, street motors, or where slippery or greasy rails are to be expected, the driving weight may, with good results, be close to five times the tractive force. When the water is carried in a tank over the boiler the proportion of the tractive force to the weight on the driving wheels is usually calculated with reference to the water-tank being about half full. In the Tables of Hauling Capacity in this catalogue it is assumed that the proportion of driving weight to tractive force is such as to secure the best results.

Cylinders 4 x 8		SIZES OF DRIVING WHEELS							
		18	20	22	23	24	26	28	30
Boiler Pressure	120	725	650	590	565	540	500	465	435
	130	785	705	640	615	590	545	505	470
	140	845	760	690	660	635	585	540	505
	150	905	815	740	710	680	625	580	545

Cylinders 5 x 8		SIZES OF DRIVING WHEELS							
		18	20	22	23	24	26	28	30
Boiler Pressure	120	1,125	1,015	920	880	845	780	725	675
	130	1,230	1,105	1,005	960	920	850	790	735
	140	1,320	1,190	1,080	1,030	990	915	850	795
	150	1,415	1,275	1,160	1,110	1,060	980	910	850

Cylinders 5 x 10		SIZES OF DRIVING WHEELS							
		18	20	22	23	24	26	28	30
Boiler Pressure	120	1,410	1,270	1,150	1,100	1,055	975	905	845
	130	1,535	1,380	1,255	1,200	1,150	1,060	985	915
	140	1,650	1,485	1,350	1,290	1,240	1,140	1,060	990
	150	1,770	1,590	1,450	1,385	1,330	1,225	1,140	1,060
	160	1,890	1,700	1,545	1,480	1,415	1,305	1,215	1,130

Cylinders 5½ x 10		SIZES OF DRIVING WHEELS							
		18	20	22	23	24	26	28	30
Boiler Pressure	120	1,710	1,540	1,400	1,340	1,285	1,185	1,100	1,025
	130	1,855	1,670	1,515	1,450	1,390	1,285	1,190	1,115
	140	2,000	1,800	1,635	1,565	1,500	1,380	1,285	1,200
	150	2,140	1,925	1,750	1,675	1,605	1,480	1,375	1,285
	160	2,285	2,055	1,870	1,785	1,710	1,580	1,465	1,370

Cylinders 6 x 10		SIZES OF DRIVING WHEELS							
		18	20	22	23	24	26	28	30
Boiler Pressure	120	2,040	1,835	1,665	1,595	1,525	1,410	1,310	1,220
	130	2,210	1,985	1,805	1,725	1,655	1,525	1,415	1,325
	140	2,380	2,140	1,945	1,860	1,780	1,645	1,530	1,425
	150	2,550	2,290	2,085	1,995	1,910	1,765	1,640	1,530
	160	2,715	2,445	2,225	2,125	2,035	1,880	1,745	1,630

Cylinders 6 x 12

		\multicolumn{8}{c}{SIZES OF DRIVING WHEELS}
		20	22	23	24	26	28	30	33
Boiler Pressure	120	2,200	2,000	1,915	1,835	1,690	1,570	1,435	1,335
	130	2,385	2,170	2,070	1,985	1,835	1,700	1,590	1,445
	140	2,565	2,330	2,230	2,140	1,975	1,830	1,710	1,555
	150	2,755	2,500	2,395	2,295	2,120	1,965	1,835	1,670
	160	2,935	2,670	2,555	2,445	2,260	2,100	1,955	1,780

Cylinders 6½ x 10

		\multicolumn{8}{c}{SIZES OF DRIVING WHEELS}
		18	20	22	23	24	26	28	30
Boiler Pressure	130	2,590	2,330	2,120	2,025	1,945	1,795	1,665	1,555
	140	2,790	2,510	2,285	2,185	2,090	1,930	1,795	1,675
	150	2,990	2,690	2,445	2,340	2,240	2,070	1,920	1,790
	160	3,190	2,870	2,610	2,495	2,395	2,210	2,050	1,915

Cylinders 7 x 10

		\multicolumn{8}{c}{SIZES OF DRIVING WHEELS}
		20	22	23	24	26	28	30	33
Boiler Pressure	130	2,700	2,460	2,350	2,250	2,080	1,930	1,805	1,640
	140	2,915	2,650	2,535	2,425	2,240	2,080	1,940	1,765
	150	3,120	2,840	2,720	2,605	2,400	2,230	2,080	1,895
	160	3,330	3,030	2,900	2,775	2,560	2,380	2,220	2,020

Cylinders 7 x 12

		\multicolumn{8}{c}{SIZES OF DRIVING WHEELS}
		22	23	24	26	28	30	33	36
Boiler Pressure	130	2,950	2,820	2,700	2,500	2,315	2,165	1,970	1,810
	140	3,180	3,040	2,915	2,690	2,500	2,330	2,120	1,945
	150	3,420	3,265	3,125	2,885	2,680	2,500	2,275	2,085
	160	3,640	3,480	3,330	3,075	2,855	2,660	2,425	2,225

Cylinders 7 x 14

		\multicolumn{8}{c}{SIZES OF DRIVING WHEELS}
		22	23	24	26	28	30	33	36
Boiler Pressure	130	3,445	3,295	3,160	2,920	2,710	2,530	2,300	2,105
	140	3,710	3,550	3,400	3,145	2,920	2,730	2,480	2,270
	150	3,980	3,800	3,640	3,365	3,120	2,920	2,650	2,430
	160	4,240	4,060	3,885	3,590	3,330	3,110	2,830	2,590

Cylinders 8 x 12	SIZES OF DRIVING WHEELS						
	23	24	26	28	30	33	36
Boiler Pressure 130	3,690	3,530	3,260	3,030	2,825	2,570	2,355
140	3,970	3,810	3,520	3,260	3,045	2,770	2,540
150	4,250	4,075	3,765	3,490	3,260	2,965	2,720
160	4,540	4,350	4,020	3,730	3,480	3,165	2,900

Cylinders 8 x 14	SIZES OF DRIVING WHEELS						
	23	24	26	28	30	33	36
Boiler Pressure 130	4,300	4,120	3,800	3,530	3,290	2,990	2,745
140	4,630	4,440	4,100	3,805	3,550	3,230	2,960
150	4,965	4,760	4,390	4,075	3,810	3,460	3,175
160	5,290	5,070	4,680	4,350	4,055	3,690	3,385

Cylinders 8 x 16	SIZES OF DRIVING WHEELS						
	24	26	28	30	33	36	40
Boiler Pressure 130	4,720	4,350	4,040	3,770	3,430	3,145	2,830
140	5,080	4,685	4,350	4,065	3,690	3,385	3,045
150	5,450	5,025	4,660	4,360	3,960	3,630	3,265
160	5,810	5,360	4,980	4,650	4,220	3,870	3,485

Cylinders 9 x 12	SIZES OF DRIVING WHEELS						
	24	26	28	30	33	36	40
Boiler Pressure 130	4,475	4,130	3,835	3,580	3,255	2,985	2,685
140	4,820	4,450	4,130	3,855	3,505	3,210	2,890
150	5,170	4,770	4,425	4,135	3,760	3,445	3,100
160	5,515	5,085	4,720	4,410	4,010	3,675	3,305

Cylinders 9 x 14	SIZES OF DRIVING WHEELS						
	24	26	28	30	33	36	40
Boiler Pressure 130	5,220	4,820	4,475	4,175	3,795	3,480	3,130
140	5,620	5,190	4,820	4,500	4,080	3,750	3,370
150	6,020	5,560	5,160	4,820	4,375	4,020	3,610
160	6,420	5,925	5,500	5,135	4,670	4,280	3,850

Cylinders 9 x 16	SIZES OF DRIVING WHEELS						
	28	30	33	36	40	42	44
Boiler Pressure 130	5,115	4,770	4,335	3,980	3,580	3,410	3,250
140	5,510	5,135	4,670	4,280	3,850	3,670	3,500
150	5,900	5,505	5,000	4,585	4,125	3,930	3,750
160	6,290	5,875	5,330	4,890	4,400	4,190	4,000

Cylinders 9½ x 14	SIZES OF DRIVING WHEELS						
	24	26	28	30	33	36	40
Boiler Pressure 130	5,820	5,365	4,980	4,650	4,225	3,875	3,490
140	6,270	5,780	5,370	5,015	4,550	4,175	3,760
150	6,720	6,200	5,760	5,375	4,880	4,475	4,030
160	7,160	6,610	6,135	5,730	5,210	4,775	4,300

Cylinders 10 x 14	SIZES OF DRIVING WHEELS						
	24	26	28	30	33	36	40	44
Boiler Pressure 130	6,450	5,950	5,525	5,160	4,685	4,300	3,870	3,515
140	6,950	6,410	5,955	5,560	5,050	4,630	4,170	3,790
150	7,440	6,870	6,375	5,960	5,415	4,960	4,465	4,060
160	7,935	7,330	6,800	6,350	5,775	5,290	4,765	4,330
170	8,435	7,800	7,230	6,750	6,140	5,625	5,065	4,605

Cylinders 10 x 16	SIZES OF DRIVING WHEELS						
	28	30	33	36	40	44	48
Boiler Pressure 130	6,320	5,890	5,355	4,915	4,425	4,020	3,685
140	6,800	6,350	5,775	5,290	4,765	4,330	3,970
150	7,285	6,800	6,180	5,670	5,100	4,635	4,250
160	7,765	7,250	6,585	6,040	5,440	4,940	4,530
170	8,260	7,710	7,000	6,420	5,780	5,250	4,820

Cylinders 11 x 14	SIZES OF DRIVING WHEELS						
	26	28	30	33	36	40	44
Boiler Pressure 130	7,200	6,685	6,240	5,675	5,200	4,680	4,255
140	7,750	7,200	6,720	6,110	5,600	5,035	4,580
150	8,310	7,720	7,200	6,550	6,000	5,400	4,915
160	8,860	8,230	7,680	6,980	6,400	5,760	5,235
170	9,420	8,750	8,160	7,420	6,800	6,120	5,570

Cylinders 11 x 16		SIZES OF DRIVING WHEELS						
		28	30	33	36	40	44	48
Boiler Pressure	130	7,640	7,125	6,480	5,940	5,350	4,860	4,460
	140	8,230	7,680	6,980	6,400	5,760	5,235	4,800
	150	8,820	8,230	7,480	6,860	6,170	5,610	5,140
	160	9,400	8,770	7,970	7,315	6,580	5,980	5,480
	170	9,985	9,320	8,470	7,770	6,990	6,355	5,825

Cylinders 11 x 18		SIZES OF DRIVING WHEELS						
		30	33	36	40	44	48	50
Boiler Pressure	130	8,025	7,295	6,690	6,020	5,470	5,020	4,815
	140	8,640	7,855	7,200	6,480	5,890	5,400	5,185
	150	9,265	8,425	7,725	6,950	6,320	5,790	5,560
	160	9,885	8,990	8,240	7,415	6,740	6,175	5,930
	170	10,500	9,550	8,750	7,875	7,160	6,560	6,300

Cylinders 12 x 14		SIZES OF DRIVING WHEELS						
		28	30	33	36	40	44	48
Boiler Pressure	140	8,575	8,000	7,270	6,670	6,000	5,455	5,000
	150	9,185	8,565	7,790	7,145	6,430	5,840	5,360
	160	9,800	9,135	8,310	7,620	6,850	6,230	5,715
	170	10,410	9,715	8,830	8,100	7,285	6,625	6,075
	180	11,015	10,280	9,340	8,575	7,715	7,010	6,430

Cylinders 12 x 16		SIZES OF DRIVING WHEELS						
		28	30	33	36	40	44	48
Boiler Pressure	140	9,800	9,150	8,320	7,625	6,855	6,230	5,720
	150	10,500	9,800	8,915	8,170	7,350	6,675	6,130
	160	11,195	10,450	9,495	8,710	7,835	7,120	6,530
	170	11,900	11,100	10,080	9,250	8,330	7,570	6,940
	180	12,600	11,750	10,680	9,800	8,820	8,020	7,350

Cylinders 12 x 18		SIZES OF DRIVING WHEELS						
		30	33	36	40	44	48	50
Boiler Pressure	140	10,280	9,350	8,575	7,720	7,020	6,425	6,180
	150	11,010	10,010	9,180	8,265	7,520	6,885	6,615
	160	11,750	10,680	9,800	8,820	8,015	7,340	7,050
	170	12,490	11,350	10,420	9,370	8,520	7,810	7,490
	180	13,220	12,020	11,030	9,920	9,020	8,270	7,930

Cylinders 13 x 16	SIZES OF DRIVING WHEELS						
	30	33	36	40	44	48	50
Boiler Pressure 140	10,730	9,750	8,940	8,040	7,315	6,710	6,440
150	11,490	10,450	9,580	8,620	7,840	7,180	6,900
160	12,260	11,150	10,225	9,200	8,360	7,660	7,360
170	13,030	11,850	10,860	9,775	8,880	8,140	7,820
180	13,785	12,550	11,490	10,340	9,400	8,620	8,270

Cylinders 13 x 18	SIZES OF DRIVING WHEELS						
	30	33	36	40	44	48	50
Boiler Pressure 140	12,080	10,975	10,060	9,060	8,235	7,550	7,245
150	12,940	11,770	10,800	9,710	8,830	8,100	7,770
160	13,800	12,550	11,500	10,350	9,410	8,625	8,280
170	14,670	13,340	12,230	11,000	10,000	9,175	8,800
180	15,530	14,130	12,955	11,650	10,590	9,715	9,320

Cylinders 13 x 20	SIZES OF DRIVING WHEELS						
	33	36	40	44	46	48	50
Boiler Pressure 140	12,200	11,175	10,055	9,150	8,750	8,385	8,050
150	13,070	11,970	10,780	9,800	9,375	8,990	8,625
160	13,930	12,780	11,500	10,450	9,990	9,580	9,200
170	14,800	13,580	12,210	11,100	10,620	10,170	9,780
180	15,675	14,380	12,930	11,760	11,250	10,775	10,350

Cylinders 14 x 16	SIZES OF DRIVING WHEELS						
	33	36	40	44	46	48	50
Boiler Pressure 140	11,300	10,360	9,320	8,475	8,115	7,770	7,460
150	12,110	11,100	9,990	9,085	8,690	8,330	7,990
160	12,920	11,850	10,650	9,700	9,275	8,890	8,530
170	13,740	12,595	11,330	10,300	9,850	9,450	9,065
180	14,550	13,330	11,980	10,900	10,420	9,995	9,600
190	15,355	14,070	12,660	11,500	11,005	10,550	10,130

Cylinders 14 x 18	SIZES OF DRIVING WHEELS						
	33	36	40	44	46	48	50
Boiler Pressure 140	12,715	11,660	10,500	9,540	9,125	8,750	8,400
150	13,630	12,500	11,250	10,225	9,780	9,375	9,000
160	14,540	13,330	11,995	10,900	10,430	9,995	9,595
170	15,450	14,170	12,750	11,590	11,080	10,620	10,200
180	16,360	15,000	13,500	12,265	11,730	11,240	10,800
190	17,260	15,840	14,250	12,950	12,385	11,870	11,400

Cylinders 14 x 20		SIZES OF DRIVING WHEELS							
		33	36	38	40	44	46	48	50
Boiler Pressure	140	14,130	12,950	12,275	11,650	10,600	10,125	9,720	9,320
	150	15,140	13,880	13,145	12,490	11,350	10,850	10,415	9,995
	160	16,145	14,800	14,025	13,330	12,110	11,585	11,100	10,655
	170	17,160	15,735	14,905	14,170	12,875	12,315	11,800	11,330
	180	18,170	16,655	15,775	15,000	13,640	13,030	12,500	12,000
	190	19,180	17,575	16,645	15,840	14,400	13,750	13,185	12,650

Cylinders 14 x 22		SIZES OF DRIVING WHEELS							
		36	38	40	44	46	48	50	52
Boiler Pressure	140	14,250	13,500	12,820	11,650	11,150	10,680	10,250	9,870
	150	15,260	14,470	13,740	12,490	11,950	11,450	10,990	10,570
	160	16,275	15,430	14,650	13,330	12,750	12,210	11,720	11,265
	170	17,300	16,400	15,570	14,155	13,550	12,975	12,460	11,970
	180	18,325	17,360	16,480	14,980	14,340	13,740	13,190	12,680
	190	19,350	18,330	17,400	15,820	15,130	14,500	13,930	13,390

Cylinders 14 x 24		SIZES OF DRIVING WHEELS							
		36	38	40	44	46	48	50	52
Boiler Pressure	140	15,550	14,730	14,000	12,730	12,170	11,660	11,200	10,760
	150	16,670	15,780	15,000	13,640	13,040	12,500	12,000	11,530
	160	17,780	16,840	16,000	14,550	13,900	13,330	12,800	12,300
	170	18,890	17,900	17,000	15,450	14,770	14,160	13,600	13,070
	180	20,000	18,950	18,000	16,350	15,640	15,000	14,400	13,830
	190	21,105	20,000	19,000	17,260	16,500	15,840	15,200	14,600

Cylinders 15 x 18		SIZES OF DRIVING WHEELS							
		33	36	38	40	42	44	46	48
Boiler Pressure	150	15,630	14,350	13,590	12,900	12,295	11,720	11,220	10,750
	160	16,680	15,300	14,500	13,770	13,105	12,520	11,970	11,470
	170	17,710	16,250	15,400	14,630	13,930	13,300	12,720	12,180
	180	18,760	17,210	16,300	15,480	14,750	14,070	13,470	12,900
	190	19,800	18,170	17,200	16,340	15,560	14,860	14,210	13,620
	200	20,850	19,110	18,100	17,190	16,370	15,630	14,940	14,330

Cylinders 15 x 20		SIZES OF DRIVING WHEELS							
		36	38	40	42	44	46	48	50
Boiler Pressure	150	15,950	15,120	14,360	13,670	13,050	12,480	11,970	11,490
	160	17,020	16,130	15,320	14,590	13,930	13,325	12,760	12,250
	170	18,090	17,140	16,260	15,500	14,800	14,150	13,550	13,030
	180	19,150	18,140	17,220	16,410	15,660	14,980	14,360	13,790
	190	20,200	19,150	18,180	17,330	16,540	15,820	15,170	14,560
	200	21,270	20,150	19,140	18,230	17,400	16,650	15,960	15,320

Cylinders 15 x 22	SIZES OF DRIVING WHEELS							
	38	40	42	44	46	48	50	52
Boiler Pressure 150	16,610	15,780	15,030	14,340	13,720	13,150	12,620	12,130
160	17,725	16,825	16,030	15,300	14,630	14,020	13,470	12,950
170	18,840	17,880	17,030	16,270	15,550	14,910	14,310	13,770
180	19,940	18,940	18,030	17,220	16,470	15,780	15,150	14,570
190	21,030	19,980	19,030	18,170	17,370	16,650	15,980	15,370
200	22,120	21,040	20,030	19,120	18,280	17,530	16,820	16,170

Cylinders 15 x 24	SIZES OF DRIVING WHEELS							
	40	42	44	46	48	50	52	56
Boiler Pressure 150	17,210	16,370	15,650	14,960	14,350	13,770	13,250	12,290
160	18,350	17,460	16,680	15,950	15,300	14,680	14,120	13,100
170	19,510	18,570	17,730	16,960	16,250	15,600	15,000	13,910
180	20,650	19,660	18,770	17,950	17,200	16,510	15,890	14,730
190	21,790	20,750	19,820	18,950	18,160	17,440	16,770	15,560
200	22,950	21,860	20,850	19,950	19,110	18,350	17,650	16,390

Cylinders 16 x 20	SIZES OF DRIVING WHEELS							
	36	38	40	42	44	46	48	50
Boiler Pressure 150	18,130	17,175	16,320	15,540	14,835	14,190	13,600	13,055
160	19,340	18,320	17,405	16,575	15,825	15,135	14,505	13,925
170	20,550	19,470	18,495	17,615	16,815	16,080	15,410	14,795
180	21,760	20,610	19,580	18,650	17,800	17,025	16,320	15,665
190	22,965	21,760	20,670	19,685	18,790	17,975	17,225	16,535
200	24,175	22,905	21,760	20,720	19,780	18,920	18,130	17,405

Cylinders 16 x 22	SIZES OF DRIVING WHEELS							
	38	40	42	44	46	48	50	52
Boiler Pressure 150	18,895	17,950	17,095	16,315	15,610	14,955	14,360	13,805
160	20,155	19,150	18,235	17,405	16,650	15,955	15,315	14,730
170	21,415	20,345	19,375	18,495	17,690	16,955	16,275	15,650
180	22,675	21,540	20,515	19,580	18,730	17,950	17,230	16,570
190	23,935	22,735	21,655	20,670	19,770	18,945	18,190	17,490
200	25,195	23,935	22,795	21,760	20,810	19,945	19,145	18,410

Cylinders 16 x 24	SIZES OF DRIVING WHEELS							
	40	42	44	46	48	50	52	56
Boiler Pressure 150	19,580	18,650	17,800	17,025	16,320	15,665	15,060	13,985
160	20,885	19,895	18,990	18,165	17,405	16,710	16,065	14,920
170	22,195	21,135	20,175	19,300	18,495	17,755	17,070	15,850
180	23,500	22,380	21,360	20,435	19,580	18,800	18,075	16,785
190	24,805	23,625	22,550	21,570	20,670	19,845	19,080	17,715
200	26,110	24,865	23,735	22,705	21,760	20,885	20,085	18,650

Cylinders 17 x 20		SIZES OF DRIVING WHEELS							
		36	38	40	42	44	46	48	50
Boiler Pressure	150	20,470	19,390	18,420	17,545	16,745	16,015	15,350	14,735
	160	21,835	20,685	19,650	18,715	17,865	17,085	16,335	15,720
	170	23,200	21,975	20,880	19,885	18,980	18,150	17,400	16,700
	180	24,565	23,270	22,105	21,055	20,095	19,220	18,420	17,685
	190	25,925	24,565	23,335	22,225	21,215	20,290	19,445	18,665
	200	27,290	25,855	24,560	23,395	22,330	21,360	20,470	19,650

Cylinders 17 x 22		SIZES OF DRIVING WHEELS							
		38	40	42	44	46	48	50	52
Boiler Pressure	150	21,330	20,265	19,300	18,420	17,620	16,885	16,210	15,585
	160	22,740	21,615	20,585	19,650	18,795	18,010	17,290	16,625
	170	24,175	22,965	21,870	20,880	19,970	19,140	18,370	17,665
	180	25,595	24,315	23,160	22,105	21,145	20,265	19,455	18,705
	190	27,020	25,670	24,445	23,335	22,320	21,390	20,535	19,745
	200	28,440	27,020	25,735	24,565	23,495	22,515	21,615	20,785

Cylinders 17 x 24		SIZES OF DRIVING WHEELS							
		40	42	44	46	48	50	52	56
Boiler Pressure	150	22,105	21,055	20,095	19,225	18,420	17,685	17,005	15,790
	160	23,580	22,455	21,435	20,505	19,650	18,865	18,140	16,845
	170	25,055	23,860	22,775	21,785	20,880	20,045	19,270	17,895
	180	26,535	25,265	24,115	23,065	22,105	21,220	20,405	18,950
	190	28,000	26,670	25,455	24,350	23,335	22,400	21,540	20,000
	200	29,475	28,070	26,795	25,630	24,565	23,580	22,675	21,055

Hauling Capacity

With the description of each locomotive in this catalogue its **hauling capacity on a level**, and on grades of ½ per cent, 1 per cent, 2 per cent and 3 per cent, is stated in tons of 2,000 pounds, and based on a resistance of rolling friction of 6½ pounds per ton of 2,000 pounds.

RULE FOR CALCULATION OF HAULING CAPACITY. In each case the hauling capacity is computed by dividing the tractive force of the locomotive by the rate of resistance per ton due to gravity and to rolling friction, and then deducting the weight of the locomotive (and tender, if any). This gives the weight in tons of 2,000 pounds of the train (including weight of cars and of lading, if cars are to be hauled loaded) which the locomotive can haul.

The resistance of **gravity** increases in exact proportion to the steepness of the grade; is always 20 pounds per ton of 2,000 pounds for each 1 foot per 100 rise; *i. e.*, if there is an elevation of 1 foot in a distance of 100 feet, the locomotive must exert enough force to lift one one-hundredth of the weight of the train (itself included), or, what amounts to the same thing, to exert a tractive force enough to overcome a resistance of 20 pounds per ton of 2,000 pounds. For a grade of ½ per cent the resistance of gravity is 10 pounds per ton; for 2 per cent, 40 pounds per ton, and so on for any practicable grade.

The resistance due to **rolling friction** varies with the character and condition of rolling stock and track. With extra good cars and track it may be as low as 5 pounds per ton of 2,000 pounds; but 6½ pounds may be taken as a fair average for first-class cars and track, 8 to 12 pounds for reasonably good conditions, and as high as 20 to 40 pounds for bad cars and track, and 60 to 80 pounds, or even more, for excessively hard-running cars and very rough track. Cars with fixed axles and suitable bearings and oil boxes should not exceed 8 to 12 pounds; logging cars may run 6½ to 15 pounds if of good construction, up to 20 or even 40 pounds if with poor arrangement for oiling. Contractors' dump cars are usually hard-running, say 10 to 25 pounds; coal-mine wagons, with loose wheels, are seldom less than 15 pounds, and often exceed 30 pounds; and with the holes in the wheels worn out of true, and the wheels scraping against the sides of the car, may develop 60 to 80 pounds, or even greater resistance. Street cars may be reckoned at 15 to 25 pounds. The resistance of flange friction on wooden rails is an indeterminate quantity, but usually twice the resistance on steel rails. Poorly laid track and crooked rails increase the resistance indefinitely.

Overloading cars also increases the resistance greatly. The resistance is greater in cold weather. The resistance of rolling friction per ton is greater for empty cars than for loaded cars.

THE ACTUAL RESISTANCE OF ROLLING FRICTION MAY BE DETERMINED by noting down what grade a car once started will just keep in motion. If a car will barely keep in motion if started down a 1 per cent grade, its frictional resistance is just about equal to 20 pounds per ton.

In computing the hauling capacity of any locomotive, the resistance due to gravity and the resistance due to rolling friction must be added, and the tractive force divided by this total resistance. For example: With cars and track involving $6\frac{1}{2}$ pounds per ton resistance, the hauling capacity on a level is found by dividing the tractive force by $6\frac{1}{2}$, and deducting the weight of the locomotive; but with the same cars on a grade of 2 per cent the tractive force must be divided by $46\frac{1}{2}$ ($6\frac{1}{2}$ + 40), and the weight of the locomotive deducted. It is easily seen that poorly constructed cars are very costly to operate; it is easier, for example, to haul cars of 10 pounds frictional resistance up a $1\frac{1}{2}$ per cent grade than to haul cars of 40 pounds frictional resistance up a $\frac{1}{2}$ per cent grade, the total resistance in one case being 40 pounds and in the other case 50 pounds per ton. Similarly, it is as easy to haul cars of 10 pounds per ton resistance up a 1 per cent grade as to haul cars of 50 pounds resistance down a 1 per cent grade.

When trains are hauled on curved track the resistance due to the curve should be considered, as explained on pages 177 and 178.

In any practical determination of the proper hauling capacity advisable in any special case, some suggestions by way of caution are shown by experience to be worthy of consideration:

1. It is always desirable to provide a reasonable amount of surplus power, and not to work a locomotive regularly too close to its full capacity. A reserve of power is economical, because it cuts down the cost of repairs, and also of fuel and oil, to the lowest point, and lengthens the useful lifetime of the machine, and also provides for emergencies and increase of output.

2. It is not safe to figure on a grade as "level" because the land is quite flat. In such cases the so-called "level" grade may prove to be 1 per cent or possibly more, and a grade of only $\frac{1}{4}$ of 1 per cent, or 13 feet per mile, may cut down the hauling capacity of a locomotive to but little more than one-half its capacity on a perfect level.

This is clearly seen by examination of the following tables of hauling capacities.

3. The statement is sometimes made that a geared locomotive can haul a heavier train and "climb" steeper grades than a direct-acting locomotive of **the same weight.** This is incorrect unless the direct-acting locomotive has only part of its weight on the driving wheels or is equipped with a separate tender. If two machines weigh the same and have all their weight on the driving wheels, and are properly designed, the loads they can start are absolutely identical, —*i. e.*, the introduction of gears has no effect upon the proportion of weight on driving wheels that is useful for adhesion on the rail. A direct-acting locomotive on account of the position of the crank-pins has more tendency to slip its wheels in starting trains. A geared locomotive cannot make the same mileage or handle as great daily tonnage and has less advantage from train momentum in overcoming grades.

4. It pays to buy a locomotive of proper design for the requirements and cars properly constructed, and it pays to keep the rolling stock in good order. It pays to avoid bad grades and sharp curves if it can be done at reasonable cost. It does not pay to let road-bed and track get into bad condition through neglect. In such cases as contractor's service, temporary logging spurs, tramways in quarries, dumps at furnaces, collieries, etc., where the track must be shifted frequently, ideal conditions are impracticable; but it pays to pay good wages to a foreman with brains who with the least cost of maintenance and repairs and least time lost will get the most results out of the plant.

Percentage Tables for Computing the Hauling Capacity (see next two pages)

Of any locomotive on any practicable grade and with cars of varying resistance of rolling friction.

Owing to the lack of space, it was found impossible to state with the descriptive text and illustration of each size and design the hauling capacity of each locomotive on all practicable grades, or for more than one rate of resistance of rolling friction.

By the following tables, by using the hauling capacity on a level with $6\frac{1}{2}$ pounds frictional resistance, as stated for each locomotive, as a basis, and reckoning this amount as 100 per cent, the hauling capacity on grades up to 580 feet per mile (*i. e.*, 11 per cent), and with resistances of rolling friction up to 40 pounds per ton of 2,000 pounds, may readily be calculated. The results are not absolutely exact, but are closely approximate.

NOTE.—These tables are on the basis of including tenders as a part of the train to be hauled on grades, and for minute accuracy any weight carried on engine trucks should be considered as a part of the train.

NOTE.—In the application of these tables it must be borne in mind that on very steep grades, *i. e.*, over about 8 per cent, slippery or wet rails, or failure to use sand, may prevent any safe, practical, or economical use of any locomotive. A locomotive can climb a steeper grade than it is safe for it to come down, since any acceleration of speed down an excessively steep grade may result in the engine sliding with all wheels locked.

EXAMPLE ILLUSTRATING THE USE OF THE FOLLOWING TABLES OF PERCENTAGES.—The hauling capacity of the locomotive code word HETMAN (page 38, 12 x 18 cylinders), at $6\frac{1}{2}$ pounds rate of frictional resistance on a level, is stated at 1,470 tons of 2,000 pounds. What can it haul on a grade of 4 per cent, and with cars and track involving 10 pounds per ton rolling friction? By turning to the tables below, at the intersection of the column for 10 pounds rate of friction with the horizontal line for 4 feet per 100—*i. e.*, 4 per cent grade—is found the figure $5\frac{6}{10}$, and $5\frac{6}{10}$ per cent of 1,470 is 82 tons; deducting from this 14 tons the weight of the tender of this locomotive, 68 tons is left, which is the heaviest train (lading of cars, if cars are loaded, and weight of cars included) this locomotive can start under the given conditions.

Percentage Tables for Computation of Hauling Capacity
With Grades and Frictional Resistances as noted below

GRADES	Percentages figured to include Frictional Resistances per ton of 2,000 lbs.										
	6½ lbs.	7 lbs.	8 lbs.	9 lbs.	10 lbs.	11 lbs.	12 lbs.	15 lbs.	20 lbs.	25 lbs.	30 lbs.	40 lbs.
On absolute level the percentage of hauling capacity is	100	93	81	72	64	58	53	42	31	24.5	20	14.5
1 foot per mile	94	87	77	69	62	56	52	41	31	24	20	14.5
2 feet " "	91	83	74	66	60	54	50	40	30	24	20	14.5
3 " " "	85	79	70	63	57.5	53	48.5	39	29.5	23.5	19.5	14
5 " " "	77	72	65	59	54	49	46	37	29	23	19	14
8 " " "	67.5	64	58	53	49	45	42	35	27	22	18	14
10 " " "	60.5	59	54	50	46	43	40	33	26	21	18	13
13 2/10 " " " (= 3 inches per 100 feet)	56	53	49	45	42	40	37	31	24.5	20	17	13
15 " " "	52	50	46	43	40	38	36	30	24	19.5	17	13
20 " " "	45	43	41	38	36	34	32	27.5	22	18.5	16	12
25 " " "	40	38	36	34	32	30.5	29	25	21	17	15	12
26 4/10 " " " (= 6 inches per 100 feet)	38	37	35	33	31	30	28	24.5	20	17	14.5	11.5
30 " " "	35	34	32	31	29	28	26.5	24	19	16	14	11
35 " " "	32	31	29	28	27	25.5	24.5	22	18	15.5	14	11
30 6/10 " " " (= 9 inches per 100 feet)	29	28	27	26	25	24	23	20	17	14.5	13	10
45 " " "	26	25	24	23	22	21.5	21	19	16	14	12	10
52 7/10 " " " (= 1 foot per 100)	23	22.5	22	21	20.4	19.5	19	17	14.5	13	11.5	9.3
55 " " "	22.5	22	21	20.5	20	19	18.5	17	14.5	12.5	11	9.2
60 " " "	21.5	20.5	20	19	18.5	18	17	16.5	13.5	12	10.5	8.8
66 " " " (= 1¼ feet per 100)	19.5	19	18.5	17.5	17	16.5	16	14.5	13	11.5	10.5	8.4
70 " " "	18.5	18	17.5	17	16.5	16	15.5	14	12.5	11	10	8.2
79 2/10 " " " (= 1½ feet per 100)	17.5	16	15.5	15.2	14.8	14.4	14	13	11.5	10.3	9.3	7.7
85 " " "	15.3	15.1	14.7	14.4	13.9	13.6	13.2	12.3	10.9	9.8	8.7	7.4
90 " " "	14.5	14.4	14	13.6	13.3	12.9	12.6	11.7	10.5	9.5	8.6	7.2
92 4/10 " " " (= 1¾ feet per 100)	14.2	14	13.6	13.3	13	12.6	12.3	11.5	10.3	9.3	8.4	7.1
100 " " "	13.2	13	12.7	12.4	12.1	11.8	11.5	10.8	9.7	8.8	8	6.8
105 6/10 " " " (= 2 feet per 100)	12.5	12.3	12	11.7	11.5	11.2	11	10.3	9.3	8.5	7.7	6.6
110 " " "	12	11.8	11.6	11.4	11.1	10.8	10.6	9.9	9	8.2	7.5	6.4
118 8/10 " " " (= 2¼ feet per 100)	11.1	11	10.7	10.5	10.3	10.1	9.9	9.3	8.4	7.7	7.1	6.1
120 " " "	11	10.9	10.6	10.4	10.2	10	9.8	9.2	8.4	7.7	7.1	6

	6½ lbs.	7 lbs.	8 lbs.	9 lbs.	10 lbs.	11 lbs.	12 lbs.	15 lbs.	20 lbs.	25 lbs.	30 lbs.	40 lbs.
130 feet per mile............	10.2	10	9.8	9.6	9.4	9.3	9.1	8.5	7.8	7.2	6.6	5.7
132 " " (= 2½ feet per 100)...	10	9.9	9.7	9.5	9.3	9.1	8.9	8.4	7.7	7.1	6.5	5.6
140 " "	9.4	9.3	9.1	8.9	8.7	8.6	8.4	8.0	7.4	6.8	6.3	5.4
145 2/10 " " (= 2¾ feet per 100)...	9.1	9.0	8.8	8.6	8.5	8.3	8.2	7.7	7.1	6.6	6.1	5.2
150 " "	8.7	8.6	8.5	8.3	8.2	8	7.9	7.5	6.9	6.4	5.9	5.1
158 4/10 " " (= 3 feet per 100)....	8.3	8.2	8.1	7.9	7.7	7.6	7.5	7.1	6.6	6.1	5.6	4.9
160 " "	8.1	8.0	7.9	7.8	7.6	7.5	7.4	7.0	6.5	6.0	5.6	4.8
170 " "	7.6	7.5	7.4	7.3	7.2	7.1	6.9	6.6	6.1	5.7	5.3	4.6
180 " "	7.2	7.1	7.0	6.9	6.7	6.6	6.5	6.2	5.8	5.4	5.0	4.4
184 8/10 " " (= 3½ feet per 100)...	6.9	6.8	6.8	6.7	6.5	6.5	6.4	6.1	5.6	5.3	4.9	4.3
190 " "	6.7	6.6	6.5	6.4	6.3	6.2	6.1	5.9	5.5	5.1	4.8	4.2
200 " "	6.4	6.3	6.2	6.1	6.0	5.9	5.8	5.6	5.2	4.8	4.5	4.0
211 2/10 " " (= 4 feet per 100)....	6.0	5.9	5.8	5.7	5.6	5.5	5.5	5.3	4.9	4.6	4.3	3.8
220 " "	5.6	5.7	5.6	5.5	5.4	5.3	5.2	5.0	4.8	4.4	4.1	3.6
230 " "	5.4	5.4	5.3	5.2	5.1	5.0	5.0	4.8	4.5	4.2	3.9	3.5
237 6/10 " " (= 4½ feet per 100)...	5.2	5.2	5.1	5.0	4.9	4.8	4.8	4.6	4.4	4.0	3.8	3.4
240 " "	5.1	5.1	5.0	4.9	4.8	4.8	4.7	4.5	4.3	3.9	3.7	3.3
250 " "	4.8	4.8	4.7	4.6	4.6	4.5	4.5	4.3	4.0	3.8	3.6	3.2
260 " "	4.6	4.6	4.5	4.5	4.4	4.3	4.3	4.1	3.9	3.7	3.4	3.1
264 " " (= 5 feet per 100)....	4.5	4.5	4.4	4.4	4.3	4.3	4.2	4.0	3.8	3.6	3.4	3.0
270 " "	4.4	4.4	4.3	4.3	4.2	4.2	4.1	3.9	3.8	3.5	3.3	3.0
280 " "	4.2	4.2	4.1	4.1	4.0	4.0	3.9	3.7	3.6	3.4	3.2	2.9
290 4/10 " " (= 5½ feet per 100)...	4.0	4.0	3.9	3.9	3.8	3.8	3.7	3.6	3.4	3.2	3.0	2.7
300 " "	3.8	3.8	3.7	3.7	3.7	3.6	3.6	3.4	3.3	3.1	2.9	2.6
316 8/10 " " (= 6 feet per 100)....	3.6	3.6	3.5	3.5	3.4	3.4	3.4	3.2	3.0	2.9	2.8	2.5
325 " "	3.5	3.4	3.4	3.4	3.3	3.3	3.2	3.1	2.9	2.8	2.7	2.4
350 " "	3.1	3.1	3.0	3.0	3.0	3.0	2.9	2.8	2.7	2.6	2.4	2.2
369 6/10 " " (= 7 feet per 100)....	2.9	2.8	2.8	2.8	2.8	2.7	2.7	2.6	2.5	2.4	2.2	2.0
375 " "	2.8	2.8	2.8	2.7	2.7	2.7	2.6	2.6	2.4	2.3	2.2	2.0
400 " "	2.5	2.5	2.5	2.5	2.4	2.4	2.4	2.3	2.2	2.1	2.0	1.8
422 4/10 " " (= 8 feet per 100)....	2.3	2.3	2.3	2.3	2.2	2.2	2.2	2.1	2.0	1.9	1.8	1.6
450 " "	2.1	2.1	2.1	2.0	2.0	2.0	2.0	1.9	1.8	1.7	1.6	1.5
475 2/10 " " (= 9 feet per 100)....	1.9	1.9	1.9	1.8	1.8	1.8	1.8	1.7	1.6	1.6	1.5	1.4
500 " "	1.7	1.7	1.7	1.7	1.7	1.6	1.6	1.6	1.5	1.4	1.4	1.2
528 " " (= 10 feet per 100)...	1.5	1.5	1.5	1.5	1.5	1.5	1.5	1.4	1.4	1.3	1.2	1.1
550 " "	1.4	1.4	1.4	1.4	1.4	1.4	1.4	1.3	1.3	1.2	1.1	1.1
580 8/10 " " (= 11 feet per 100)...	1.3	1.3	1.2	1.2	1.2	1.2	1.2	1.2	1.1	1.0	1.0	.9

TABLE showing how many times its weight on driving wheels any locomotive can haul on straight track up various grades, at different allowances for frictional resistances. The tractive power is assumed to be equal to one-fifth of the weight on the driving wheels. Tenders and weight on pony trucks must be considered as if part of train weight.

Frictional Resistances of Train in pounds per ton of 2,000 pounds

	6½	7	8	9	10	11	12	15	20	25	30	40
Number of times its weight on driving wheels any locomotive can haul on absolute level	60.5	56	49	43.5	39	35.3	32.3	25.7	19	15	13.3	9
On grade ¼ per cent = 13 2/10 feet per mile	33.8	32.3	29.7	27.6	25.7	24	22.5	19	15	12.3	10.4	7.9
" ½ " = 26 4/10 "	23.3	22.5	21.2	20	19	18	17.2	15	12.3	10.4	9	7
" ¾ " = 39 6/10 "	17.6	17.2	16.4	15.6	15	14.4	13.8	12.3	10.4	9	7.9	6.25
" 1 " = 52 8/10 "	14.1	13.8	13.3	12.8	12.3	11.9	11.5	10.4	9	7.9	7	5.6
" 1¼ " = 66 "	11.7	11.5	11.1	10.8	10.4	10.1	9.8	9	7.9	7	6.3	5.1
" 1½ " = 79 2/10 "	10	9.8	9.5	9.2	9	8.7	8.5	7.9	7	6.3	5.6	4.7
" 1¾ " = 92 4/10 "	8.65	8.5	8.3	8.1	7.9	7.7	7.5	7	6.25	5.6	5.15	4.3
" 2 " = 105 6/10 "	7.6	7.5	7.3	7.1	7	6.8	6.7	6.25	5.6	5	4.7	4
" 2¼ " = 118 8/10 "	6.77	6.7	6.5	6.4	6.25	6.1	6	5.6	5.1	4.7	4.3	3.7
" 2½ " = 132 "	6.08	6	5.9	5.78	5.68	5.55	5.46	5.15	4.7	4.32	4	3.45
" 2¾ " = 145 2/10 "	5.5	5.45	5.35	5.25	5.16	5.07	4.97	4.71	4.33	4	3.7	3.22
" 3 " = 158 4/10 "	5.02	4.97	4.88	4.8	4.71	4.64	4.56	4.34	4	3.71	3.45	3
" 3½ " = 184 8/10 "	4.23	4.2	4.13	4.07	4	3.94	3.88	3.7	3.45	3.22	3	2.64
" 4 " = 211 2/10 "	3.62	3.6	3.55	3.5	3.45	3.4	3.35	3.21	3	2.81	2.64	2.33
" 4½ " = 237 6/10 "	3.15	3.12	3.08	3.04	3	2.96	2.92	2.81	2.64	2.48	2.34	2.08
" 5 " = 264 "	2.75	2.74	2.7	2.67	2.64	2.61	2.57	2.48	2.33	2.2	2.08	1.86
" 5½ " = 290 4/10 "	2.43	2.41	2.39	2.36	2.33	2.31	2.28	2.2	2.08	1.96	1.86	1.66
" 6 " = 318 8/10 "	2.16	2.15	2.12	2.1	2.08	2.05	2.03	1.96	1.86	1.76	1.66	1.5
" 7 " = 369 6/10 "	1.73	1.72	1.7	1.68	1.66	1.65	1.63	1.58	1.5	1.42	1.35	1.22
" 8 " = 422 4/10 "	1.4	1.39	1.38	1.37	1.35	1.34	1.32	1.28	1.22	1.16	1.1	1
" 9 " = 475 2/10 "	1.15	1.14	1.13	1.12	1.1	1.09	1.08	1.05	1	.95	.9	.82
" 10 " = 528 "	.94	.93	.92	.91	.9	.89	.88	.86	.82	.78	.74	.67
" 11 " = 580 8/10 "	.77	.76	.76	.75	.74	.73	.72	.7	.67	.63	.6	.54

The above table is useful for the selection of a locomotive of suitable weight to do any given work, since it shows the relative power of a locomotive on any practicable grade and with varying allowance for frictional resistance. Example: How heavy a locomotive is needed to start 50 tons on a 3 per cent grade with contractors' cars and poor track involving a frictional resistance of 20 pounds per ton? By following the column for 20 pounds resistance to the intersection of the horizontal line for 3 per cent grade, the figure 4 is noted, i.e., a locomotive under these conditions can haul four times its weight on driving wheels; since 4 times 12½ = 50, a locomotive 12½ tons, or 25,000 pounds in weight, with all the weight on driving wheels, would be needed.

Memoranda as to Tables of Hauling Capacity
(see pages 162 to 169)

The following series of four Tables of Hauling Capacity is convenient for quick approximate selection of a locomotive to do any required work. The Hauling Capacity of locomotives ranging from 4,000 to 80,000 pounds weight on driving wheels, and on grades from level to 11 per cent, is stated in each table. The tractive force is assumed to be equivalent to one-fifth the weight of the locomotive, (the weight being all on the driving wheels.)

TABLE I is based on a resistance of rolling friction of **6½ pounds per ton of 2,000 pounds,** and is to be used where the track and rolling stock are of good construction and in good condition. This would usually apply to passenger and freight roads, wide or narrow gauge, also to many roads for various industrial and special purposes where proper attention is given to maintenance.

TABLE II is based on a resistance of rolling friction of **8 pounds per ton of 2,000 pounds,** and is applicable to passenger and freight roads, and to roads used for a wide range of purposes, such as plantations, logging, coal and ore haulage, where the track may be expected to be in fair condition, and where the cars, if not in the best order and of the best construction, are not defective nor specially in need of repair.

TABLE III is based on a resistance of rolling friction of **15 pounds per ton of 2,000 pounds,** and is applicable to industrial tramways, coal and ore roads, plantations, logging roads, etc., where the track is in somewhat poor condition, and the cars not of the best construction or not in thoroughly good order.

TABLE IV is based on a resistance of rolling friction of **30 pounds per ton of 2,000 pounds,** and applies to cases where the service is such that the track cannot be kept in good order, and where the construction of the cars involves extra friction, or where repairs are needed. This includes contractors' tramways where cars and track cannot be kept in good order; coal and ore roads where cars with loose wheels are used; street railways where it is impossible to keep the track in proper condition; logging roads where four-wheel cars of imperfect design are used. A resistance of 30 pounds per ton is usually a proof of lack of reasonable care of track and cars. In the case of steel works or furnaces, where hot material requires very clumsy cars and renders it difficult to give proper lubrication to car journals, also in contractors' work, or at brick yards where the track is frequently shifted, it may be impossible to avoid a greater resistance than 30 pounds per ton.

No account is taken in these tables of the resistance of curves or of speed.

The weights of the trains that can be hauled are stated in tons of 2,000 pounds, and include cars and lading (except where only empty cars are to be hauled). Except for passenger service, it is usually safe to allow the weight of an empty car to be about four-tenths its carrying capacity.

The weights of trains are in addition to the locomotive; but if the locomotive has a tender, the tender is considered as a part of the train. (For minute accuracy or on excessive grades, any portion of the weight of the locomotive that may be carried on front or rear trucks should be considered also as a part of the train.)

In the practical application of these tables, it is well to bear in mind that it is most economical to operate locomotives regularly at not more than about two-thirds or three-fourths of their full power, according to circumstances; that for saddle-tank locomotives it is safest to reckon the weight with tanks about half full, to allow for average conditions; that in determining the weight a locomotive can haul, the steepest grade and not the average grade must be taken; also that for short grades, where curves or other reasons do not prevent approaching the grade at a fair rate of speed, a locomotive can take about 50 per cent more up the grade than it can start on the grade

Practical Illustrations of the Use of the Following Four Tables (see pages 162 to 169)

EXAMPLE 1.—How heavy a train can a contractors' saddle-tank locomotive, weighing 24,000 pounds, all on the driving wheels, resistance of rolling friction assumed at 15 pounds per ton, start on a grade of 3 per cent?

Making allowance of 1,000 pounds for tank of locomotive being only part full, Table III, under the column heading for 23,000 pounds, and along the horizontal line for 3 per cent grade, gives the answer 49 tons; or reckoning regular work at two-thirds to three-fourths of full capacity, say 32 to 37 tons as the weight of train which this locomotive, with somewhat poor track and cars, can start constantly with desirable reserve power on a 3 per cent grade. Or if the grade is short, and can be approached at a good rate of speed, the locomotive may be able to take up about 74 tons by taking advantage of momentum.

EXAMPLE 2.—What should be the weight on driving wheels of a locomotive with pony truck and separate tender for it to be able on special test to start 40 tons on a 4 per cent grade, the conditions involving a resistance of rolling friction of 8 pounds per ton?

Turning to Table II, and following the horizontal line for 4 per cent grade, it is evident that—not allowing for weight of tender nor for weight on pony truck—a locomotive with 23,000 pounds on the driving wheels is required. Allowing 10 tons to cover weight of tender and weight on pony truck, and considering this weight as practically part of the train, a total weight of 50 tons is to be provided for, and this is seen to require a locomotive with 28,000 pounds on the driving wheels.

EXAMPLE 3.—It is desired to haul a train of 50 tons, with conditions involving 30 pounds per ton resistance of rolling friction, with a saddle-tank locomotive, which, under average conditions, is 30,000 pounds total weight, of which 22,000 pounds is on the driving wheels and the remainder on pony truck; how steep a grade is practicable, running the engine at three-fourths its full power?

To the 50-ton train the 4 tons carried on the engine truck is added, making a total of 54 tons; this is increased by one-third, making 72 tons, to cover the weight of train that could be hauled with the engine working at full power. Turning to Table IV, under the column for 22,000 pounds on driving wheels it is seen that a locomotive of this weight can start 77 tons on a grade of 1 per cent, or 69 tons on a grade of 1¼ per cent. The steepest practicable grade would therefore be between 1 per cent and 1¼ per cent; or, if the engine should be used at its full power and a load of not over 54 tons be considered, it will be noted that a grade of very nearly 2 per cent would be practicable.

Table I. Approximate Hauling Capacity, Extra Good Cars, 6½ Pounds per Ton Resistance of Rolling Friction

Showing weight in tons of 2,000 pounds of heaviest trains, exclusive of the locomotive; inclusive of weight of cars and lading (and tender if any); which locomotives with 4 000 to 80,000 pounds on the driving wheels can haul on straight track in good order on grades from **Absolute Level** to **11 feet per 100.** The **Tractive Force** is assumed to be one-fifth of the weight on driving wheels

	TOTAL WEIGHTS ON DRIVING WHEELS IN POUNDS																											
	4,000	5,000	6,000	7,000	8,000	9,000	10,000	11,000	12,000	13,000	14,000	15,000	16,000	17,000	18,000	19,000	20,000	21,000	22,000	23,000	24,000	26,000	28,000	30,000	32,000	34,000	36,000	38,000
Absolute level..........	121	151	181	212	242	272	302	332	363	393	423	453	483	513	544	574	605	635	665	696	726	786	847	907	968	1029	1089	1150
¼ per cent = 13 2/10 ft. per mile	67	84	101	118	135	152	169	186	202	219	236	253	270	287	304	321	338	355	371	388	405	439	473	507	540	574	608	642
½ " = 26 4/10 "	46	58	69	81	93	104	116	128	139	151	163	174	186	197	209	221	232	244	255	267	279	302	325	348	372	395	418	442
¾ " = 39 6/10 "	35	44	52	61	70	79	88	96	105	114	123	132	141	149	158	167	176	185	193	202	211	229	246	264	282	299	317	334
1 " = 52 8/10 "	28	35	42	49	56	63	70	77	84	91	98	105	112	119	127	134	141	148	155	162	169	183	197	211	225	239	253	267
1¼ " = 66 "	23	29	35	41	46	52	58	64	70	76	82	87	93	99	105	111	117	123	128	134	140	152	164	175	187	199	210	222
1½ " = 79 2/10 "	19	24	29	34	39	44	49	54	59	64	69	74	79	84	89	94	99	104	109	114	119	129	139	149	159	169	179	189
1¾ " = 92 4/10 "	17	21	25	30	34	38	43	47	51	56	60	64	69	73	77	82	86	90	95	99	103	112	121	129	138	147	155	164
2 " = 105 6/10 "	15	19	22	26	30	34	38	41	45	49	53	57	60	64	68	72	76	79	83	87	91	98	106	114	121	129	136	144
2¼ " = 118 8/10 "	13	16	20	23	27	30	33	37	40	44	47	50	54	57	60	64	67	71	74	77	81	88	94	101	108	115	121	128
2½ " = 132 "	12	15	18	21	24	27	30	33	36	39	42	45	48	51	54	57	60	63	66	69	73	79	85	91	97	103	109	115
2¾ " = 145 2/10 "	11	13	16	19	22	24	27	30	33	35	38	41	44	46	49	52	55	57	60	63	66	71	77	82	88	93	99	104
3 " = 158 4/10 "	10	12	15	17	20	22	25	27	30	32	35	37	40	42	45	47	50	52	55	57	60	65	70	75	80	85	90	95
3½ " = 184 8/10 "	8	10	12	14	16	19	21	23	25	27	29	31	33	35	38	40	42	44	46	48	50	54	59	63	67	71	76	80
4 " = 211 2/10 "	7	9	10	12	14	16	18	19	21	23	25	27	29	30	32	34	36	38	39	41	43	47	50	54	58	61	65	68
4½ " = 237 6/10 "	6	7	9	11	12	14	15	17	18	20	22	23	25	26	28	29	31	33	34	36	37	40	44	47	50	53	56	59
5 " = 264 "	5	6	8	9	11	12	13	15	16	17	19	20	22	23	24	26	27	28	30	31	33	35	38	41	44	46	49	52
5½ " = 290 4/10 "	4	6	7	8	9	10	11	12	14	15	17	18	19	20	21	23	24	25	26	27	29	31	34	36	38	41	43	46
6 " = 316 8/10 "	4	5	6	7	8	9	10	11	12	14	15	16	17	18	19	20	21	22	23	24	25	28	30	32	34	36	38	41
7 " = 369 6/10 "	3	4	5	6	6	7	8	9	10	11	12	12	13	14	15	16	17	18	19	19	20	22	24	25	27	29	31	32
8 " = 422 4/10 "	2	3	4	4	5	6	7	7	8	9	9	10	11	11	12	13	14	14	15	16	16	18	19	21	22	23	25	26
9 " = 475 2/10 "	2	2	3	4	4	5	5	6	6	7	8	8	9	9	10	10	11	12	12	13	13	14	16	17	18	19	20	21
10 " = 528 "	1	2	2	3	3	4	4	5	5	6	6	7	7	7	8	8	9	9	10	10	11	12	13	14	15	15	16	17
11 " = 580 8/10 "	1	1	2	2	3	3	3	4	4	4	5	5	6	6	6	7	7	8	8	8	9	9	10	11	12	13	13	14

Continuation of Table I on opposite page

	TOTAL WEIGHTS ON DRIVING WHEELS IN POUNDS																				
	40,000	42,000	44,000	46,000	48,000	50,000	52,000	54,000	56,000	58,000	60,000	62,000	64,000	66,000	68,000	70,000	72,000	74,000	76,000	78,000	80,000
Absolute level..................	1210	1270	1330	1390	1450	1510	1570	1630	1690	1750	1810	1875	1935	1995	2055	2115	2175	2235	2300	2360	2420
¼ per cent = $13\frac{2}{10}$ ft. per mile	675	710	743	777	810	845	878	912	946	980	1013	1047	1080	1115	1149	1183	1216	1250	1285	1317	1350
½ " = $26\frac{4}{10}$ " "	465	487	511	534	557	581	604	627	651	674	697	720	744	767	790	813	837	860	883	907	930
¾ " = $39\frac{6}{10}$ " "	352	369	387	405	422	440	457	475	493	511	528	546	563	581	598	616	633	651	669	687	705
1 " = $52\frac{8}{10}$ " "	282	296	310	324	338	352	366	380	394	408	422	437	451	465	479	493	507	521	535	550	564
1¼ " = 66 " "	234	246	257	269	281	292	304	316	328	339	351	363	374	386	398	409	421	433	445	457	468
1½ " = $79\frac{2}{10}$ " "	199	209	219	229	239	249	259	269	278	288	298	308	318	328	338	348	358	368	378	388	398
1¾ " = $92\frac{4}{10}$ " "	173	181	190	199	207	216	224	233	242	250	259	268	276	285	294	302	311	320	328	337	346
2 " = $105\frac{6}{10}$ " "	152	159	167	174	182	190	197	205	212	220	227	235	243	250	255	266	273	281	288	296	304
2¼ " = $118\frac{8}{10}$ " "	135	142	148	155	162	169	176	182	189	196	203	209	216	223	230	236	243	250	257	264	270
2½ " = 132 " "	121	127	133	139	146	152	158	164	170	176	182	188	194	200	206	212	218	225	231	237	243
2¾ " = $145\frac{2}{10}$ " "	110	115	121	126	132	137	143	148	154	159	165	170	176	181	187	192	198	203	209	214	220
3 " = $158\frac{4}{10}$ " "	100	105	110	115	120	125	130	135	140	145	150	155	160	165	170	175	180	185	190	195	200
3½ " = $184\frac{8}{10}$ " "	84	88	93	97	101	105	109	114	118	122	126	131	135	139	143	147	152	156	160	164	169
4 " = $211\frac{2}{10}$ " "	72	76	79	83	87	90	94	97	101	105	108	112	115	119	123	126	130	134	137	141	144
4½ " = $237\frac{6}{10}$ " "	62	66	69	72	75	78	81	84	88	91	94	97	100	103	107	110	113	116	119	122	125
5 " = 264 " "	55	57	60	63	66	69	71	74	77	80	82	85	88	91	93	96	99	101	104	107	110
5½ " = $290\frac{4}{10}$ " "	48	51	53	55	58	60	63	65	68	70	73	75	77	80	82	85	87	90	92	94	97
6 " = $316\frac{8}{10}$ " "	43	45	47	49	51	54	56	58	60	62	64	66	69	71	73	75	77	79	82	84	86
7 " = $369\frac{6}{10}$ " "	34	36	38	39	41	43	45	46	48	50	51	53	55	57	58	60	62	64	65	67	69
8 " = $422\frac{4}{10}$ " "	28	29	30	32	33	35	36	37	39	40	42	43	44	46	47	49	50	51	53	54	56
9 " = $475\frac{2}{10}$ " "	22	23	25	26	27	28	29	30	32	33	34	35	36	37	38	40	41	42	43	44	45
10 " = 528 " "	18	19	20	21	22	23	24	25	26	27	28	29	30	31	31	32	33	34	35	36	37
11 " = $580\frac{8}{10}$ " "	15	16	16	17	18	19	19	20	21	22	22	23	24	25	26	26	27	28	29	29	30

The above table is especially valuable for determining at a glance approximately the weight of locomotive needed to haul stated loads up stated grades. The exact weight and the design may then be determined according to the kind of traffic, exact frictional resistance, curves and other conditions.

NOTE.—In the case of saddle-tank engines, it is well to make a deduction from the weight on driving wheels to allow for the tank being only partly full under average conditions. In the case of locomotives with separate tender, the tender must be reckoned as a part of the train to be hauled. Also for engines with trucks, the weight on truck should be deducted to arrive at net weight of train, particularly on very steep grades. Speed is not taken into account.

Table II. Approximate Hauling Capacity, Average Good Cars, 8 Pounds per Ton Resistance of Rolling Friction

Showing weight in tons of 2,000 pounds of heaviest trains, exclusive of the locomotive; inclusive of weight of cars and lading (and tender, if any); which locomotives with 4,000 to 80,000 pounds on the driving wheels can haul on straight track in good order on grades from **Absolute Level** to **11 feet per 100**. The **Tractive Force** is assumed to be one-fifth of the weight on driving wheels.

TOTAL WEIGHTS ON DRIVING WHEELS IN POUNDS

Grade	ft per mile	4,000	5,000	6,000	7,000	8,000	9,000	10,000	11,000	12,000	13,000	14,000	15,000	16,000	17,000	18,000	19,000	20,000	21,000	22,000	23,000	24,000	26,000	28,000	30,000	32,000
Absolute level.......		98	122	147	171	196	220	245	269	294	318	343	367	392	417	441	466	490	514	539	563	588	637	686	735	784
¼ per cent	= $13\frac{2}{10}$	59	74	89	104	119	133	148	163	178	193	208	223	238	253	268	282	297	312	327	342	357	387	417	447	476
½ "	= $26\frac{4}{10}$	42	53	63	74	84	95	106	116	127	138	148	159	169	180	191	201	212	223	233	244	254	276	297	318	339
¾ "	= $39\frac{6}{10}$	32	41	49	57	65	74	82	90	98	106	114	123	131	139	147	156	164	172	180	188	196	213	229	246	262
1 "	= $52\frac{8}{10}$	26	33	39	46	53	59	66	73	79	86	93	100	106	113	119	126	133	139	146	153	159	173	186	199	212
1¼ "	= 66	22	27	33	39	44	50	55	61	66	72	77	83	89	94	100	105	111	116	122	128	133	144	156	167	178
1½ "	= $79\frac{2}{10}$	19	24	28	33	38	42	47	52	57	62	66	71	76	81	85	90	95	100	104	109	114	124	133	143	152
1¾ "	= $92\frac{4}{10}$	16	20	24	29	33	37	41	45	49	54	58	62	66	70	74	78	83	87	91	95	99	108	116	124	132
2 "	= $105\frac{6}{10}$	14	18	22	25	29	33	36	40	44	47	51	55	58	62	66	70	73	77	80	84	88	95	102	110	117
2¼ "	= $118\frac{8}{10}$	13	16	19	22	26	29	32	35	39	42	45	49	52	55	59	62	65	68	72	75	78	85	91	98	104
2½ "	= 132	12	14	17	20	23	26	29	32	35	38	41	44	47	50	53	56	59	62	65	68	70	76	82	88	94
2¾ "	= $145\frac{2}{10}$	11	13	16	18	21	24	26	29	32	34	37	40	42	45	48	51	53	56	59	61	64	69	75	80	84
3 "	= $158\frac{4}{10}$	9	11	14	17	19	22	24	26	29	31	34	36	39	41	44	46	48	51	53	56	58	63	68	73	78
3½ "	= $184\frac{8}{10}$	8	10	12	14	16	18	20	22	24	26	28	31	33	35	37	39	41	43	45	47	49	53	57	62	66
4 "	= $211\frac{2}{10}$	7	8	10	12	14	15	17	19	21	23	24	26	28	30	31	33	35	37	39	40	42	46	50	53	56
4½ "	= $237\frac{6}{10}$	6	7	9	10	12	13	15	16	18	20	21	23	25	26	27	29	30	32	33	35	37	40	43	46	50
5 "	= 264	5	6	8	9	10	12	13	14	16	17	18	20	21	23	24	25	27	28	29	30	32	35	37	40	42
5½ "	= $290\frac{4}{10}$	4	5	7	8	9	10	11	13	14	15	16	17	19	20	21	22	23	25	26	27	28	31	33	35	38
6 "	= $316\frac{8}{10}$	4	5	6	7	8	9	10	11	12	13	14	15	16	18	19	20	21	22	23	24	25	27	29	31	32
7 "	= $369\frac{6}{10}$	3	4	5½	5	6	7	8	9	10	11	11	12	13	14	15	16	17	17	18	19	20	22	23	25	26
8 "	= $422\frac{4}{10}$	3	3½	4	5	6	6½	7	7½	8	8½	9	10	11	11	12	13	13	14	15	16	16	17	19	21	22
9 "	= $475\frac{2}{10}$	2	2½	3	3½	4	4½	5	5½	6	6½	7	8	9	9½	10	10	11	11	12	12	13	14	15	16	18
10 "	= 528	2	2	2½	3	3½	4	4½	5	5½	6	6½	7	7½	8	8	8½	9	9½	10	10	11	12	13	14	14
11 "	= $580\frac{8}{10}$	1	1½	2	2½	3	3	3½	4	4	4½	5	5½	6	6	6½	7	7	7½	8	8½	9	9½	10	11	12

Continuation of Table II on opposite page

TOTAL WEIGHTS ON DRIVING WHEELS IN POUNDS

per cent	ft. per mile	34,000	36,000	38,000	40,000	42,000	44,000	46,000	48,000	50,000	52,000	54,000	56,000	58,000	60,000	62,000	64,000	66,000	68,000	70,000	72,000	74,000	76,000	78,000	80,000
Absolute level		833	882	931	980	1029	1078	1127	1176	1225	1274	1323	1372	1421	1470	1519	1568	1617	1666	1715	1764	1813	1862	1917	1966
1/4	13 2/10	506	536	566	596	626	655	685	715	744	774	804	833	863	893	922	952	982	1012	1042	1072	1102	1132	1162	1192
1/2	26 4/10	301	382	403	424	445	467	488	509	531	552	573	594	616	637	658	679	701	722	743	764	786	807	828	849
3/4	39 6/10	278	294	312	328	344	360	376	392	410	426	442	458	475	492	508	524	540	556	572	588	606	623	639	656
1	52 8/10	226	240	254	266	278	292	306	318	330	345	359	372	385	398	411	424	438	452	465	478	491	504	518	532
1 1/4	66	188	200	210	222	232	244	256	266	276	288	300	312	323	334	345	356	367	377	388	400	411	422	433	444
1 1/2	79 2/10	162	170	180	190	200	208	218	228	238	248	257	266	276	286	295	304	314	324	333	342	352	362	371	380
1 3/4	92 4/10	140	148	156	166	174	182	190	198	207	216	224	232	240	248	257	265	273	282	290	298	307	315	323	332
2	105 6/10	124	132	139	146	154	161	168	176	183	190	198	205	213	220	227	234	241	248	256	264	271	279	286	293
2 1/4	118 8/10	110	118	124	130	136	144	150	156	164	170	176	184	190	196	203	210	216	223	229	236	242	248	254	260
2 1/2	132	100	106	112	118	124	130	136	141	147	153	159	164	170	176	182	188	194	200	206	212	218	224	230	236
2 3/4	145 2/10	90	96	102	106	112	118	122	128	133	138	144	150	155	160	165	171	176	181	187	192	198	204	209	214
3	158 4/10	82	88	92	97	102	106	112	116	122	126	132	136	141	146	151	156	161	166	171	176	181	186	191	196
3 1/2	184 8/10	70	74	78	82	86	90	94	98	102	106	111	115	120	124	128	132	136	140	144	148	152	156	161	166
4	211 2/10	60	63	66	70	74	78	81	84	88	92	96	100	103	106	109	112	116	120	123	126	130	134	138	141
4 1/2	237 6/10	52	55	58	61	63	66	70	74	77	80	83	86	89	92	95	98	101	104	108	111	114	117	120	123
5	264	46	48	52	54	56	58	60	64	67	70	73	75	78	80	83	86	89	92	94	96	100	102	105	108
5 1/2	290 4/10	40	42	45	47	50	52	54	56	59	62	64	66	68	70	73	76	78	80	83	86	88	90	93	95
6	316 8/10	36	38	40	42	44	46	48	50	52	54	56	58	61	63	65	68	70	72	74	76	78	80	82	84
7	369 6/10	28	30	32	34	35	36	38	40	42	44	46	47	49	51	52	54	56	57	59	61	63	64	66	68
8	422 4/10	23	24	26	27	28	30	32	33	34	35	37	38	40	41	42	44	45	47	48	49	51	52	53	55
9	475 2/10	19	20	21	22	23	24	25	26	28	29	30	31	32	33	35	36	37	38	39	40	41	42	43	44
10	528	15	16	17	18	19	20	21	22	23	24	25	26	26	27	28	29	30	31	32	33	34	35	36	37
11	580 8/10	12	13	14	15	15	16	17	18	18	19	20	21	21	22	23	24	25	25	26	27	28	28	29	30

The above table is especially valuable for determining at a glance approximately the weight of locomotive needed to haul stated loads up stated grades. The exact weight and the design may then be determined according to the kind of traffic, exact frictional resistance, curves and other conditions.

NOTE.—In the case of saddle-tank engines, it is well to make a deduction from the weight on driving wheels to allow for the tank being only partly full under average conditions. In the case of locomotives with separate tender, the tender must be reckoned as part of the train to be hauled. Also for engines with trucks, the weight on truck should be deducted to arrive at net weight of train, particularly on very steep grades. Speed is not taken into account.

Table III. Approximate Hauling Capacity, Poor Cars, 15 Pounds per Ton Resistance of Rolling Friction

Showing weight in tons of 2,000 pounds of heaviest trains, exclusive of the locomotive; inclusive of weight of cars and lading (and tender, if any); which locomotives, with 4,000 to 80,000 pounds on the driving wheels, can haul on straight track in good order on grades from Absolute Level to 11 feet per 100. The Tractive Force is assumed to be one-fifth of the weight on driving wheels.

TOTAL WEIGHTS ON DRIVING WHEELS IN POUNDS

Grade	ft/mile	4,000	5,000	6,000	7,000	8,000	9,000	10,000	11,000	12,000	13,000	14,000	15,000	16,000	17,000	18,000	19,000	20,000	21,000	22,000	23,000	24,000	26,000
Absolute level	—	51	63	76	89	102	114	127	140	153	166	179	192	205	218	231	244	257	269	282	295	308	334
1/4 percent	13 2/10	38	47	57	66	76	85	95	104	114	123	133	142	152	161	171	180	190	199	209	218	228	247
1/2 "	26 6/10	30	37	45	52	60	67	75	82	90	97	105	112	120	127	135	143	150	157	165	172	180	195
3/4 "	39 9/10	24	30	37	43	49	55	61	67	74	80	86	92	98	104	111	117	123	129	135	141	147	160
1 "	52 8/10	20	25	31	36	41	46	52	57	62	67	73	78	83	89	93	98	104	109	115	120	125	135
1 1/4 "	66	18	22	27	31	36	40	45	49	54	58	63	67	72	76	81	85	90	94	99	103	108	117
1 1/2 "	79 2/10	16	19	23	27	31	35	39	43	47	51	55	59	63	67	71	75	79	83	87	91	95	103
1 3/4 "	92 4/10	14	17	21	24	28	31	35	38	42	45	49	52	56	59	63	66	70	73	77	80	84	91
2 "	105 6/10	12	15	18	21	25	28	31	34	37	40	43	46	50	53	56	59	62	65	68	71	74	81
2 1/4 "	118 8/10	11	14	17	20	23	25	28	31	34	36	39	42	45	48	51	53	56	59	62	65	68	73
2 1/2 "	132	10	13	15	18	20	23	25	28	30	33	36	38	41	43	46	49	51	53	56	59	62	67
2 3/4 "	145 2/10	9	11	14	16	18	21	23	26	28	30	33	35	38	40	42	44	47	49	51	53	56	61
3 "	158 4/10	8	10	13	15	17	19	21	23	26	28	30	32	34	36	39	41	43	45	47	49	52	56
3 1/4 "	171 6/10	7	9	11	13	15	16	18	20	22	24	26	27	29	31	33	35	37	38	40	42	44	48
3 1/2 "	184 8/10	6	8	10	11	13	14	16	18	19	21	22	24	25	27	28	30	32	33	35	36	38	41
3 3/4 "	198	5	7	8	10	11	12	14	15	16	18	19	20	22	23	25	26	28	29	31	32	33	36
4 "	211 2/10	5	6	7	8	10	11	12	13	14	16	17	18	19	21	22	23	24	26	27	28	29	32
4 1/2 "	237 6/10	4	5	6	7	8	9	10	12	13	14	15	16	17	18	19	20	22	23	24	25	26	28
5 "	264	3	4	5	6	7	8	9	10	11	12	13	14	15	16	17	18	19	20	21	22	23	25
5 1/2 "	290 4/10	3 1/2	4	5	5	6	7	8	9	9 1/2	10 1/2	11	12 1/2	13 1/2	14 1/2	15	16	17	18	19	20	21	23
6 "	316 8/10	3	3 1/2	4	5	5 1/2	6	7	8	8 1/2	9	10	10 1/2	11 1/2	12	13	13 1/2	15	15	17	17	19	20
7 "	369 6/10	2 1/2	3	3 1/2	4	4 1/2	5	6	7	7	7 1/2	8	9 1/2	10	10 1/2	11	12	13	13	14	15	16
8 "	422 4/10	2	2 1/2	3	3	3 1/2	4	5	5	6	6 1/2	7	7 1/2	8	8 1/2	9 1/2	10	10	11	12	12	13
9 "	475 2/10	1 1/2	2	2 1/2	3	3	3 1/2	4	5	5	5 1/2	6	6 1/2	7	7 1/2	7 1/2	8 1/2	8 1/2	9	9 1/2	10	10	11
10 "	528	1	1 1/2	2	2 1/2	2 1/2	3	3 1/2	4	4	5	5	5 1/2	6	6 1/2	7	7 1/2	7 1/2	7 1/2	7 1/2	8	10	10
11 "	580 8/10	1	1 1/2	2	2	2 1/2	3	3	3 1/2	4	4 1/2	5	5	5 1/2	6	6	6 1/2	7	7 1/2	7 1/2	8	8	9

Continuation of Table III on opposite page

TOTAL WEIGHT ON DRIVING WHEELS

Grade	28,000	30,000	32,000	34,000	36,000	38,000	40,000	42,000	44,000	46,000	48,000	50,000	52,000	54,000	56,000	58,000	60,000	62,000	64,000	66,000	68,000	70,000	72,000	74,000	76,000	78,000	80,000
Absolute level	359	385	410	436	462	488	514	540	565	591	617	643	668	693	718	744	770	796	822	847	872	898	924	950	976	1002	1028
¼ per cent = $13\frac{2}{10}$ ft. per mile	266	285	304	323	342	361	380	399	418	437	456	475	494	513	532	551	570	589	608	627	646	665	684	703	722	741	760
½ " = $26\frac{4}{10}$ "	210	225	240	255	270	285	300	315	330	345	360	375	390	405	420	435	450	465	480	495	510	525	540	555	570	585	600
¾ " = $39\frac{6}{10}$ "	172	185	197	209	222	234	247	259	271	284	296	308	321	333	345	358	370	382	395	407	419	432	444	456	469	481	493
1 " = $52\frac{8}{10}$ "	146	156	166	177	188	198	208	219	230	240	250	261	271	281	292	303	313	323	334	344	355	365	375	386	397	407	417
1¼ " = 66 "	126	135	144	153	162	171	180	189	198	207	216	225	234	243	252	261	270	279	288	297	306	315	324	333	342	351	360
1½ " = $79\frac{2}{10}$ "	111	119	126	134	142	150	157	165	173	181	189	197	205	213	220	228	236	244	252	260	268	276	284	292	300	308	316
1¾ " = $92\frac{4}{10}$ "	98	105	112	119	126	133	140	147	154	161	168	175	182	189	196	203	210	217	224	231	238	245	252	259	266	273	280
2 " = $105\frac{6}{10}$ "	87	94	100	106	112	119	125	131	138	144	150	157	163	169	175	182	188	194	201	207	213	219	226	232	238	244	251
2¼ " = $118\frac{2}{10}$ "	79	85	90	96	102	107	113	119	124	130	136	141	147	153	158	164	170	176	181	187	192	198	204	210	215	221	227
2½ " = 132 "	72	77	82	87	93	98	103	108	113	118	123	128	134	139	144	149	154	160	165	170	175	180	185	191	196	201	206
2¾ " = $145\frac{2}{10}$ "	66	70	75	80	85	89	94	99	103	108	113	118	122	127	132	136	141	146	151	155	160	165	170	175	179	184	188
3 " = $158\frac{4}{10}$ "	60	65	69	74	78	82	86	91	95	99	103	108	112	117	121	125	130	134	138	143	147	151	156	160	165	169	173
3½ " = $184\frac{8}{10}$ "	51	55	59	63	66	70	74	77	81	85	89	92	96	100	103	107	111	115	118	122	126	129	133	137	140	144	148
4 " = $211\frac{2}{10}$ "	45	48	51	54	57	61	64	67	70	73	77	80	83	86	90	93	96	99	103	106	109	112	115	119	122	125	128
4½ " = $237\frac{6}{10}$ "	39	42	45	48	50	53	56	59	62	64	67	70	73	76	78	81	84	87	90	93	95	98	101	104	106	109	112
5 " = 264 "	34	37	39	42	44	47	49	52	54	57	59	62	64	67	69	72	74	77	79	82	84	87	89	92	94	97	99
5½ " = $290\frac{4}{10}$ "	30	33	35	37	39	42	44	46	48	50	53	55	57	59	61	63	66	68	70	72	74	77	79	81	83	85	88
6 " = $316\frac{8}{10}$ "	27	29	31	33	35	37	39	41	43	45	47	49	51	53	55	57	59	61	63	65	67	69	71	73	75	77	79
7 " = $369\frac{6}{10}$ "	22	23	25	27	28	30	32	33	35	36	38	39	41	42	44	45	47	48	50	51	53	55	56	58	59	61	63
8 " = $422\frac{4}{10}$ "	18	19	20	21	23	24	25	27	28	29	31	32	33	34	36	37	38	40	41	42	43	45	46	47	49	50	51
9 " = $475\frac{2}{10}$ "	14	15	16	17	19	20	21	22	23	24	25	26	27	28	29	30	31	32	33	34	35	36	37	39	40	41	42
10 " = 528 "	12	13	13	14	15	16	17	18	19	19	20	21	22	23	24	25	26	26	27	28	29	30	31	32	32	33	34
11 " = $580\frac{8}{10}$ "	9½	10	11	12	12	13	14	14	15	16	16	17	18	19	19	20	21	21	22	22	23	24	25	26	26	27	28

The above table is especially valuable for determining at a glance approximately the weight of locomotive needed to haul stated loads up stated grades. The exact weight and the design may then be determined according to the kind of traffic, exact frictional resistance, curves and other conditions.

NOTE.—In the case of saddle-tank engines it is well to make a deduction from the weight on driving wheels to allow for the tank being only partly full under average conditions. In the case of locomotives with separate tender, the tender must be reckoned as part of the train to be hauled. Also, for engines with trucks the weight on truck should be deducted to arrive at the net weight of train, particularly on very steep grades. Speed is not taken into account.

Table IV. Approximate Hauling Capacity, Very Poor Cars, 30 Pounds per Ton Resistance of Rolling Friction

Showing weight in tons of 2,000 pounds of heaviest train, exclusive of the locomotive; inclusive of weight of cars and lading (and tender, if any); which locomotives with 4,000 to 80,000 pounds on the driving wheels can haul on straight track in good order, on grades from **Absolute Level** to **11 feet per 100.** The **Tractive Force** is assumed to be one-fifth of the weight on driving wheels.

	TOTAL WEIGHTS ON DRIVING WHEELS IN POUNDS																				
	4,000	5,000	6,000	7,000	8,000	9,000	10,000	11,000	12,000	13,000	14,000	15,000	16,000	17,000	18,000	19,000	20,000	21,000	22,000	23,000	24,000
Absolute level	24	31	37	43	49	56	62	68	74	80	86	92	98	104	110	117	123	129	135	142	148
¼ per cent = 13$\frac{2}{10}$ ft. per mile	21	26	31	36	41	47	52	57	62	67	73	78	83	88	93	99	104	109	115	120	125
½ " = 26$\frac{4}{10}$ " "	18	23	27	32	36	41	45	50	54	58	63	67	72	76	81	85	90	94	99	103	108
¾ " = 39$\frac{6}{10}$ " "	16	20	23	27	31	35	39	43	47	51	55	59	63	67	71	75	79	83	87	91	95
1 " = 52$\frac{8}{10}$ " "	14	17	21	24	28	31	35	38	42	45	49	52	56	59	63	66	70	73	77	80	84
1¼ " = 66 " "	12	15	18	21	25	28	31	34	37	40	44	47	50	53	56	59	62	65	69	72	75
1½ " = 79$\frac{2}{10}$ " "	11	14	17	20	23	26	28	31	34	37	40	42	45	48	51	54	57	59	62	65	68
1¾ " = 92$\frac{4}{10}$ " "	10	13	15	18	21	23	26	28	31	34	36	39	41	44	46	49	52	54	57	60	62
2 " = 105$\frac{6}{10}$ " "	9	12	14	17	19	21	24	26	28	31	33	35	38	40	43	45	47	50	52	55	57
2¼ " = 118$\frac{8}{10}$ " "	8½	11	13	15	17	19	22	24	26	28	30	32	34	37	39	41	43	46	48	50	52
2½ " = 132 " "	8	10	12	14	16	18	20	22	24	26	28	30	32	34	36	38	40	42	44	46	48
2¾ " = 145$\frac{2}{10}$ " "	7	9	11	13	15	17	19	20	22	24	26	28	30	32	34	35	37	39	41	43	45
3 " = 158$\frac{4}{10}$ " "	6½	8½	10	12	14	15	17	19	20	22	24	26	28	29	31	33	35	36	38	40	41
3½ " = 184$\frac{8}{10}$ " "	6	7½	9	11	12	14	15	16	18	19	21	22	24	25	27	28	30	32	33	34	36
4 " = 211$\frac{2}{10}$ " "	5	6½	7½	9	11	12	13	14	16	17	18	20	21	22	24	25	26	28	29	30	32
4½ " = 237$\frac{6}{10}$ " "	4½	5½	7	8	9	10	11	13	14	15	16	17	18	20	21	22	23	24	25	27	28
5 " = 264 " "	4	5	6	7	8	9	10	11	12	13	14	15	16	17	19	20	21	22	23	24	25
5½ " = 290$\frac{4}{10}$ " "	3½	4½	5½	6½	7	8	9	10	11	12	13	14	15	16	17	18	19	20	21	21	22
6 " = 316$\frac{8}{10}$ " "	3	4	5	5½	6½	7½	8	9	10	11	11	12	13	14	15	16	17	17	18	19	20
7 " = 369$\frac{6}{10}$ " "	2½	3	4	4½	5	6	6½	7	8	8½	9	10	11	11	12	13	13	14	15	15	16
8 " = 422$\frac{4}{10}$ " "	2	2½	3	3½	4	5	5½	6	6½	7	7½	8	8½	9½	10	10	11	11	12	13	13
9 " = 475$\frac{2}{10}$ " "	1½	2	2½	3	3½	4	4½	5	5	5½	6	6½	7	7½	8	8½	9	9½	10	10	10½
10 " = 528 " "	1	1½	2	2½	3	3	3½	4	4½	5	5	5½	6	6	6½	7	7	7½	8	8½	8½
11 " = 580$\frac{8}{10}$ " "	0	1	1½	2	2	2½	3	3	3½	3½	4	4½	4½	5	5	5½	6	6	6½	6½	7

Continuation of Table IV on opposite page

TOTAL WEIGHTS ON DRIVING WHEELS IN POUNDS

	26,000	28,000	30,000	32,000	34,000	36,000	38,000	40,000	42,000	44,000	46,000	48,000	50,000	52,000	54,000	56,000	58,000	60,000	62,000	64,000	66,000	68,000	70,000	72,000	74,000	76,000	78,000	80,000
Absolute level	160	172	185	197	210	222	234	247	259	271	284	296	308	321	333	345	358	370	382	395	407	419	432	444	456	469	481	493
$\tfrac{1}{4}$ per cent $= 13\tfrac{2}{10}$ ft. per mile	135	146	157	167	177	187	198	208	219	230	240	250	261	271	281	292	302	313	324	334	344	354	365	376	386	397	407	417
$\tfrac{1}{2}$ " $= 26\tfrac{4}{10}$ "	117	126	135	144	153	162	171	180	189	198	207	216	225	234	243	252	261	270	279	288	297	306	315	324	333	342	351	360
$\tfrac{3}{4}$ " $= 39\tfrac{6}{10}$ "	102	110	118	126	134	142	150	158	166	173	181	189	197	205	213	221	228	236	244	252	260	268	276	284	292	300	308	316
1 " $= 52\tfrac{8}{10}$ "	91	98	105	112	119	126	133	140	147	154	161	168	175	182	189	196	203	210	217	224	231	238	245	252	259	266	273	280
$1\tfrac{1}{4}$ " $= 66$ "	81	87	94	100	106	113	119	125	131	138	144	150	157	163	169	176	182	188	195	201	207	213	219	226	232	238	245	251
$1\tfrac{1}{2}$ " $= 79\tfrac{2}{10}$ "	74	80	85	90	96	102	107	113	118	124	130	136	141	147	153	158	164	170	175	181	187	192	198	204	209	215	221	226
$1\tfrac{3}{4}$ " $= 92\tfrac{4}{10}$ "	67	72	77	82	87	92	98	103	108	113	118	124	129	134	139	144	149	154	159	165	170	175	180	185	190	195	200	206
2 " $= 105\tfrac{6}{10}$ "	61	66	71	75	80	85	89	94	99	103	108	113	118	122	127	132	137	141	146	151	155	160	165	170	175	179	184	189
$2\tfrac{1}{4}$ " $= 118\tfrac{8}{10}$ "	56	60	65	69	73	78	82	86	91	95	99	104	108	113	117	121	125	130	134	139	143	147	151	156	160	165	169	173
$2\tfrac{1}{2}$ " $= 132$ "	52	56	60	64	68	72	76	80	84	88	92	96	100	104	108	112	116	120	124	128	132	136	140	144	148	152	156	160
$2\tfrac{3}{4}$ " $= 145\tfrac{2}{10}$ "	48	52	56	59	63	66	70	74	78	81	85	89	92	96	100	104	107	111	115	119	123	126	130	134	137	141	145	148
3 " $= 158\tfrac{4}{10}$ "	45	48	52	55	58	62	65	69	72	76	79	83	86	90	93	97	100	104	107	110	113	117	120	124	127	131	135	138
$3\tfrac{1}{2}$ " $= 184\tfrac{8}{10}$ "	39	42	45	48	51	54	57	60	63	66	69	72	75	78	81	84	87	90	93	96	99	102	105	108	111	114	117	120
4 " $= 211\tfrac{2}{10}$ "	34	37	39	42	45	47	50	53	55	58	61	63	66	68	71	74	76	79	82	84	87	90	92	95	97	100	103	105
$4\tfrac{1}{2}$ " $= 237\tfrac{6}{10}$ "	30	33	35	37	39	42	44	46	49	51	53	56	58	60	63	65	67	70	72	74	77	79	81	84	86	88	91	93
5 " $= 264$ "	27	29	31	33	35	37	39	41	43	45	48	50	52	54	56	58	60	62	64	67	68	70	72	75	77	79	81	83
$5\tfrac{1}{2}$ " $= 290\tfrac{4}{10}$ "	24	26	28	29	31	33	35	37	39	41	42	44	46	48	50	52	54	55	57	59	61	63	65	67	68	70	72	74
6 " $= 316\tfrac{8}{10}$ "	22	23	25	26	28	30	31	33	35	36	38	40	41	43	45	46	48	50	51	53	55	56	58	60	61	63	65	66
7 " $= 369\tfrac{6}{10}$ "	17	19	20	22	23	24	25	27	28	29	30	32	33	34	36	37	39	40	42	43	44	46	47	48	50	51	52	54
8 " $= 422\tfrac{4}{10}$ "	14	15	16	18	19	20	21	22	23	24	25	26	27	28	30	31	32	33	34	35	36	37	38	40	41	42	43	44
9 " $= 475\tfrac{2}{10}$ "	$11\tfrac{1}{2}$	$12\tfrac{1}{2}$	$13\tfrac{1}{2}$	14	15	16	17	18	19	20	21	22	23	24	25	26	27	28	29	30	30	31	32	33	34	34	35	36
10 " $= 528$ "	$9\tfrac{1}{2}$	10	11	12	13	13	14	15	15	16	17	18	18	19	20	20	21	22	23	23	24	25	25	26	27	28	29	30
11 " $= 580\tfrac{8}{10}$ "	$7\tfrac{1}{2}$	8	9	10	11	11	12	12	13	13	14	14	15	15	16	17	17	18	19	19	20	20	21	21	22	23	23	24

The above table is especially valuable for determining at a glance approximately the weight of locomotive needed to haul stated loads up stated grades. The exact weight and the design may then be determined according to the kind of traffic, exact frictional resistance, curves and other conditions.

NOTE.—In the case of saddle-tank engines it is well to make a deduction from the weight on driving wheels to allow for the tank being only partly full under average conditions. In the case of locomotives with separate tender, the tender must be reckoned as a part of the load to be hauled. Also, for engines with trucks the weight on truck should be deducted to arrive at the net weight of train, particularly on very steep grades. Speed is not taken into account.

Grades

Grades are stated in various ways

1st. The usual engineer's method by per cent, or the number of feet rise per 100 feet of track, fractions of a foot being expressed generally in tenths of a foot instead of in inches.

To reduce grade stated in per cent (or feet rise per 100 feet of length) to feet per mile, multiply by $52\frac{8}{10}$.

EXAMPLE.—3 per cent, or 3 per 100, is equivalent to 3 x 52.8 = $158\frac{4}{10}$ feet per mile.

2d. The American railroad method is to state the number of feet rise in a distance of 1 mile.

To reduce grade stated in feet per mile to grade stated in feet per 100 or per cent, divide by 52.8.

EXAMPLE.—396 feet per mile ÷ 52.8 = $87\frac{1}{2}$ feet per 100, or $7\frac{1}{2}$ per cent.

3d. The English method is to state in feet the distance in which the grade rises 1 foot.

To reduce grade stated in the English method of a certain number of feet length per one foot rise, to grade in feet per mile, divide 5,280 by the given number.

EXAMPLE.—A grade of 1 in 20 is equivalent to 5,280 ÷ 20 = 264 feet per mile.

To reduce grades stated in the English method to grades in per cent or feet per 100, divide 100 by the given number.

EXAMPLE.—A grade of 1 in 40 is equivalent to 100 ÷ 40 = $2\frac{1}{2}$ per cent, or $2\frac{1}{2}$ feet per 100.

4th. Grades may be stated as a rise of so many feet or inches in a number of yards or rods or feet, as 2 inches per rod, 2 feet in 150 yards, etc.

To reduce grades irregularly stated to grades in feet per mile, multiply the rise in inches by 5,280, and divide by the length of the grade in inches.

EXAMPLE.—A grade of 5 inches in $1\frac{1}{2}$ rods. Multiply 5 by 5,280 = 26,400; divide by 297 (the number of inches in $1\frac{1}{2}$ rods) = $88\frac{9}{10}$ feet per mile.

To reduce grades irregularly stated to grades in feet per 100 or per cent, multiply the rise in inches by 100, and divide by the length of the grade in inches.

EXAMPLE.—A grade of 6 inches in 10 yards. Multiply 6 by 100 = 600; divide by 360 the number of inches in 10 yards) = 1.66 +, or $1\frac{2}{3}$ feet per 100, or $1\frac{2}{3}$ per cent grade.

5th. Grades are sometimes stated in degrees, or the amount of angle which the incline makes from the level, and measured in degrees of a circle, 360 degrees to the entire circle, an angle of 45 degrees, or half-way between horizontal and perpendicular, being one-eighth of an entire circle. This is a very inconvenient method of stating railroad grades. The rise of the grade is the sine of the angle, and must be figured out by tables of the length of sines of angles in proportion to the radius, the length of the grade being represented as the radius. Consequently, if the grade be taken as 100 feet long, the sine of the angle will state the grade in feet per 100.

Easy Method of Measuring Heavy Grades

Of course, the proper way of determining grades is by surveyor's instruments. But where the grade varies many times in a distance of a few hundred feet, it is quite as important to know the maximum as the average grade. In such cases it is sufficiently accurate to use a straight edge 100 inches long, and, leveling it with an ordinary spirit level, to measure in inches from bottom of straight edge to top of rail. This gives the grade in per cent, which can be reduced to feet per mile by multiplying by 52.8. A few trials in different places will readily determine the ruling grades. On very low grades this method is not practicable, but it is useful on most of the roads where our special-service engines are running, the grades varying from 1 to 10 per 100.

Comparison of Different Methods of Designating the Same Grades

Engineers' Method	English Method	American Railroad Method
⅛ of 1 per cent or 1½ inches per 100 feet	= 1 in 800	= 6 6/10 ft. per mile
¼ of 1 " 3 " 100 "	= 1 in 400	= 13 2/10 "
½ of 1 " 6 " 100 "	= 1 in 200	= 26 4/10 "
¾ of 1 " 9 " 100 "	= 1 in 150	= 39 6/10 "
1 per cent or 1 foot 0 " 100 "	= 1 in 100	= 52 8/10 "
1¼ " 1 " 3 " 100 "	= 1 in 80	= 66 "
1½ " 1 " 6 " 100 "	= 1 in 66	= 79 2/10 "
1¾ " 1 " 9 " 100 "	= 1 in 54+	= 92 4/10 "
2 " 2 feet 0 " 100 "	= 1 in 50	= 105 6/10 "
2¼ " 2 " 3 " 100 "	= 1 in 44+	= 118 8/10 "
2½ " 2 " 6 " 100 "	= 1 in 40	= 132 "
2¾ " 2 " 9 " 100 "	= 1 in 36+	= 145 2/10 "
3 " 3 " 0 " 100 "	= 1 in 33⅓	= 158 4/10 "
3¼ " 3 " 3 " 100 "	= 1 in 31−	= 171 6/10 "
3½ " 3 " 6 " 100 "	= 1 in 28+	= 184 8/10 "
3¾ " 3 " 9 " 100 "	= 1 in 26+	= 198 "
4 " 4 " 0 " 100 "	= 1 in 25	= 211 2/10 "
4½ " 4 " 6 " 100 "	= 1 in 22+	= 237 6/10 "
5 " 5 " 0 " 100 "	= 1 in 20	= 264 "
5½ " 5 " 6 " 100 "	= 1 in 18+	= 290 4/10 "
6 " 6 " 0 " 100 "	= 1 in 16⅔	= 316 8/10 "
6½ " 6 " 6 " 100 "	= 1 in 15+	= 343 2/10 "
7 " 7 " 0 " 100 "	= 1 in 14+	= 369 6/10 "
7½ " 7 " 6 " 100 "	= 1 in 13+	= 396 "
8 " 8 " 0 " 100 "	= 1 in 12½	= 422 4/10 "
8½ " 8 " 6 " 100 "	= 1 in 12−	= 448 8/10 "
9 " 9 " 0 " 100 "	= 1 in 11+	= 475 2/10 "
9½ " 9 " 6 " 100 "	= 1 in 10+	= 501 6/10 "
10 " 10 " 0 " 100 "	= 1 in 10	= 528 "
10½ " 10 " 6 " 100 "	= 1 in 9½+	= 554 4/10 "
11 " 11 " 0 " 100 "	= 1 in 9+	= 580 8/10 "
11½ " 11 " 6 " 100 "	= 1 in 8⅔+	= 607 2/10 "
12 " 12 " 0 " 100 "	= 1 in 8+	= 633 6/10 "

Curves

The simplest way of designating a railroad curve is by giving the length of the radius—*i. e.*, the distance from the center to the outside of the circle, or one-half the diameter. The shorter the radius the sharper the curve. The length of the radius is usually stated in feet; but English engineers often state the radius in chains (one chain=66 feet). The length of the radius of a railroad curve is measured to the center of the track.

Civil engineers designate railway curves by degrees (using the sign ° for degrees and " for minutes, there being 60 minutes in one degree). The sharpness of the curve is determined by the "degree of curve," or the number of degrees of the central angle subtended by a chord of 100 feet. Or, in other words, let two lines start from the center of a circle in the shape of a V, so that the angle at the point of the V is one degree (equivalent to $\frac{1}{360}$ of a complete circle), then, if the two sides of the V are prolonged until they are 100 feet apart, any part of a circle made by using one of these lines for its radius is a "one-degree curve." The exact length of radius which with an angle of one degree has a chord of 100 feet is found to be 5,729.65 feet. For sake of convenience 5,730 feet is usually taken as the radius of a one-degree curve. If the angle at the point of the V is two degrees and the sides are prolonged until 100 feet apart, the length of each side is (almost exactly) one-half as long as when the angle is one degree, or one-half of 5,730=2,865 feet. For a three-degree curve the radius is one-third of 5,730; for a four-degree curve one-fourth of 5,730; and so on. For perfect exactness the length of 100 feet should be measured not along a straight line connecting the ends of the V, but along the line of the circle of which the sides of the V are radii—*i. e.*, the arc should be used and not the chord. The difference, however, is so slight for any curves ordinarily used on main lines of standard gauge railroad as to be ignored in practice. But for extremely sharp curves, such as our locomotives both wide and narrow gauge are built for, a considerable mathematical error would be involved by the use of 100-foot chords and calculating the length of the radius by dividing 5,730 by the degree of curve. The ratio of this error increases with the degree of curve, since the error is caused by neglecting the difference between the length of the chord and of the arc (*e. g.*, a 60-degree curve and 100-foot chord mathematically compels 100 feet radius instead of 95½ feet; a 90-degree curve and 100-foot chord, 71+ feet radius instead of 63.6 feet).

In practice, however, the formula of dividing 5,730 by the degree of curve ($R=\frac{5730}{D}$) is almost universally used, and the mathematical error is avoided by using two 50-foot chords for curves ranging from 10 to 16 degrees, and four

25-foot chords for curves ranging from 17 to 30 degrees, and further subdividing for sharper curves, since this almost exactly balances the error, and it is also a practical necessity in laying out sharp curves to use short chords.

For extremely sharp curves, or say 100 feet radius or less, it is usual to express the curve by feet radius rather than by degrees. The table following is computed by the formula $R = \frac{5730}{D}$, and fractions of feet are not taken into account.

NOTE.—The above engineers' method of designating the rate of curvature of a railway curve must not be confounded with the number of degrees of a circle occupied by the curved portion of the track; thus a curved track making a quarter turn, equivalent to a right angle, will always be 90 degrees of a circle (360 degrees = the whole circle) no matter whether the curve is an easy one with a long radius or a sharp one with a short radius.

Table Showing Lengths of Radius in Feet (Fractions Disregarded) for Curves from One to Sixty Degrees

Degrees	Radius	Degrees	Radius	Degrees	Radius
1 =	5730 feet	21 =	273 feet	41 =	140 feet
2 =	2865 "	22 =	260 "	42 =	136 "
3 =	1910 "	23 =	249 "	43 =	133 "
4 =	1432 "	24 =	239 "	44 =	130 "
5 =	1146 "	25 =	229 "	45 =	127 "
6 =	955 "	26 =	220 "	46 =	125 "
7 =	819 "	27 =	212 "	47 =	122 "
8 =	717 "	28 =	205 "	48 =	119 "
9 =	637 "	29 =	198 "	49 =	117 "
10 =	573 "	30 =	191 "	50 =	115 "
11 =	521 "	31 =	185 "	51 =	112 "
12 =	478 "	32 =	179 "	52 =	110 "
13 =	441 "	33 =	174 "	53 =	108 "
14 =	410 "	34 =	169 "	54 =	106 "
15 =	382 "	35 =	163 "	55 =	104 "
16 =	358 "	36 =	159 "	56 =	102 "
17 =	337 "	37 =	155 "	57 =	100 "
18 =	318 "	38 =	151 "	58 =	99 "
19 =	302 "	39 =	147 "	59 =	97 "
20 =	287 "	40 =	143 "	60 =	95 "

Rule for Measuring the Radius of a Sharp Curve

Stretch a string, say 20 feet long, or longer if the curve is not a sharp one, across the curve corresponding to the line from A to C in the diagram. Then measure from B, the center of the line A C, and at right angles with it, to the rail at D.

Multiply the distance A to B, or one-half the length of the string in inches, by itself; measure the distance D to B in inches, and multiply it by itself. Add these two products and divide the sum by twice the distance from B to D, measured exactly in inches and fractional parts of inches. This will give the radius of the curve in inches.

It may be more convenient to use a straight edge instead of a string. Care must be taken to have the ends of the string or straight edge touch the same part of the rail as is taken in measuring the distance from the center. If the string touches the bottom of the rail flange at each end, and the center measurement is made to the rail head, the result will not be correct.

In practice it will be found best to make trials on different parts of the curve to allow for irregularities. It is best not to measure across from one end of the curved track to the other even when the curve is so located that this is possible, since if any portion of the straight track at either end of the curve is included the results will be incorrect. This rule does not apply to curves of over one-half circle if the line is drawn connecting the two ends of the curve. It is a good plan to make the measurement on the **inside of the outer rail of the curve,** as this is often more convenient. In this case one-half of the width of gauge should be deducted from the radius when calculated, as the radius of the curve should be measured to the center of the track.

EXAMPLE.—Let A C be a 20-foot string; half the distance, or A B, is then 10 feet, or 120 inches. Suppose B D is found on measurement to be 3 inches. Then 120 multiplied by 120 is 14,400, and 3 multiplied by 3 is 9; 14,400 added to 9 is 14,409, which, divided by twice 3, or 6, equals 2,401½ inches, or 200 feet 1½ inches, which is the radius of the curve.

The formula is thus stated: $\dfrac{AB^2 + BD^2}{2\,BD} = R.$

Or applied to the above example, $\dfrac{120^2 + 3^2}{2 \times 3} = 2{,}401\tfrac{1}{2}$ in. = 200 ft. 1½ in.

Laying Out Curves

It is hardly within the limits of a condensed catalogue of locomotives to cover fully a subject so technical as the laying out of railroad curves. In cases where the services of a professional surveyor cannot be obtained it is possible to lay out curves without surveyors' instruments.

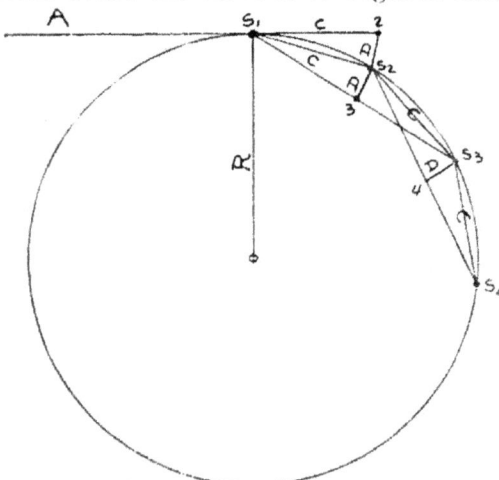

In the diagram the straight track is represented by the line A—S1. The point where the curve is to begin is noted as Station One (S1). Continue the straight line beyond S1, as shown by line C (*i. e.*, from S1 to 2), a distance of 100, 50, or 25 feet, according to how sharp a curve is to be laid out or whether the situation is cramped or not, as shown by the table below. Start from Station S1 with a line or chain of length C, as given by the table. From the end of this line C measure the offset D, of length as given in the table, to Station Two (S2), so that its distance from Station S1 is also measured by the line C. Then measure from S2 the same offset D to point 3, making distance from point 3 to S1 also the same as line C. A line drawn from S1 to point 3 and continued in the same direction an additional distance C fixes the next point, Station Three (S3). Making from S3 another offset D, so that the distance S2 to S3 and S2 to 4 are each the length of line C, and prolonging the line S2—4 in a straight line an additional distance C, fixes Station Four (S4). Thus the points on the curve have been fixed S1, S2, S3, and S4. The same process is continued until a point is reached where it is desired to discontinue the curve and lay straight track.

In cramped locations the length of the line C (which is the chord of the arc) can be decreased to one-half or one-quarter of the lengths given in the table below, and the corresponding offset D will be respectively one-quarter and one-sixteenth of the lengths given in the table. In the table the length of the line C is taken at 100 feet for curves 1 to 12 degrees; 50 feet for curves of 13 to 24 degrees, and 25 feet for sharper curves; and for the reason that for the sharper curves the situation is usually so cramped that measuring the longer distances is impracticable. In the diagram the line R is the radius of the curve, but the formation of the ground where the curved track is to be laid is supposed to be such that it is impossible to fix a pin at the center of the circle, and in this way, by using a line of the proper length, to describe the circle.

Table of Radii and Deflections for Curves

Curve in Degrees	Radius R in Feet	Offset D in Feet C=100 Feet	Curve in Degrees	Radius R in Feet	Offset D in Feet C=50 Feet	Curve in Degrees	Radius R in Feet	Offset D in Feet C=25 Feet
1	5,730	.87	13	441	2.83	25	229	1.362
2	2,865	1.74	14	410	3.05	26	220	1.405
3	1,910	2.62	15	382	3.27	28	205	1.51
4	1,433	3.49	16	358	3.48	30	191	1.615
5	1,146	4.36	17	337	3.7	32	179	1.72
6	955	5.23	18	318	3.92	36	159	1.935
7	819	6.10	19	302	4.13	40	143	2.14
8	717	6.98	20	287	4.35	44	130	2.34
9	637	7.85	21	273	4.56	50	115	2.64
10	573	8.72	22	260	4.77	60	95	3.125
11	521	9.58	23	249	4.98			
12	478	10.45	24	239	5.2			

The offset D for given radius R and chord C is found from formula $D = \dfrac{C^2}{2R}$

NOTE.—For extremely sharp curves, say 20 to 50 feet radius, it is practicable to lay off the curve by the above method at one-twelfth the usual scale by using inches throughout instead of feet; for example, in case of a 30-foot radius curve (radius 360 inches) the formula for 16-degree curve, substituting inches for feet, using a 50-inch chord and 3.48-inch offset, will give sufficiently close results.

The Resistance of Curves

The frictional resistance to the passage of trains around curves is very considerable, and is also extremely variable. The shorter the radius of the curve the greater is the resistance; also the length of the wheel-bases of locomotive and of the cars, the elevation of the outer rail, the speed, the condition of track and rolling stock, the length of the train and the length of the curved track, and other matters influence the resistance, so that no one formula will apply to all cases. If the gauge of track on curves is not sufficiently widened to prevent the wheels from binding against the rails the resistance may be excessive.

Excessive or irregular curves, and especially sharp curves in connection with steep grades, are to be avoided, as they greatly decrease the loads which locomotives can handle, limit the amount of business practicable, and increase the cost of operation and the repairs required for track and rolling stock. It is preferable to increase the distance or the expense of track construction, rather than for sake of saving in first cost to lose continuously in operating expenses.

Compensation, or Reduction of Grade on Curves

It is customary, when a curve occurs on a grade, to reduce the grade on the curved part of the track so that the combined resistance of the flattened grade and the curve will not exceed the resistance of the steeper grade on the straight part of the track.

In practice most engineers compensate for curves on grades at the rate of **two one-hundredths of a foot** grade in each 100 feet for **each degree of curvature**.

> EXAMPLE.—If a 20-degree curve comes on a grade of 5 feet per 100, the grade is reduced $20 \times \frac{2}{100} = \frac{4}{10}$ of 1 foot, which, subtracted from the original grade of 5 feet per 100, leaves $4\frac{6}{10}$ feet per 100 as the compensated grade on the curve; or, in other words, a grade of 5 feet in 100 coming on a straight track offers the same resistance as a grade of $4\frac{6}{10}$ feet in 100 coming on a 20-degree curve.

Where the grade is stated in feet per mile the equivalent reduction for each degree of curvature is $1\frac{56}{100}$ feet per mile.

> EXAMPLE.—A 20-degree curve coming on a grade of 264 feet per mile, the grade is reduced $20 \times 1\frac{56}{100} = 21\frac{13}{100}$ feet, which, subtracted from 264, leaves $242\frac{55}{100}$ feet per mile as the compensated grade on the curved track.

The above rule works well within the limits of ordinary railroad practice where excessive grades and curves are not required. For short local roads, such as are used for mining and industrial purposes, where very heavy grades and very sharp curves are necessary, the rate of compensation should be increased. On narrow gauge **three one-hundredths of a foot** per degree of curvature gave the best results with 40-degree curves on 4 per cent grades.

Sharper curves may be used on narrow gauge than on wide gauge, because there is less difference between the length of the inner and outer rails on curves of the same radius, and because narrow-gauge rolling stock usually has a shorter wheel-base.

Gauge of Track Widened on Curves

Theoretically, in order to pass around curves perfectly, every axle in the train should point to the center of the curve, and the outside wheels should be larger than the inner wheels. In practice, the difference in size of the wheels is supposed to be accomplished by coning the tread of each wheel so that the diameter close to the flange is greater than at the front face. But the radial position of the axles is impracticable, as cars and locomotives are built so that two or more axles are parallel. On sharp curves this arrangement of the axles causes the cars and locomotive to bind, a four-wheel car or truck having a tendency to press the front wheel against the outside rail and the rear wheel against the inside rail. On this account the usual amount of clearance between the rails and wheel flanges must be increased. The exact amount of additional width of gauge required on a curve depends on the radius of the curve, the gauge of track, and the wheel-bases of the rolling stock, and no rule can be given which will apply to all cases. The width of the tread of the wheels limits the amount of extra width of gauge practicable. Actual trial has proved that on narrow gauge, with locomotives and cars of short wheel-base and with sharp curves, that a good rule is to widen the gauge of track **one-sixteenth of an inch** for each $2\frac{1}{2}$ degrees of curvature; *i. e.*, a 40-degree curve calls for one inch increase in gauge of track. On extremely sharp curves, such as are often used about manufactories, mines, etc., it is well to widen the gauge as much as can be done and still secure a safe amount of bearing on the rail for the car wheels, allowing for wear of flanges and for wheels hugging one rail. When a six-driver locomotive, with the center drivers flangeless, is used on an extremely sharp curve, it may be advisable to lay extra rails inside of the outer rail and outside the inner rail.

Elevation of Outer Rail on Curves

In passing around curves the centrifugal force tends to tip over the rolling stock and to crowd the wheels against the outer rail. This tendency increases with increased speed, and is greater in the case of a sharp curve than an easy curve. To counteract this tendency—which at a very high rate of speed might derail the train—it is desirable to elevate the outer rail of a curved track so that the train will lean inward to such an extent that at the desired rate of speed there will be no more pressure against one rail than against the other. Where the same track is used for both slow and fast trains it is usual to elevate the outer rail to suit the fast train. Excessive speeds around very sharp curves are altogether impossible.

It is customary to elevate the outer rail one-half inch for each degree of curvature on roads of 56½-inch gauge of track, and for speeds of 25 to 35 miles per hour. For narrower gauges the elevation is proportionately less. Thus, if on standard (56½-inch) gauge with a speed of 30 miles per hour on a 10-degree (573 feet radius) curve the outer rail is elevated 5 inches, on a gauge of track 28¼ inches the elevation would be 2½ inches. The elevation of the outer rail on 36-inch gauge should be very nearly two-thirds of the elevation for 56½-inch gauge for the same speed around the same curve. The above rule is only approximate and requires modification for curves much sharper than 10 degrees and for speeds much less than 15 to 20 miles per hour. If the outer rail is elevated exactly the proper amount it will be impossible for a passenger to feel any sensation of tipping or rocking motion while the train is on the curve. The exact elevation to secure this result can only be arrived at in each case by very abstruse calculations. It is considered the best practice in approaching a curve to begin to make a difference in the level of the two rails some distance—say 50 or 100 feet—before the curve is reached, and to elevate the outer rail and depress the inner rail so that the center of the track is level. The best difference in level between the two rails on curved track can only be determined by actual trial after the track is complete.

We submit, however, a **Diagram for Elevation of outer rail on curves up to 70 degrees and for speeds up to 60 miles per hour for a standard (56½-inch) gauge track.**

EXAMPLE.—What should be the elevation of the outer rail for standard gauge track on a 20-degree curve for a speed of 25 miles per hour?

The rates of speed are noted at top line of diagram; follow down the line for 25 mile per hour speed until it intersects the curved line for 20-degree curve—noted on bottom line of diagram; follow from this intersection to the left-hand margin, which gives the required elevation at 8½ inches.

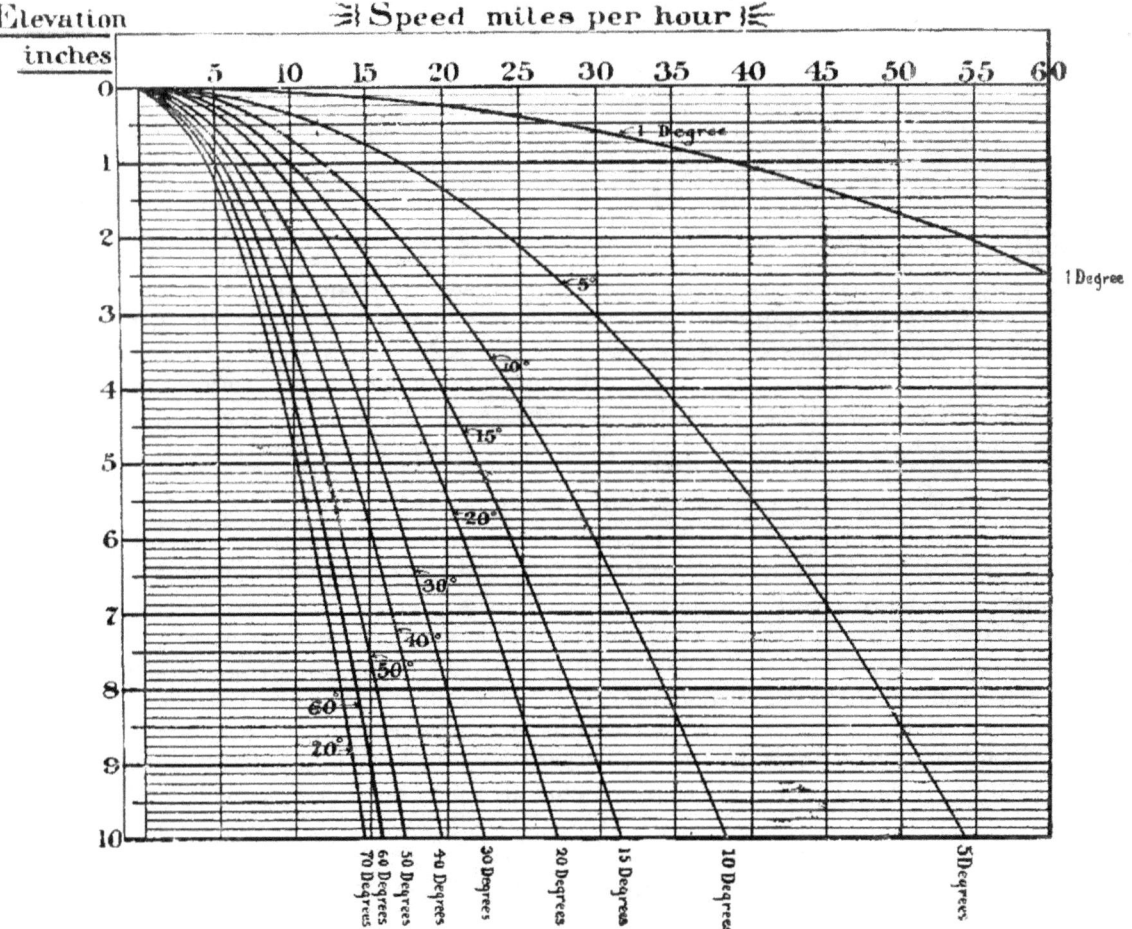

NOTE.—The elevation for other gauges of track will be in the same proportion, or for

24	inch gauge,	$42\frac{5}{10}$,	or say	40	per cent of elevation	for	$56\frac{1}{2}$-inch gauge
30	" "	$53\frac{1}{10}$,	"	50	" " "	"	" " " "
36	" "	$63\frac{7}{10}$,	"	60	" " "	"	" " " "
$39\frac{3}{8}$	" "	$69\frac{7}{10}$,	"	$66\frac{2}{3}$	" " "	"	" " " "
42	" "	$74\frac{3}{10}$,	"	70	" " "	"	" " " "

NOTE.—The above diagram does not cover unreasonably fast speeds on sharp curves, and does not provide for any elevation in excess of 10 inches on standard gauge.

In average practice, if any variation is found advisable from the results obtained from the above diagram, it will probably be in the direction of reduced rather than of increased heights. The diagram is as nearly accurate as practicable for track laying, and modifications may be made after practical tests.

Speed

In most instances, the daily mileage which our locomotives can be relied upon to maintain is determined more by local conditions— such as the length of the haul and the time required to exchange trains at each end of the road — than by the ability of the locomotive to make excessive speed. In any case, the speed at which a locomotive can haul a given load is dependent upon many factors, most of which are too variable to be covered by any formula. For these reasons we have refrained from any mention of speed in connection with our figures of hauling capacities on level and on grades. We would prefer to ask our correspondents to furnish us with a memorandum of their requirements as explained on page 17 of this catalogue, which will enable us to suggest such sizes and designs of locomotives as will in our judgment cover the best selection.

Some general facts as to speed may be of interest.

It requires more power to start a train than to keep it in motion after it has been started. This is due to the fact that the resistances of axle friction and of flange friction are greatest in starting and diminish very rapidly as the train first acquires motion, and then continue to diminish, but less rapidly, as the train speed accelerates. Journal lubrication is more perfect at high speed than at slow, and in cold weather when oil congeals the difference is greatest. The lessening of flange friction with increase of speed is believed to be due largely to the increase of momentum and to the tendency of a body in motion to move in a straight line. For these reasons a locomotive may be relied upon to haul any train it can start.

The resistance of the atmosphere is practically zero at slow speed, but is excessive at extreme speed; but the old idea that the resistance increases as the square of the speed appears to be an error.

Sharp or badly laid out curves or uneven track may wholly prevent a rate of speed which would be considered moderate on good straight track.

Car trucks out of square, wheels out of center, wheels mismatched on axles, and other rolling-stock defects are accentuated at fast speed.

The resistance caused by a strong side wind may be negligible with small cars at slow speed, but a considerable factor with large cars at high speed.

The resistance due to grade is absolutely constant whether speed is fast or slow, but the momentum of fast speed will take a train up a grade of considerable length with but little retarding, while the same grade may stall a slow-moving train.

No locomotive can at the same time haul its heaviest load and make its fastest speed. As speed increases the available tractive force decreases. At slow speed the mean effective pressure is estimated at 85 per cent of the boiler pressure. Steam requires time to move, and as piston speed is increased the steam from the boiler cannot get into the cylinders quick enough nor the exhaust steam be expelled quick enough to maintain the same mean effective pressure as at slow speed, and from mechanical as well as economic reasons steam must be used expansively. Together with the loss of mean effective pressure at high speed a greater amount of power is absorbed in forcing exhaust steam through the exhaust nozzles. At extreme speeds the best designed fast passenger engines, using steam expansively in the most efficient manner, will for an instant compress the exhaust steam to a very much higher pressure than the boiler pressure. The ratio of loss of effective tractive power to increase of speed varies greatly with the design of the locomotive. A better proportion of its maximum load at maximum speed can be hauled by a passenger locomotive than by a freight locomotive, each machine being well designed for its distinctive service. This is because the passenger locomotive with its large driving wheels has a more moderate and effective piston speed when developing high train speed than the freight engine with small drivers at less train speed. This results in the apparent paradox that a passenger locomotive can haul a heavier train at fast speed and can develop more horsepower than a much heavier freight locomotive with larger cylinders and greater tractive force.

Gauge of Track

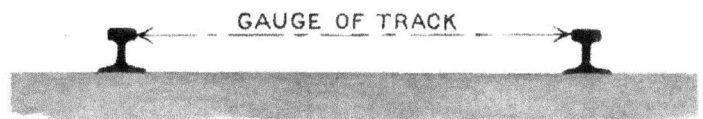

The gauge of track of a railroad is always the distance measured in the clear between the rails, as shown by the above sketch. A three-foot gauge track should measure exactly 36 inches in the clear between rails on straight track. (There are, however, some tracks, chiefly for industrial purposes, laid with the gauge measured from outside to outside of rail heads, and with rolling stock having wheel-flanges outside instead of inside.) The gauge of track is not measured between the flanges of rolling-stock wheels, and it is a mistake to increase the track gauge for sake of "clearance." (But see page 179 as to widening track gauge on curves.) In the construction of locomotive and car wheels the proper amount of clearance or side-play is provided, as shown by the accompanying sketch, one-half actual size, showing a rail with a wheel of the standard flange and tread. The position of the gauge-line is $1\frac{7}{8}$ inches from the back face of the tire; the width of tread is $3\frac{9}{16}$ inches measured from the gauge-line; the width over all is 5 inches; the depth of flange, $1\frac{3}{32}$ inches; the taper of the tread is $\frac{1}{32}$ per inch.

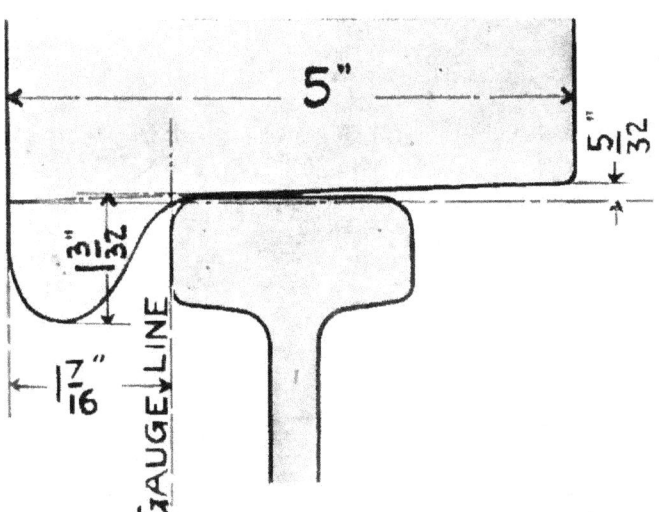

Customers in putting on new tire are cautioned to locate the position by the gauge-lines (or by the back faces of the tires), and not by making the front faces of tire and wheel center come flush, since these are often faced off for sake of finish.

Comparative Cost of Operating Animals and Light Locomotive

Cost per year of operating 3 mules and 3 drivers

Where Feed and Labor are at	Low Prices	Average Prices	High Prices
3 mules' feed, harness, shoeing, care, etc., for 365 days, each per day	At 40c.=$438.00	At 75c.=$821.25	$1.25=$1,368.75
3 drivers' wages, 300 days, each per day	At $1.00= 900.00	At $1.50=1,350.00	2.25= 2,025.00
6 per cent interest, mules worth $100 each	18.00	18.00	18.00
Total	$1,356.00	$2,189.25	$3,411.75

Cost per year of operating one of our light locomotives capable of doing the work of 10 to 40 mules or horses

Where Fuel and Labor are at	Low Prices	Average Prices	High Prices
Oil and repairs, per year	$50.00	$100.00	$200.00
Fuel, 400 to 1,000 pounds coal, or ¼ to ¾ cord wood. Costs almost nothing at coal mines, lumber mills, etc., per day	At 20c.=$ 60.00	At $1.00=$300.00	At $3.00=$900.00
Engineer's wages, 300 days, per day	At $1.75= 525.00	At 2.50= 750.00	At 3.25= 975.00
Boy to switch, couple, etc	At 75c.= 225.00	At 1.00= 300.00	At 1.50= 450.00
Interest, 6 per cent, say	150.00	150.00	150.00
Total	$1,010.00	$1,600.00	$2,675.00

The above calculations demonstrate that on an average where three animals and three drivers, or animals and drivers in different proportion but at about the same daily expense, are used, it is cheaper to operate a light locomotive. From $5 to $6 per day, or $1,500 to $1,800 per year, is a reasonable allowance for the cost of operating a light locomotive to take the place of 10 to 40 animals. It is not unusual for an engine to save its cost in less than a year. When through strikes or dullness of trade an engine is idle it saves money as well as when it is busy; only a few cents' worth of white lead and tallow are needed for it, while mules, whether idle or not, must be fed.

There are a number of items which must be considered in a fair comparison of animals with locomotives, which vary too much with each individual case to be noted in the table given on page 184.

A locomotive makes so much quicker time than animals that fewer cars are required to carry a greater daily total of tonnage. This effects a reduction in original investment that may nearly amount to the cost of the locomotive, and also reduces materially the running expenses. This reduction in the number of cars—the engine, with quick trips, replacing a number of teams making slow trips—reduces the number of turnouts needed. In one case, one of our engines was mostly paid for by the sale of rails from extra track that was no longer of any use.

The keeping up of a path between the rails for animals to work on, the renewing of ties worn out by constant trampling over them, is a vexatious expense avoided by the use of a locomotive. This item often amounts to one man's continuous time, or $1 to $2 per day.

Even where a large sum is spent in keeping up a footway, the chance of accident and wear and tear of animals is greater and the average useful life is less than that of a locomotive.

The relative economy increases rapidly with the length of the road. On a track of a quarter of a mile or less in length, the locomotive, although much preferable, would not have so much advantage as on a road half a mile long. While it is almost impracticable to haul with mules much over half a dozen miles, freight can be hauled ten miles by the locomotive cheaper than by mules two or three miles.

These incidental savings, which are not included in the table, will usually cover the additional cost if heavier rails are required, and also of any changes of grades, curves, mine headings, etc., as may be advisable for the most economical use of the locomotive.

We recommend that an engineer be also enough of a mechanic to do all light repairs and keep the locomotive in good order. With such a man the item of repairs, unless the engine is overworked, should not average for say twenty years over $50 to $100 per year. The amount of fuel used is also considerably dependent on the engineer. We believe a liberal salary to a good, competent engineer the best policy. Our system of standard templets enables us to express duplicate parts on telegraphic orders.

We believe that if parties who are doing hauling on tramways by animals will calculate for themselves the cost of operating, their own figures will show more than ours the advantages and economy of substituting light locomotives.

Estimates of Cost of One Mile of Railroad Track

Laid with Steel Rails Weighing 16, 20, 25, 30, 35, 40, and 45 Pounds per Yard

The following estimates are for the track ready for rolling stock, not including survey, right of way, buildings, tunnels, bridges, etc. They are intended merely to give a basis for more exact calculations, and will require modification to conform to variations in prices of material, freight charges, etc. The item of grading is very variable, and the lowest figures for this are for easy country or where steep grades and sharp curves are used to avoid expense in grading. These estimates are for single track (*i. e.*, two rails), and no allowance is made for sidings, switches, frogs, crossings, culverts, etc.

I.—Estimate of cost of one mile of track with 16-pound steel rails

	Rails at $31 per Ton	Rails at $36 per Ton	Rails at $41 per Ton
$25\frac{320}{2240}$ tons of 16-pound steel rails..	At $31 = $779.43	At $36 = $905.14	At $41 = $1,030.86
1,690 pounds of 3½ x ⅜ spikes....	At 2½c. = 42.25	At 2¾c. = 46.52	At 3c. = 50.70
357 splice joints...	At 22c. = 78.54	At 25c. = 89.25	At 27c. = 96.39
2,640 crossties.....	At 15c. = 396.00	At 20c. = 528.00	At 25c. = 660.00
Grading and laying track...........	= 300.00	= 500.00	= 700.00
Total per mile....	$1,596.22	$2,068.91	$2,537.95

MEMO.—Each $1 per ton variation in the price of 16-pound rails will make a difference of $25.14 per mile.

II.—Estimate of cost of one mile of track with 20-pound steel rails

	Rails at $31 per Ton	Rails at $36 per Ton	Rails at $41 per Ton
$31\frac{960}{2240}$ tons of 20-pound steel rails...	At $31 = $974.29	At $36 = $1,131.42	At $41 = $1,288.57
2,710 pounds of 4 x 7/16 spikes......	At 2 4/10c. = 65.04	At 2 6/10c. = 70.46	At 2 9/10c. = 78.59
357 splice joints...	At 27c. = 96.39	At 30c. = 107.10	At 33c. = 117.81
2,640 crossties.....	At 15c. = 396.00	At 20c. = 528.00	At 25c. = 660.00
Grading and laying track...........	= 300.00	= 500.00	= 700.00
Total per mile....	$1,831.72	$2,336.98	$2,844.97

MEMO.—Each $1 per ton variation in the price of 20-pound rails will make a difference of $31.43 per mile.

III.—Estimate of cost of one mile of track with 25-pound steel rails

	Rails at $30 per Ton	Rails at $35 per Ton	Rails at $40 per Ton
39$\frac{640}{2240}$ tons of 25-pound steel rails...	At $30 = $1,178.57	At $35 = $1,375.00	At $40 = $1,571.43
3,495 pounds of 4x½ spikes......	At 2$\frac{35}{100}$c. = 82.13	At 2$\frac{55}{100}$c. = 89.12	At 2$\frac{85}{100}$c. = 99.61
357 splice joints....	At 32c. = 114.24	At 35c. = 124.95	At 38c. = 135.66
2,640 crossties	At 20c. = 528.00	At 25c. = 660.00	At 30c. = 792.00
Grading and laying track............	= 400.00	= 600.00	= 800.00
Total per mile...	$2,302.94	$2,849.07	$3,398.70

MEMO.—Each $1 per ton variation in the price of 25-pound rails will make a difference of $39.28 per mile.

IV.—Estimate of cost of one mile of track with 30-pound steel rails

	Rails at $30 per Ton	Rails at $35 per Ton	Rails at $40 per Ton
47$\frac{320}{2240}$ tons of 30-pound steel rails...	At $30 = $1,414.28	At $35 = $1,650.00	At $40 = $1,885.71
3,950 pounds of 4½x½ spikes.....	At 2$\frac{35}{100}$c. = 92.82	At 2$\frac{55}{100}$c. = 100.72	At 2$\frac{85}{100}$c. = 112.57
357 splice joints....	At 37c. = 132.09	At 40c. = 142.80	At 43c. = 153.51
2,640 crossties	At 20c. = 528.00	At 25c. = 660.00	At 30c. = 792.00
Grading and laying track............	= 400.00	= 600.00	= 800.00
Total per mile...	$2,567.19	$3,153.52	$3,743.79

MEMO.—Each $1 per ton variation in the price of 30-pound rails will make a difference of $47.14 per mile.

V.—Estimate of cost of one mile of track with 35-pound steel rails

	Rails at $30 per Ton	Rails at $35 per Ton	Rails at $40 per Ton
55 tons of 35-pound steel rails........	At $30 = $1,650.00	At $35 = $1,925.00	At $40 = $2,200.00
3,950 pounds of 4½x½ spikes.....	At 2$\frac{35}{100}$c. = 92.82	At 2$\frac{55}{100}$c. = 100.72	At 2$\frac{85}{100}$c. = 112.57
357 splice joints....	At 42c. = 149.94	At 45c. = 160.65	At 48c. = 171.36
2,640 crossties	At 20c. = 528.00	At 25c. = 660.00	At 30c. = 792.00
Grading and laying track............	= 500.00	= 600.00	= 800.00
Total per mile...	$2,920.76	$3,446.37	$4,075.93

MEMO.—Each $1 per ton variation in the price of 35-pound rails will make a difference of $55 per mile.

VI.—Estimate of cost of one mile of track with 40-pound steel rails

	Rails at $30 per Ton	Rails at $35 per Ton	Rails at $40 per Ton
$62\frac{1920}{2240}$ tons of 40-pound steel rails	At $30 = $1,885.71	At $35 = $2,200.00	At $40 = $2,514.28
4,185 pounds of 5x½ spikes	At $2\frac{35}{100}$c. = 98.35	At $2\frac{55}{100}$c. = 106.71	At $2\frac{85}{100}$c. = 119.27
357 splice joints	At 45c. = 160.65	At 50c. = 178.50	At 55c. = 196.35
2,640 crossties	At 25c. = 660.00	At 30c. = 792.00	At 35c. = 924.00
Grading and laying track	= 500.00	= 700.00	= 1000.00
Total per mile	$3,304.71	$3,977.21	$4,753.90

MEMO.—Each $1 per ton variation in price of 40-pound rails will make a difference of $62.86 per mile.

VII.—Estimate of cost of one mile of track with 45-pound steel rails

	Rails at $30 per Ton	Rails at $35 per Ton	Rails at $40 per Ton
$70\frac{1600}{2240}$ tons of 45-pound steel rails	At $30 = $2,121.43	At $35 = $2,475.00	At $40 = $2,828.57
5,215 pounds of 5x⅜ spikes	At 2¼c. = 117.34	At $2\frac{35}{100}$c. = 122.55	At $2\frac{6}{100}$c. = 135.59
357 splice joints	At 50c. = 178.50	At 60c. = 214.20	At 70c. = 249.90
2,348 crossties	At 30c. = 704.40	At 40c. = 939.20	At 50c. = 1174.00
Grading and laying track	= 500.00	= 700.00	= 1000.00
Total per mile	$3,621.67	$4,450.95	$5,388.06

MEMO.—Each $1 per ton variation in price of 40-pound rails will make a difference of $70.71 per mile.

Memorandum of Weights and Capacities of Cars for Use in Estimating Weights of Trains

	Narrow Gauge		Wide Gauge	
	Weight of Car Pounds	Weight of Load Pounds	Weight of Car Pounds	Weight of Load Pounds
8-wheel flat car	9,500 to 11,000	25,000	18,000 to 20,000	40,000
	10,000 " 12,000	30,000	20,000 " 22,000	50,000
	15,500 " 18,000	40,000	22,000 " 24,000	60,000
			26,000 " 28,000	70,000
			28,000 " 30,000	80,000
			32,000 " 36,000	100,000
8-wheel gondola car	15,000 to 16,500	30,000	19,000 " 23,000	40,000
	21,000 " 23,000	44,000	26,000 " 28,000	60,000
	22,000 " 24,000	50,000	34,000 " 38,000	80,000
			36,000 " 42,000	100,000
8-wheel box car	14,000 to 15,000	20,000	33,000 " 36,000	60,000
	19,000 " 21,000	30,000	34,000 " 36,000	70,000
	20,000 " 22,000	40,000	38,000 " 40,000	80,000
	22,000 " 23,000	50,000	40,000 " 46,000	100,000
4-wheel flat car	5,000	12,000		
4-wheel gondola car	6,000	12,000	9,000	20,000
4-wheel box car	6,500	12,000		

	Weight of Car Pounds	Number Passengers Seated	Weight of Car Pounds	Number Passengers Seated
8-wheel passenger coach	26,000	52	90,000	62
12-wheel Pullman	....	....	117,500	....
Light 8-wheel open excursion coach	9,700	60	18,000	80
Light 8-wheel coach for motor lines, suburban roads, etc.	10,000	40	10,000	40

Weights and Capacities of Street Cars

Usual gauges of track, 56½, 60, and 62½ inches.
4-wheel, 1-horse street car, 16 to 18 ft. long, 3,500 lbs., seating 16 passengers.
  "   2- "   "   "   23 " 25 "   "   5,000 "   "   28   "

NOTE.—Passengers average 15 per ton of 2,000 pounds.

Weights and Capacities of Logging Cars

36 to 56½ inches gauge of track.

MEMO.—The bunks of logging cars for narrow gauge are shorter than for wide gauge and logs must be piled higher than for wide gauge; for this reason standard gauge is usually preferable to narrow for logging.

	Weight	Capacity, White Pine 8,000 Lbs., Yellow Pine 10,000 Lbs., per 1,000 Feet
4-wheel logging cars	3,000 lbs.	1,000 ft. of logs = 8,000 to 10,000 lbs.
" " "	5,000 "	2,000 " " " = 16,000 " 20,000 "
" " "	6,000 "	2,500 " " " = 20,000 " 25,000 "
8-wheel " "	6,900 "	2,500 to 3,000 ft. of logs = 20,000 to 30,000 lb.
" " "	8,400 "	3,500 " 4,000 " " = 28,000 " 40,000 "
" " "	9,600 "	4,500 " 5,000 " " = 36,000 " 50,000 "
" " "	11,000 "	5,500 " 6,000 " " = 44,000 " 60,000 "

Weights and Capacities of Contractors' Cars and Industrial Dump Cars

Four wheels; usual gauge of track, 36 inches

	Weight of Empty Car	Average Weight of Load
1 cubic yard capacity............	1,400 lbs.	3,000 lbs.
1½ " " "	2,500 "	4,500 "
2 " " "	3,000 "	6,000 "
2½ " " "	3,500 "	7,500 "
3 " " "	4,500 "	9,000 "
4 " " "	6,000 "	12,000 "
5 " " "	6,800 "	15,000 "

Weights and Capacities of Colliery Cars

Four wheels; usual gauge of track, 36 to 44 inches

Approximate Capacity	Weight of Empty Car	Average Weight of Load
15 bushels "run of mine" coal....	500 lbs.	1,200 lbs. bituminous coal
20 " " " " "	600 "	1,500 " " "
25 " " " " "	850 "	1,900 " " "
30 " " " " "	950 "	2,300 " " "
33 " " " " "	1,050 "	2,500 " " "
35 " " " " "	1,150 "	2,700 " " "
40 " " " " "	1,250 "	3,000 " " "
46 " " " " "	1,400 "	3,500 " " "
54 " " " " "	1,700 "	4,100 " " "
2½ "long" tons coal.	2,000 "	5,700 " anthracite coal
3 " " "	2,500 "	6,700 " " "

Miscellaneous

A bushel of bituminous coal weighs 76 pounds, and contains 2,688 cubic inches.

A bushel of hard coke weights 40 pounds.

A bushel of soft or gas-house coke weighs 32 pounds.

One acre of bituminous coal contains 1,600 tons of 2,240 pounds per foot of thickness of coal worked. Fifteen to 25 per cent must be deducted for waste in mining.

One ton, 2,000 pounds, of bituminous coal requires for storage 40 cubic feet, or one ton of 2,240 pounds 45 cubic feet.

One ton, 2,000 pounds, of anthracite coal requires for storage 33 cubic feet, or one ton of 2,240 pounds 37 cubic feet.

A cubic yard of loose earth weighs 2,200 to 2,600 pounds.

A cubic yard of wet sand weighs 3,000 to 3,500 pounds.

A cubic yard of broken rock weighs 2,600 to 3,000 pounds.

Water weighs about $8\frac{1}{3}$ pounds per gallon, and one gallon contains 231 cubic inches.

One cubic foot contains almost exactly $7\frac{1}{2}$ gallons.

The circumference of a circle is about $3\frac{1}{7}$ times its diameter.

One acre contains 43,560 square feet.

A square of $208\frac{71}{100}$ feet contains one acre = 43,560 square feet.

A square of $147\frac{51}{100}$ feet contains $\frac{1}{2}$ acre = 21,780 square feet.

A square of $104\frac{355}{1000}$ feet contains $\frac{1}{4}$ acre = 10,890 square feet.

One square mile contains 640 acres.

To find the number of gallons in a circular tank, multiply the diameter in feet by itself, then multiply by the depth in feet, then by 6, and from this sum deduct 2 per cent.

EXAMPLE.—A tank 14 feet diameter and 9 feet deep. $14 \times 14 = 196 \times 9 = 1,764 \times 6 = 10,584$ less 2 per cent $(= 210) = 10,374$ gallons. (This is very nearly exact.)

One barrel is rated at $31\frac{1}{2}$ gallons.

Cast iron weighs about one pound per 4 cubic inches.

Wrought iron weighs about one pound per $3\frac{1}{2}$ cubic inches.

Steel weighs about 2 per cent more than wrought iron.

To ascertain the weight in pounds per running foot of round steel, multiply the diameter in inches (using decimals to express fractions most conveniently) by 4; square this; divide by 6; add 1 per cent.

To ascertain the weight in pounds per running foot of square steel, multiply the size in inches (using decimals to express fractions most conveniently) by 4; square this; divide by 5; add $\frac{1}{16}$.

To ascertain the weight in pounds per running foot of flat steel, multiply the width by the thickness in inches (using decimals to express fractions most conveniently); multiply by 10; divide by 3; add 2 per cent.

Steel boiler plate weighs per square foot approximately $2\frac{1}{2}$ pounds (more exactly $2\frac{55}{100}$ pounds) for each $\frac{1}{16}$ inch of thickness.

Copper plate weighs $2\frac{73}{100}$ pounds, and brass plate $2\frac{60}{100}$ pounds per square foot of $\frac{1}{16}$ inch thickness.

Weights of Logs and Lumber

Weight of Green Logs to Scale 1,000 Feet Board Measure

Yellow Pine (Southern)	8,000 to 10,000	pounds
Norway Pine (Michigan)	7,000 to 8,000	"
White Pine (Michigan) { off of stump	6,000 to 7,000	"
{ out of water	7,000 to 8,000	"
White Pine (Pennsylvania), bark off	5,000 to 6,000	"
Hemlock (Pennsylvania), bark off	6,000 to 7,000	"

Four acres of water are required to store 1,000,000 feet of logs.

Weight of 1,000 Feet of Lumber Board Measure

Yellow or Norway Pine ... Dry, 3,000 pounds; Green, 4,000 to 4,500 pounds
White Pine . . . . Dry, 2,500 " ; Green, 3,500 to 4,000 "

Weight of One Cord of Seasoned Wood, 128 Cubic Feet per Cord

Hickory or Sugar Maple	4,500	pounds
White Oak	3,850	"
Beech, Red Oak, or Black Oak	3,250	"
Poplar, Chestnut, or Elm	2,350	"
Pine (White or Norway)	2,000	"
Hemlock Bark, Dry (1 cord bark got from 1,500 feet logs)	2,000	"

MEMORANDUM.—When wood is cut in 4 feet lengths, a pile 4 feet high and 8 feet long contains one full cord of 128 cubic feet. Wood for locomotive fuel is cut in 2 feet lengths and a pile 4 feet high and 8 feet long is reckoned as a locomotive cord. For our small locomotives wood should be cut about 18 inches long.

To Find the Size of Rail Needed for a Locomotive

Multiply the number of tons (of 2,000 pounds) on one driving wheel by eight, and the result is the number of pounds per yard of the lightest rail advisable.

This rule is only approximate, and is subject to modification in practice.

NOTE.—If, as is often the case with four-wheel-connected locomotives, the weight on front and back driving wheels is not the same, the heavier weight must be taken.

To Find the Number of Tons of Rail per Mile of Road

Multiply weight of rail per yard by 11, and divide by 7. This does not include sidings, and a ton is reckoned at 2,240 pounds.

EXAMPLE.—The number of tons of 28 pounds per yard rail required for one mile is 11 x 28 = 308; divided by 7 = 44 tons.

The number of tons of 2,000 pounds required per mile is very nearly 1¾ times the weight per yard.

EXAMPLE.—1¾ times 28 gives 49 tons per mile required of 28-pound rail.

Rails are regularly sold by the ton of 2,240 pounds.

Table of Tons per Mile Required of Rails of Following Weights per Yard

Weight per Yard	Tons of 2,240 Lb. per Mile	Weight per Yard	Tons of 2,240 Lb. per Mile
16 lb.	25 tons, 320 lb.	35 lb.	55 tons, 0 lb.
20 "	31 " 960 "	40 "	62 " 1,920 "
25 "	39 " 640 "	45 "	70 " 1,600 "
28 "	44 " 0 "	56 "	88 " 0 "
30 "	47 " 320 "	60 "	94 " 640 "

Railroad Spikes, made by Dilworth, Porter & Co., (Limited), Pittsburgh, Pa.

Size Measured Under Head	Average Number per Keg of 200 lb.	Ties 2 Ft. between Centers, 4 Spikes per Tie, makes per Mile	Rail Used, Weight per Yard
5½ x 9/16	360	5,870 lbs. = 29 1/3 kegs	45 to 100
5 x 9/16	405	5,215 " = 26 "	40 to 56
5 x ½	505	4,185 " = 21 "	35 to 40
4½ x ½	535	3,950 " = 19¾ "	28 to 35
4 x ½	605	3,495 " = 17½ "	24 to 35
4½ x 7/16	690	3,065 " = 15 1/3 "	20 to 30
4 x 7/16	780	2,710 " = 13½ "	
3½ x 7/16	890	2,375 " = 11¾ "	16 to 25
4 x 3/8	1,025	2,065 " = 10 1/3 "	
3½ x 3/8	1,250	1,690 " = 8½ "	16 to 20
3 x 3/8	1,380	1,530 " = 7 2/3 "	
2½ x 3/8	1,650	1,280 " = 6 1/5 "	12 to 16

Crossties per Mile

Center to Center	Ties	Center to Center	Ties
1½ feet	3,520	2¼ feet	2,348
1¾ "	3,017	2½ "	2,113
2 "	2,640		

Splice Joints per Mile

2 Bars and 4 Bolts and Nuts to each Joint		2 Bars and 4 Bolts and Nuts to each Joint	
Rails 20 feet long	528 joints	Rails 28 feet long	378 joints
" 24 " "	440 "	" 30 " "	352 "
" 26 " "	406 "		

The length of rails as usually sold is 90 per cent 30 feet long, and 10 per cent 24 to 28 feet long, requiring 357 splice joints per mile. The average weight of splice joints (complete with 2 bars and 4 bolts and nuts) is as follows:

For rails of 16 to 20 pounds per yard, each joint weighs   5 to 6 pounds.
"   "   24 to 28   "   "   "   "   6 to 8   "
"   "   30 to 35   "   "   "   "   10 to 12   "
"   "   40 to 50   "   "   "   "   12 to 16   "
"   "   56 to 60   "   "   "   "   18 to 24   "

Comparison of Weights of Rail—American and Metric Standards

1 lb. per yd.	= 0.496 kilog. per metre	1 kilog. per metre	= 2.016 lb. per yd.
8 "	= 3.968 "	4 "	= 8.064 "
10 "	= 4.960 "	5 "	= 10.080 "
12 "	= 5.952 "	6 "	= 12.096 "
16 "	= 7.936 "	8 "	= 16.128 "
20 "	= 9.920 "	10 "	= 20.160 "
25 "	= 12.400 "	12 "	= 24.192 "
30 "	= 14.880 "	14 "	= 28.224 "
35 "	= 16.960 "	16 "	= 32.256 "
40 "	= 19.840 "	20 "	= 40.320 "
45 "	= 22.320 "	22 "	= 44.352 "
50 "	= 24.800 "	24 "	= 48.384 "
55 "	= 27.280 "	26 "	= 52.416 "
60 "	= 29.760 "	30 "	= 60.480 "

To change pounds per yard to kilograms per metre: Divide by 2, and then subtract $\tfrac{8}{10}$ of 1 per cent (.008).

EXAMPLE.—60 pounds per yard, divided by 2=30; 1 per cent of 30=.3; $\tfrac{8}{10}$ of 1 per cent (.008) of 30=.24; 30—.24=29.76 kilograms per metre.

To change kilograms per metre to pounds per yard: Multiply by 2, and then add $\tfrac{8}{10}$ of 1 per cent (.008).

EXAMPLE.—24 kilograms per metre multiplied by 2=48; $\tfrac{8}{10}$ of 1 per cent (.008) of 48=.384, which added to 48 makes 48.384 pounds per yard.

NOTE.—Approximately each 1,000 pounds weight resting on four wheels requires one pound per yard weight of T rail; *i. e.*, a locomotive with 20,000 pounds on four wheels needs a rail 20 pounds per yard.

American and Metric Standards of Length

1 millimetre = $\frac{1}{1000}$ metre = 0.03937 (nearly $\frac{2}{51}$) inch = 0.00328 foot
1 centimetre = $\frac{1}{100}$ metre = 0.3937 (full ⅜) inch = 0.0328 foot

1 metre
= 1000 millimetres = 39.37079 (about 39⅜) inches
= 100 centimetres = 3.2809 feet = 1.0936 yard

1 kilometre 1000 metres
= 3280$\frac{9}{10}$ feet = 1093$\frac{6}{10}$ yards
= 0.62138 (about ⅝) mile

1 inch = 2.5399 centimetres = 25.3995 millimetres
1 foot = 30.4794 centimetres = 304.7944 millimetres
1 yard = 91.4383 centimetres = 914.3835 millimetres
1 mile = 1.6094 kilometres = 1609$\frac{4}{10}$ metres

American and Metric Square Measure

1 square millimetre = 0.00155 square inch
1 square centimetre = 100 square millimetres = 0.155 sq. inch

1 square metre = 1000000 square millimetres =
  1550 sq. inches
  10.7641 sq. feet
  1.1960 sq. yard

1 hectare = 10000 square metres =
  107641 sq. feet
  2.4711 acres
  0.003861 sq. mile

1 sq. in. = 645.16 sq. mm. = 6.4516 sq. centimetres
1 sq. ft. = 144 sq. in. = 92903 sq. mm. = 929.03 sq. centimetres
1 sq. yard = 9 sq. ft. = 836127 sq. mm. = 0.8361 sq. metre
1 acre = 43560 sq. ft. = 4047 sq. metres = 0.4047 hectare
1 sq. mile = 27878400 sq. ft. = 2589945 sq. metres = 258.99 hectares

American and Metric Cubic Measure

1 cubic millimetre = 0.000061 cubic inch
1 cubic centimetre = 1000 cubic mm. = 0.061023 cubic inch

1 cubic metre = 1000000000 cubic mm. =
  610230 cubic inches
  35.3156 cubic feet
  1.3080 cubic yard
  0.88 cu. ton of 40 cu. ft.

1 litre = 1000000 cubic mm. =
  2.11342 pt., liquid measure
  1.05671 qt., liquid measure
  0.26417 gal., liquid measure
  61.023 cubic inches

American and Metric Cubic Measure—*Continued*

1 cubic inch	=16387 cubic millimetres	
1 cubic ft. =1728 cubic in.	=0.02832 cubic metre	= 283200 cu. centimetres
1 cubic yd.= 27 cubic ft.	=0.7645 cubic metre	= 764500 cu. centimetres
1 cubic ton of 40 feet	=1.1328 cubic metre	=1132800 cu. centimetres
1 pint =28.9 cubic in.	=0.47315 litre	= 473.15 cu. centimetres
1 quart =57.75 cubic in.	=0.9463 litre	= 946.3 cu. centimetres
1 gallon =231. cubic in.	=3.7852 litre	= 3785.2 cu. centimetres

American and Metric Standards of Weight

1 kilogram	=2.2046 lb. (usually reckoned as $2\frac{2}{10}$ lb.)
1 pound	=0.45359 kilograms
1 metric ton (1000 kilograms)	=2204$\frac{6}{10}$ lb. (usually reckoned as 2200 lb.)
1 ton of 2000 pounds	= 907.2 kilograms
1 ton of 2240 pounds	=1016. kilograms

NOTE.—In ocean shipments it is customary for the vessel to have the option of reckoning each box or piece at 2,000 pounds, or at 40 cubic feet per ton. In computing the cubic measurements extreme dimensions are taken, and the width, length, and height multiplied together to arrive at the cubic contents of a rectangular figure which would contain any irregularly shaped piece. It is our practice to pack so as to secure economy of space, and to mark each piece with dimensions in feet and tenths of feet.

Distances in Miles and in Kilometres for Comparison of Lengths of Railroads, Speed per Hour, etc.

(5,280 feet=1 mile.   1,000 metres=1 kilometre.)

1 mile = 1.61 kilometres.	1 kilometre = 0.62 miles.
2 miles= 3.22 "	2 kilometres= 1.24 "
3 " = 4.83 "	3 " = 1.86 "
4 " = 6.44 "	4 " = 2.48 "
5 " = 8.05 "	5 " = 3.10 "
6 " = 9.66 "	6 " = 3.73 "
7 " =11.26 "	7 " = 4.34 "
8 " =12.88 "	8 " = 4.97 "
9 " =14.49 "	9 " = 5.59 "
10 " =16.09 "	10 " = 6.21 "
11 " =17.70 "	11 " = 6.83 "
12 " =19.31 "	12 " = 7.45 "
13 " =20.92 "	13 " = 8.08 "
14 " =22.53 "	14 " = 8.70 "
15 " =24.94 "	15 " = 9.32 "
20 " =32.19 "	20 " =12.43 "
25 " =40.24 "	25 " =15.53 "
30 " =48.28 "	30 " =18.64 "
35 " =56.33 "	35 " =21.75 "
40 " =64.37 "	40 " =24.85 "
50 " =80.47 "	50 " =31.07 "

Comparison of Measurements in Inches and Millimetres

Sufficiently accurate for use in connection with gauges of track, heights of car coupling, lengths of wheel-base, width of locomotives, etc.

½ inch	=	12 7/10 millimetres.	31 inches	= 0 metre	787 millimetres.	
1 "	=	25 4/10 "	31½ "	= 0 "	800 "	
2 inches	=	50 8/10 "	32 "	= 0 "	813 "	
3 "	=	76 2/10 "	33 "	= 0 "	838 "	
3 15/16 "	=	100 "	34 "	= 0 "	863 "	
4 "	=	102 "	35 "	= 0 "	889 "	
5 "	=	127 "	35½ "	= 0 "	900 "	
6 "	=	153 "	36 "	= 0 "	914 "	
7 "	=	178 "	37 "	= 0 "	940 "	
7 7/8 "	=	200 "	38 "	= 0 "	965 "	
8 "	=	203 "	39 "	= 0 "	990 "	
9 "	=	229 "	39 3/8 "	= 1 "	0 "	
10 "	=	254 "	40 "	= 1 "	16 "	
11 "	=	280 "	41 "	= 1 "	41 "	
11 3/16 "	=	300 "	42 "	= 1 "	66 "	
12 "	=	305 "	43 "	= 1 "	91 "	
13 "	=	330 "	44 "	= 1 "	116 "	
14 "	=	355 "	45 "	= 1 "	143 "	
15 "	=	381 "	46 "	= 1 "	168 "	
15 ¾ "	=	400 "	47 "	= 1 "	184 "	
16 "	=	407 "	48 "	= 1 "	219 "	
17 "	=	432 "	49 "	= 1 "	244 "	
18 "	=	457 "	49 ¼ "	= 1 "	250 "	
19 "	=	483 "	50 "	= 1 "	270 "	
19 5/8 "	=	500 "	51 "	= 1 "	295 "	
20 "	=	508 "	52 "	= 1 "	321 "	
21 "	=	533 "	53 "	= 1 "	347 "	
22 "	=	559 "	54 "	= 1 "	372 "	
23 "	=	584 "	55 "	= 1 "	397 "	
23 5/8 "	=	600 "	56 "	= 1 "	422 "	
24 "	=	609 "	56½ "	= 1 "	435 "	
25 "	=	635 "	57 "	= 1 "	448 "	
26 "	=	660 "	58 "	= 1 "	473 "	
27 "	=	685 "	59 "	= 1 "	500 "	
27 9/16 "	=	700 "	60 "	= 1 "	524 "	
28 "	=	711 "	62½ "	= 1 "	587 "	
29 "	=	736 "	66 "	= 1 "	676 "	
29½ "	=	750 "	72 "	= 1 "	828 "	
30 "	=	762 "				

Comparison of Pressures in Pounds per Square Inch and in Kilograms per Square Centimetre

Pounds per Square Inch	(=)	Kilograms per Square Centimetre	Kilograms per Square Centimetre	(=)	Pounds per Square Inch
1	=	.0703	0.10	=	1.422
2	=	.1406	0.15	=	2.133
3	=	.2109	0.20	=	2.844
4	=	.2812	0.25	=	3.556
5	=	.3515	0.50	=	7.112
6	=	.4218	0.75	=	10.668
7	=	.4921	1	=	14.224
8	=	.5624	2	=	28.448
9	=	.6327	2.50	=	35.560
10	=	.7030	3	=	42.672
15	=	1.0546	4	=	56.896
20	=	1.4061	5	=	71.120
30	=	2.1092	6	=	85.344
40	=	2.8123	7	=	99.568
50	=	3.5154	7.50	=	106.680
100	=	7.0308	8	=	113.792
110	=	7.7338	9	=	128.016
120	=	8.4369	10	=	142.241
130	=	9.1400	11	=	156.465
140	=	9.8431	12	=	170.689
150	=	10.5462	12.50	=	177.801
160	=	11.2492	13	=	184.913
170	=	11.9523	14	=	199.137
180	=	12.6564	15	=	213.361
190	=	13.3585	16	=	227.585
200	=	14.0616	17	=	241.809
250	=	17.5770	18	=	256.033
300	=	21.0924	19	=	270.257
350	=	24.6078	20	=	284.482
400	=	28.1232	25	=	355.602
450	=	31.6386	30	=	426.722
500	=	35.1540	35	=	497.843
550	=	38.6694	40	=	568.963
600	=	42.1848	45	=	640.083
650	=	45.7002	50	=	711.204
700	=	49.2156	55	=	782.324
750	=	52.7310	60	=	853.445
800	=	56.2464	65	=	924.565
1000	=	70.3080	70	=	995.686
1500	=	105.4620	75	=	1066.806
2000	=	140.6160	100	=	1422.408
2500	=	175.7700	150	=	2133.612
			200	=	2844.816

Atmospheric Pressure

Temperature 60 Degrees Fahrenheit

Altitude above Sea Level in Feet	Pressure, Pounds per Square Inch	Barometer, Inches
0	14.72	30
1,000	14.17	28.87
2,000	13.63	27.78
3,000	13.11	26.72
4,000	12.61	25.70
5,000	12.13	24.72
6,000	11.68	23.78
7,000	11.24	22.89
8,000	10.82	22.04
9,000	10.42	21.22
10,000	10.03	20.43
11,000	9.65	19.66
12,000	9.28	18.92
13,000	8.93	18.20
14,000	8.59	17.50
15,000	8.26	16.82

The pressure of one atmosphere, 14.72 pounds per square inch, is equivalent to 1.0335 kilograms pressure per square centimetre

For convenience one atmosphere is usually reckoned as 15 pounds.

Note.—To reduce Fahrenheit to Centigrade: deduct 32, divide by 2, add 1/9th.
To reduce Centigrade to Fahrenheit: multiply by 2, deduct 10%, add 32.
To reduce Fahrenheit to Reaumur: deduct 32, divide by 2, subtract 1/9th.
To reduce Reaumur to Fahrenheit: multiply by 2, add 1/8th, add 32.

Useful Data as to Wrought-Iron Pipe

Wrought-iron pipe is commercially listed by the inside diameter in inches and fractions, the actual inside diameter for most sizes being somewhat greater than the listed size.

List Size	Actual Inside Diameter	Weight per 100 Feet	Number of Feet in 2,000 Lb.	Cubic Contents of 100 Feet	Number of Ft. to Contain 100 Cubic Ft.
1 in.	1.048	167 lbs.	1,198	.60	16,690
1¼ "	1.38	225 "	889	1.04	9,625
1½ "	1.61	269 "	744	1.41	7,066
2 "	2.067	366 "	547	2.33	4,291
2½ "	2.468	577 "	347	3.32	3,012
3 "	3.067	754 "	265	5.13	1,950
3½ "	3.548	905 "	221	6.86	1,457
4 "	4.026	1,072 "	186	8.85	1,131
4½ "	4.508	1,249 "	160	11.1	902
5 "	5.045	1,456 "	137	13.9	720
6 "	6.065	1,877 "	106.4	20.1	498
7 "	7.023	2,341 "	85.4	26.9	372
8 "	7.982	2,835 "	70.5	34.7	288

Contents of Cylindrical Pipes or Tanks

Inside Diam. in Inches	Cubic Feet for each Foot in Length	Length in Feet to Contain 100 Cubic Feet	Inside Diam. in Inches	Cubic Feet for each Foot in Length	Length in Feet to Contain 100 Cubic Feet
8	.349	286.53	41	9.168	10.90
9	.442	226.6	42	9.621	10.39
10	.545	183.4	43	10.085	9.91
11	.66	151.5	44	10.559	9.47
12	.785	127.3	45	11.045	9.05
13	.922	108.5	46	11.541	8.66
14	1.069	93.54	47	12.048	8.30
15	1.227	81.49	48	12.566	7.95
16	1.396	71.63	49	13.098	7.63
17	1.576	63.45	50	13.636	7.33
18	1.768	56.56	51	14.184	7.05
19	1.969	50.77	52	14.748	6.77
20	2.182	45.83	53	15.32	6.52
21	2.405	41.57	54	15.904	6.28
22	2.64	37.87	55	16.50	6.06
23	2.885	34.66	56	17.104	5.84
24	3.142	31.82	57	17.721	5.64
25	3.409	29.33	58	18.348	5.45
26	3.687	27.13	59	18.986	5.26
27	3.976	25.15	60	19.636	5.09
28	4.276	23.38	61	20.295	4.92
29	4.587	21.80	62	20.964	4.76
30	4.909	20.37	63	21.647	4.62
31	5.241	19.08	64	22.34	4.47
32	5.584	17.79	65	23.03	4.34
33	5.94	16.83	66	23.76	4.20
34	6.305	15.86	67	24.484	4.08
35	6.681	14.97	68	25.22	3.96
36	7.069	14.14	69	25.965	3.84
37	7.467	13.38	70	26.724	3.74
38	7.876	12.70	71	27.494	3.63
39	8.296	12.05	72	28.276	3.53
40	8.727	11.46			

American and Metric Standards of Thickness
Plates, Wire, etc.

Wire Gauge	EQUIVALENT THICKNESS		Fractions of Inch	EQUIVALENT THICKNESS	
	Decimals of Inch	Millimetres and Decimals		Decimals of Inch	Millimetres and Decimals
0000	.460	11.684	1	1	25.400
000	.410	10.414	31/32	.96875	24.606
00	.365	9.291	15/16	.9375	23.812
0	.325	8.255	29/32	.90625	23.019
1	.289	7.341	7/8	.875	22.225
2	.258	6.553	27/32	.84375	21.431
3	.229	5.817	13/16	.8125	20.637
4	.204	5.182	25/32	.78125	19.844
5	.182	4.623	3/4	.75	19.050
6	.162	4.115	23/32	.71875	18.256
7	.144	3.657	11/16	.6875	17.462
8	.128	3.247	21/32	.65625	16.669
9	.114	2.896	5/8	.625	15.875
10	.101	2.565	19/32	.59375	15.081
11	.091	2.311	9/16	.5625	14.287
12	.081	2.057	17/32	.53125	13.494
13	.072	1.829	1/2	.5	12.700
14	.064	1.626	15/32	.46875	11.906
15	.057	1.428	7/16	.4375	11.112
16	.051	1.295	13/32	.40625	10.319
18	.040	1.016	3/8	.375	9.525
20	.032	0.813	11/32	.34375	8.731
22	.025	0.635	5/16	.3125	7.947
24	.021	0.533	9/32	.28125	7.154
26	.016	0.407	1/4	.25	6.350
28	.013	0.330	7/32	.21875	5.556
			3/16	.1875	4.762
			5/32	.15625	3.969
			1/8	.125	3.175
			3/32	.09375	2.381
			1/16	.0625	1.587
			3/64	.046875	1.190
			1/32	.03125	0.794
			1/64	.015625	0.397

Number of Revolutions per Mile for Driving Wheels of Different Diameters

Diameter of Wheel	Revolutions per Mile	Diameter of Wheel	Revolutions per Mile
18 inches	1,116	36 inches	558
20 "	1,005	38 "	529
22 "	914	40 "	502
23 "	874	42 "	480
24 "	837	44 "	457
26 "	773	46 "	437
28 "	718	48 "	420
30 "	672	50 "	402
32 "	628	60 "	336
33 "	609	72 "	279

Revolutions per Minute of Driving Wheels of Different Diameters at Varying Rates of Speed

NUMBER OF REVOLUTIONS PER MINUTE FOR DRIVING WHEELS

Speed per Hour = Minutes per Mile	Dia. 18 in.	Dia. 20 in.	Dia. 22 in.	Dia. 23 in.	Dia. 24 in.	Dia. 26 in.	Dia. 28 in.	Dia. 30 in.	Dia. 32 in.	Dia. 33 in.	Dia. 36 in.	Dia. 38 in.	Dia. 40 in.	Dia. 42 in.	Dia. 44 in.	Dia. 46 in.	Dia. 48 in.	Dia. 50 in.	Dia. 60 in.	Dia. 72 in.
5 miles = 12 min. 0 sec.	93	84	76	73	70	64	60	56	52	51	46	44	42	40	38	36	35	34	28	26
6 " = 10 " 0 "	111	100	91	87	84	77	72	67	63	61	56	53	50	48	46	44	42	40	34	28
8 " = 7 " 30 "	149	134	122	116	112	103	96	90	84	81	74	70	67	64	61	58	56	54	45	37
10 " = 6 " 0 "	186	168	152	146	140	129	120	112	104	102	93	88	84	80	76	73	70	67	56	46
12 " = 5 " 0 "	222	200	182	174	168	154	144	134	126	122	112	106	100	96	92	88	84	80	68	56
15 " = 4 " 0 "	279	251	228	218	209	193	179	168	157	152	139	132	125	120	114	109	105	100	84	70
18 " = 3 " 20 "	334	301	274	262	251	232	216	201	188	182	168	159	150	144	137	131	126	120	101	84
20 " = 3 " 0 "	371	335	304	291	279	257	240	224	207	203	186	176	167	160	152	145	140	134	112	93
25 " = 2 " 24 "	465	419	380	364	348	322	299	280	261	253	232	220	209	200	190	182	175	167	140	112
30 " = 2 " 0 "	558	502	457	437	418	386	359	336	314	304	279	264	251	240	228	218	210	201	168	140
36 " = 1 " 40 "	669	603	548	524	502	464	431	403	377	365	335	317	301	288	274	262	252	241	201	167
40 " = 1 " 30 "	722	670	608	583	558	515	479	448	415	406	372	353	335	320	305	291	280	268	224	186
45 " = 1 " 20 "	837	754	685	655	628	580	538	504	471	457	418	397	376	360	343	328	315	301	252	209
50 " = 1 " 12 "	930	838	761	728	697	644	598	560	523	507	465	441	418	400	381	364	350	335	280	224
60 " = 1 " 0 "	1116	1005	914	874	837	773	718	672	628	609	558	529	502	480	457	437	420	402	336	279

Horsepower of Locomotives

It is undesirable to reckon locomotives by horsepower, since this is dependent on speed, which is a variable quantity, and any figures as to horsepower of locomotives are liable to be misleading.

Locomotive horsepower may, however, be computed by the following rule: Multiply together the area of one piston in square inches, the mean effective pressure in the cylinders in pounds per square inch, twice the length of stroke in feet, the number of revolutions of the driving wheels per minute, and divide by 33,000.

If power is to be stated in equivalent of kilowatts divide by 44,236

Horsepower may be reduced to kilowatts by multiplying by .746. Kilowatts may be reduced to horsepower by multiplying by 1.34.

In computing locomotive horsepower the speed assumed must not be greater than practicable for the locomotive while hauling its heaviest loads unless a corresponding reduction is made in the estimate of mean effective pressure.

A much simpler rule for computing the horsepower of a locomotive when the tractive force is stated is to multiply the tractive force in pounds by the speed in miles per hour at which the locomotive can handle its heaviest loads, and multiply this product by .00266.

EXAMPLE.—Locomotive 7 x 12 cylinders, 24-inch drivers, 160 pounds boiler pressure has 3,330 pounds tractive force, and can do its heaviest work at about 4 miles per hour. 3,330 x 4 x .00266 = (approximately) 35 horse-power, which is a conservative estimate.

Telegraphic Correspondence Code

Cable Address: Porter, Pittsburgh

To be used in connection with **A B C** Code (4th Edition), or **A B C** Code (5th Edition), or Lieber Code, or **A1** Code, or Western Union Code, or Business Telegraph Code.

NOTE.— Code words not in previous catalogue are printed in light-face type in tables, and in italics in list of code words.

NOTE.—All of the code words in this catalogue, including the code words designating each size and design of locomotive, and the following code words for correspondence, selected from THE OFFICIAL VOCABULARY FOR CODE TELEGRAMS published by the International Bureau of Telegraphic Administrations are approved by the various telegraph and cable companies throughout the world.

The code words selected are arranged alphabetically, and begin with the following letters in the alphabetical order given: H, K, P, R, T. Words beginning H, K, and P are used to designate the designs and sizes of locomotives, and words beginning with R and T are used for the correspondence code which here follows. These letters were selected because they are found in the firm name, H. K. PoRTer co.

Boiler Construction, Material, Pressure, Lagging, etc.

Code Word	MESSAGE
RIMEUX	Boiler pressure 120 pounds per square inch.
RIMMON	" " 125 " " "
RINGLA	" " 130 " " "
RINGOT	" " 135 " " "
RINODO	" " 140 " " "
RIPELY	" " 145 " " "
RIRONT	" " 150 " " "
RISADE	" " 155 " " "
RISBAN	" " 160 " " "
RISOTA	" " 165 " " "
RISQUE	" " 170 " " "
RISUDI	" " 175 " " "
RIVOTI	" " 180 " " "
RIXOSA	" " 190 " " "
RIZINA	" " 200 " " "
RIZODE	Pressure per square inch in pounds *———.
RIZOPO	Straight style boiler.
RIZPAH	Wagon-top style boiler.
RIZZARLO	Extension-front boiler (see Illustration No. 1, page 11).
RIZZOLLO	Short-front boiler (see Illustration No. 3, page 12).
ROADMAN	Firebox between frames and partly over rear axle (s).
ROADSTEAD	Firebox between frames and behind rear axle.
ROADWAY	Firebox between frames and between axles.
ROANA	Firebox placed above frames.
ROANESES	Firebox full width placed behind rear driving wheels.
ROANOS	Crown sheet secured by crown-bars.
ROARER	Crown sheet secured by radial stay-bolts.
ROBIGO	Dome placed on wagon-top part of boiler.
ROBLON	Dome placed on cylindrical part of boiler.
ROBIJN	Dome placed centrally on cylindrical part of boiler with 2 sand-boxes—one in front and one behind dome.
ROBORO	Boiler to be tested by hot hydraulic pressure 50 per cent above working pressure.
ROBOSA	Boiler to be tested by hot hydraulic pressure *——— per cent above working pressure.
ROBUTU	Boiler to be tested by steam *——— per cent above working pressure.
ROCHAZ	Dome placed inside of cab.
RODAPE	Dome placed outside of cab.
ROEDOR	Grate area measured in square feet *———.
ROEMER	Heating surface of firebox measured in square feet *———.
ROEMOS	Heating surface of flues measured in square feet *———.
ROENNE	Total heating surface of firebox and flues measured in square feet *———.

* Any code designated on page 204 may be used to express figures.

Boiler Construction, etc.— *Continued*

Code Word	MESSAGE
ROERBAK....	Fire box of steel and flues of iron, or seamless steel.
ROEREND....	Fire box of steel and flues of seamless brass.
ROERIAN....	Fire box of steel and flues of seamless copper.
ROEROM.....	Fire box of copper plates and flues of iron, or seamless steel.
ROFFIA......	Fire box of copper plates and flues of seamless brass.
ROGADO.....	Fire box of copper plates and flues of seamless copper.
ROGALE......	Smoke-stack of copper.
ROGALIUM...	Smoke-stack for coal fuel, taper style, cast iron, like Illustration No. 1, page 11.†
ROGASEN....	Smoke-stack for coal fuel, straight style of steel plates with cast top finish, like Illustration No. 2, page 12.†
ROGBORD....	Smoke-stack for coal fuel, diamond style of steel plates with cast spark arrester and steel wire netting, like Illustration No. 3, page 12.†
ROGEN.......	Smoke-stack for wood fuel, balloon spiral cone style, like Illustration No. 4, page 12.†
ROGERIO....	Smoke-stack for wood fuel, "sunflower" style, like Illustration No. 5, page 12.†
ROGGIO......	Smoke-stack of steel plate with copper top (straight style stack).
ROGITO......	Boiler lagged with wood and cased with planished iron.
ROHUNA.....	Boiler lagged with wood over asbestos sheet and cased with planished iron.
ROJIZO.......	Boiler lagged with asbestos cement and cased with planished iron.
ROLDES......	Boiler lagged with asbestos board and cased with planished iron.
ROLENA......	Boiler lagged with sectional magnesia and cased with planished iron.
ROLHAO......	Boiler casing with brass securing bands.
ROLLOS......	Dome casing of sheet brass body with cast-iron top and base.
RONGER......	Dome casing of sheet steel body with cast-iron top and base.

Brakes

ROPAJE......	Engine to have hand lever brake to driving wheels.
RORIDA......	Engine to have hand screw brake to driving wheels.
ROSARY.....	Engine to have hand wheel brake to 4 wheels of tender.
ROSTRO.....	Engine to have hand wheel brake to 8 wheels of tender.
ROSURI......	Engine to have H. K. Porter Co.'s steam brake to driving wheels.

† Unless otherwise agreed, stacks Nos. 1 and 2 will be furnished in connection with extension-front boiler, and stacks Nos. 3, 4, and 5 with short-front boiler.

Brakes—*Continued*

Code Word	MESSAGE
ROTBAK......	Engine to have H. K. Porter Co.'s steam brake to driving and tender wheels.
ROTULO......	Engine to have American patent steam brake to driving wheels.
ROTURA......	Engine to have American patent steam brakes to driving and tender wheels.
ROTZES......	Engine to have Eames Vacuum Air Brake to driving wheels only.
ROUAGE......	Engine to have Eames Vacuum Air Brake to driving wheels and tender only.
ROUBAZ......	Engine to have Eames Vacuum Air Brake for train only.
ROUPIE......	Engine to have Eames Vacuum Air Brake to driving wheels and train.
ROXEAR......	Engine to have Eames Vacuum Air Brake to driving wheels tender, and train.
RUANEZ......	Engine to have Westinghouse Automatic Air Brake for driving wheels only.
RUARIA......	Engine to have Westinghouse Automatic Air Brake for driving wheels and tender only.
RUARON......	Engine to have Westinghouse Automatic Air Brake for train only.
RUBACE......	Engine to have Westinghouse Automatic Air Brake for driving wheels and train.
RUBBIO......	Engine to have Westinghouse Automatic Air Brake for driving wheels, tender, and train.
RUBEDO......	Engine to have water brake to cylinders.
RUBIFY......	Brake shoes to be applied to four driving wheels.
RUBION......	Brake shoes to be applied to six driving wheels.
RUBLOS......	Brake shoes to be applied to eight driving wheels.
RUBLUT	Cam style spread brake.
RUBMES	Clamp style brake.
RUBNON.....	Equalized style brake.

Cab

RUDEZA......	Wooden cab without doors, rear entrance.
RUEFUL......	Wooden cab with side doors.
RUEPEL......	Wooden cab without doors, side entrances.
RUFULI	Steel cab, similar to page 80.
RUGIDO......	Steel cab, similar to page 82 or 84.
RUGOSU......	Mine style cab, similar to page 106 or 108.
RUGUMO.....	Open sheet-steel canopy, similar to pages 76, 86, 88. etc.
RUGWOL.....	Motor style cab, similar to pages 102 and 104.
RUIFEL.......	No cab at all, similar to page 78.
RUJADA......	Front part of tender to be protected by sheet-steel canopy.

Couplings, Lettering, Etc.

Code Word	MESSAGE
RUKKEN	Lettering for cab is ——.
RULLUM	Lettering for tank is ——.
RUMEUR	Lettering for cab and tank is ——.
RUMIAR	Numeral for number-plate is ——.
RUMINO	Lettering for cab and tank and engine number are ——.
TABERD	Usual American style coupling for link and pin.
TABIDO	Automatic patent coupling, name of patent is ——.
TABIEL	Master Car Builder type of automatic coupler, full size.
TABINS	Master Car Builder type of automatic coupler, narrow gauge or three-quarter size.
TABIOR	Master Car Builder type of automatic coupler, pivoted.
TABLON	European style coupling with two hooks and central buffer.
TABUAL	European style coupling with single hook and two buffers.
TABUDA	Screw coupling.
TACCAS	Hook coupling placed centrally, American style, as used for small cars for mines, contractors, etc.
TACHIM	Height from level of rail to center of car couplings in inches *——.
TACHYS	Height from level of rail to center of car couplings is same as usual for American standard gauge freight cars—*i. e.*, 34½ inches.
TACITA	Height from level of rail to center of car couplings is same as usual for logging cars.
TACTOS	Diameter of buffers, European style, in inches *——.
TADDEO	Distance from level of track to center of buffer in inches *——.
TADEGA	Distance apart between centers of buffers in inches *——.
TADMOR	Please telegraph height in inches from level of rail to center of car coupling, confirming by mail with description of coupling, and, if practicable, a sketch of end timbers of car, with dimensions and location.
TAFRIA	Please write fully height in inches from level of rail to center of car coupling, with description of coupling, and, if practicable, a sketch of end timbers of car, with dimensions and location.
TAGALO	Please telegraph, confirming by mail, lettering for locomotive cab and for tank, and engine number (if any) to go on engine number-plate.
TAHALI	Please write promptly instructions for lettering cab and tank, and also engine number (if any) to go on engine number-plate.
TAHENO	Please mail promptly as practicable full sketch, with dimensions and description and location, if European disc-shaped buffers, hook coupling, screw coupling, patent coupling, or any special arrangement is desired.
TAHURA	Please telegraph, confirming by mail, lettering for cab and tank.
TAIPAL	Please telegraph, confirming by mail, height of car coupling, lettering for cab and tank, and kind of fuel.
TAIXAR	Please telegraph, confirming by mail, kind of fuel and gauge of track.
TAJACU	Please write fully information as to requirements and conditions as explained on pages 16 and 17.

* Any code designated on page 204 may be used to express figures.

Construction Details

Code Word	MESSAGE
TAJEAS	Wooden pilot at front end.
TAKTIK	Wooden pilot at each end.
TALCKY	Iron pilot at front end.
TALGEN	Iron pilot at each end.
TALISCA	Metal bumper at front end.
TALITRO	Metal bumper at each end.
TALOOK	Hanging step-board with hand-rail at front end.
TALORA	Hanging step-board with hand-rail at rear end.
TALVEZ	Hanging step-board with hand-rail at each end.
TALVILLA	Snow-plow of sheet steel at front end.
TALVOLTA	Snow-plow of sheet steel at each end.
TAMARO	Angle bar each end of locomotive for removing track obstructions.
TAMBEM	Steel wire brushes each end of locomotive for cleaning track.
TAMBOR	Locomotive to be furnished with one head-light with bracket and shelf.
TAMICA	Locomotive to be furnished with two head-lights with brackets and shelves.
TAMIZO	Extra handsome finish and painting, gold lettering.
TAMPON	Very plain finish, durable, but without ornament.
TAMRAS	Bell to be omitted.

Cylinders

Code Word	MESSAGE
TAMTAM	Cylinders with sheet-brass jackets.
TAMUGE	Cylinders with sheet-steel jackets.
TAPIGO	Cylinders to be one-half inch larger diameter.
TAPITI	Cylinders to be one inch larger diameter.
TAPIZE	Cylinders to be one-half inch smaller diameter.
TAPONA	Cylinders to be one inch smaller diameter.
TAPPAL	Cylinders to be two inches longer stroke.
TAPUJO	Cylinders to be four inches longer stroke.
TAPUME	Cylinders to be two inches shorter stroke.
TARAJE	Cylinders to be four inches shorter stroke.
TARANDES	Compound cylinders, two-cylinder type.
TARANTEL	Compound cylinders, two-cylinder type, diameter of high-pressure cylinder as stated for locomotive, code word given (———);† diameter of low-pressure cylinder to be in proportion, weight of locomotive to be increased accordingly.

† Code word need not be repeated if already used in the message.

Cylinders—*Continued*

Code Word	MESSAGE
TARASANA. . .	Compound cylinders, two-cylinder type, weight of locomotive not to exceed weight stated for locomotive, code word given (———),† and diameters of high- and low-pressure cylinders of suitable size.
TARASIUS. . . .	Compound cylinders, two-cylinder type, locomotive otherwise of general design, code word given (———),† and of weight nearly the same as practicable, diameters of high- and low-pressure cylinders in inches respectively *——— and *———.
TARASPIC. . . .	Inside-connected cylinders placed between frames with main-rod connection to crank-axle, reducing width of locomotive.

Dimensions

Code Word	MESSAGE
TARAUD.	Height above rail not to exceed *——— inches.
TARAZO.	Height above rail not to exceed *——— feet.
TARBEA.	Width not to exceed *——— inches.
TARDIO	Width not to exceed *——— feet.
TARDOZ.	Length not to exceed *——— inches.
TAREFA.	Length not to exceed *——— feet.
TARGET.	Wheel-base, rigid (preferred), in inches *———.
TARGUM.	Wheel-base, total (preferred), in inches *———.
TAROTS	Wheel-base to suit turntable length, length in feet *———.

Frames

Code Word	MESSAGE
TAUDER.	Continuous forged frames of H. K. Porter Co.'s standard type of construction.
TAUMEL.	Main frames stopped at firebox with connection to rear section of frames to secure extra wide firebox for narrow gauge.
TAUPEA.	Outside frames with driving wheels placed inside of frames and with heavy steel cranks on axles for crank-pin connections.
TAUPIL	Steel castings frames.

* Any code designated on page 204 may be used to express figures.
† Code word need not be repeated if already used in the message.

Fuel

Code Word	MESSAGE
TAUPON	Fuel, bituminous coal.
TAURIM	Fuel, bituminous coal, good quality.
TAUSCH	Fuel, bituminous coal, poor quality.
TAVOUA	Fuel, bituminous coal, slack and nut size.
TAWDRY	Fuel, lignite coal, poor quality.
TAXINE	Fuel, anthracite coal.
TAYOBA	Fuel, anthracite coal, pea size or culm.
TAZANA	Fuel, pitch-pine wood.
TAZMIA	Fuel, white-pine and similar wood.
TEAGEM	Fuel, hardwood, well seasoned.
TEAPOY	Fuel, wood poorly seasoned and poor quality.
TEATRO	Fuel, sawmill slabs and refuse.
TEAZLE	Fuel, bituminous coal and wood, mostly coal.
TEBOUL	Fuel, bituminous coal and wood, mostly wood.
TECHNA	Fuel, naphtha or crude oil.
TECTLY	Fuel, bagasse.
TEFLIM	Please telegraph kind of fuel to be used.
TEGAME	Please write kind of fuel to be used.
TEGARN	Fuel capacity *—— pounds of coal.
TEGATS	Fuel capacity *—— cubic feet of wood.
TEGAUB	Fuel bunker in cab.
TEGENT	Fuel bunker at rear end.
TEGEMS	Separate four-wheel fuel car.

Gauge of Track

Code Word	MESSAGE
TEGESU	(What is) Gauge of track?
TEGORA	Gauge of track is *—— inches.
TEIFUN	" " " " *—— millimetres.
TEIMAR	" " " " 18 inches.
TEINTE	" " " " 20 "
TEJADO	" " " " 24 "
TELARY	" " " " 30 "
TELEBA	" " " " 33 "
TELHAO	" " " " 36 "
TELLER	" " " " 42 "
TELONA	" " " " 56½ "
TELPAS	" " " " 60 "
TELURO	" " " " 500 millimetres.
TEMOSO	" " " " 600 "
TENDON	" " " " 750 "
TENIDO	" " " " 1 metre.

* Any code designated on page 204 may be used to express figures.

Questions, Quotations, and Orders

Code Word	MESSAGE
TENONS......	{ Quote us **by wire,** stating earliest date of completion { We quote you.. } confirming with details by mail, delivered at Pittsburgh free on board car (or on track, if locomotive can be shipped to best advantage on own wheels), set up in usual shipping order, with small parts liable to loss or injury boxed separately, lowest price for ONE locomotive, described by code word *——, gauge of track as per code word *——.
TENREC......	{ Quote us....... } as above noted, per locomotive for { We quote you.. } order of TWO locomotives, code word *——, gauge of track as per code word *——.
TENTER......	{ Quote us....... } as above noted, per locomotive for { We quote you.. } order of THREE locomotives, code word *——, gauge of track as per code word *——.
TENZIJ......	{ Quote us....... } as above noted, per locomotive for { We quote you.. } order of FOUR locomotives, code word *——, gauge of track as per code word *——.
TEPEFY......	{ Quote us....... } as above noted, per locomotive for { We quote you.. } order of †—— locomotives, code word *——, gauge of track as per code word *——.
TEPORE......	Quote us **by mail,** with details and earliest completion, delivered at Pittsburgh free on board car (or on track, if locomotive can be shipped to best advantage on own wheels), set up in usual shipping order with small parts liable to loss or injury boxed separately, for ONE locomotive described by code word *——, gauge of track as per code word *——.
TEQUIO......	Quote us as above noted, per locomotive for order of TWO locomotives, code word *——, gauge of track as per code word *——.
TERCAS......	Quote us as above noted, per locomotive for order of THREE locomotives, code word *——, gauge of track as per code word *——.
TERCOL......	Quote us as above noted, per locomotive for order of FOUR locomotives, code word *——, gauge of track as per code word *——.

* Code word designating size and design of locomotive should follow code word for message; if quotations on several sizes and several designs are desired the code word for each should follow. The code word for gauge of track should follow code word of engine, if practicable to give it. It is desirable also to add code words for fuel and other features which affect the details of construction.

† Number required to be stated, or left unfilled if number is not decided upon.

NOTE.—All quotations, unless otherwise agreed or specified, are in accordance with standard specifications, pages 10 to 15. Special items not included in standard specifications may be furnished at extra cost. Promises of quick completion are conditioned on prompt receipt of instructions as to gauge, fuel, height, and style of couplings and lettering, and also of any special features of construction.

Questions, Quotations, and Orders—*Continued*

Code Word	MESSAGE
TEREUA......	Quote us as above noted, per locomotive for order of †——— locomotives, code word *———, gauge of track as per code word *———.
TERFEX......	{ Quote us **by wire**, stating earliest date of completion { We quote you................. } confirming with details by mail, delivery on car (or on track if shipped on own wheels), set up in usual shipping order with small parts liable to injury or loss boxed separately, including cost of delivery at ††———, for ONE locomotive designated by code word *———, gauge of track as per code word *———.
TERMLY.....	{ Quote us....... } as above noted,†† per locomotive for { We quote you.. } order of TWO locomotives, code word *———, gauge of track as per code word *———.
TERNIR.....	{ Quote us....... } as above noted,†† per locomotive for { We quote you.. } order of THREE locomotives, code word *———, gauge of track as per code word *———.
TERROR......	{ Quote us....... } as above noted,†† per locomotive for { We quote you.. } order of FOUR locomotives, code word *———, gauge of track as per code word *———.
TERTIO......	{ Quote us....... } as above noted,†† per locomotive for { We quote you.. } order of †——— locomotives, code word *———, gauge of track as per code word *———.
TESCAO......	Quote us **by mail** with earliest completion, with details. delivery on car (or on track if shipped on own wheels), set up in usual shipping order with small parts liable to injury or loss boxed separately, including cost of delivery at ††———, for ONE locomotive designated by code word *———, gauge of track as per code word *———.
TESSON......	Quote us as above noted, †† per locomotive for order of TWO locomotives, code word *———, gauge of track as per code word *———.
TETARD......	Quote us as above noted, †† per locomotive for order of THREE locomotives, code word *———, gauge of track as per code word *———.
TETCHY......	Quote us as above noted, †† per locomotive for order of FOUR locomotives, code word *———, gauge of track as per code word *———.

* Code word for locomotive should be given, and if quotations are desired for several styles or sizes code word of each should be stated. The code word for gauge of track should follow code word of engine, if practicable to give it. It is desirable also to add code words for fuel and other features which affect the details of construction.

† Number required to be stated, or left unfilled if number is not decided upon.

†† Name of point of delivery desired should follow code word of message and precede code word for size and design of locomotive.

Questions, Quotations, and Orders—*Continued*

Code Word	MESSAGE
TETRAZ......	Quote us as above noted, †† per locomotive for order of † —— locomotives, code word *——, gauge of track as per code word *——.
TETRYL......	{ Quote us **by wire**, stating earliest completion / We quote you.................................. } confirming by mail with details, for export, including taking apart, protecting from rust, securely boxing and packing; with proper shipping and rotation marks, weights and dimensions marked in indelible ink; list with contents furnished; delivered to vessel's tackle in New York harbor lighterage limits; ONE locomotive designated by code word *——, gauge of track as per code word *——.
TETTIN.......	{ Quote us....... / We quote you.. } as above noted, per locomotive for order of TWO locomotives, code word *——, gauge of track as per code word *——.
TEUCRO......	{ Quote us....... / We quote you.. } as above noted, per locomotive **for** order of THREE locomotives, code word *——, gauge of track as per code word *——.
TEUFEL......	{ Quote us....... / We quote you.. } as above noted, per locomotive for order of FOUR locomotives, code word *——, gauge of track as per code word *——.
TEURGO......	{ Quote us....... / We quote you.. } as above noted, per locomotive for order of † —— locomotives, code word *——, gauge of track as per code word *——.
TEVENS......	Quote us **by mail** with earliest completion, with details for export, including taking apart, protecting from rust, securely boxing and packing; with proper shipping and rotation marks, weights and dimensions marked in indelible ink; list with contents furnished; delivered to vessel's tackle in New York harbor lighterage limits; ONE locomotive designated by code word *——, gauge of track as per code word *——.
TEXTOS......	Quote us as above noted, per locomotive for order of TWO locomotives, code word *——, gauge of track as per code word *——.
THABIT.......	Quote us as above noted, per locomotive for order of THREE locomotives, code word *——, gauge of track as per code word *——.

*Code word for locomotives should be given, and if quotations are desired for several styles or sizes code word of each should be stated. The code word for gauge of track should follow code word of engine, if practicable to give it. It is desirable also to add code words for fuel and other features which affect the details of construction.

†Number required to be stated, or left unfilled if number is not decided upon.

††Name of point of delivery desired should follow code word of message and precede code word for size and design of locomotive.

Questions, Quotations, and Orders—*Continued*

Code Word	MESSAGE
THALNA	Quote us as above noted, per locomotive for order of FOUR locomotives, code word *———, gauge of track as per code word *———.
THAMAH	Quote us as above noted, per locomotive for order of †——— locomotives, code word *———, gauge of track as per code word *———.
THAMER	{ Quote us **by wire**, stating earliest completion / We quote you................ } confirming by mail with details, including taking apart, protecting from rust, securely boxing and packing for ocean shipment; with proper shipping and rotation marks, weights and dimensions; list with contents furnished; delivered on car at Pittsburgh.
THAMIG	{ Quote us **by wire**, stating earliest completion / We quote you................ } confirming by mail, with details, including taking apart, protecting from rust, securely boxing and packing for ocean shipment; with proper shipping and rotation marks, weights and dimensions; list with contents furnished; delivered at ———.
THAMMO	{ Quote............ / We quote you.. } additional amount to cover cost of freight and insurance by steam vessel to ††———.
THASSI	{ Quote............ / We quote you.. } additional amount to cover cost of freight and insurance by sailing vessel to ††———.
THATEN	{ Quote............ / We quote you.. } including in price freight and insurance by steam vessel to ††———.
THEBAE	{ Quote............ / We quote you.. } including in price freight and insurance by sailing vessel to ††———.
THEBEO	{ Quote us **by wire** / We quote you.. } confirming by mail, lowest price of locomotive duplicate of locomotive last furnished.
THECAL	Quote us promptly **by mail** lowest price of locomotive duplicate of locomotive last furnished.
THEMES	Quotation accompanied with full specifications and photograph or blue print.
THEOPE	Quotation accompanied with memorandum of actual or estimated dimensions, and weights of boxes and packages for export shipment.
THEORY	Quotation accompanied with list of spare parts recommended, and cost of same.
THERMAL	Quotation per locomotive including special items usually rated as extras, as follows:———.
THERMEN	Quotation per locomotive not including items as follows, ———, which may be furnished at additional cost.
THESOA	Quotation accompanied with full specifications, photograph or blue print of locomotive, memorandum of weights and dimensions of boxes and packages for export shipment, and list of spare parts recommended, and cost of same

*Code word for locomotive should be given, and if quotations are desired for several styles or sizes code word of each should be stated. The code word for gauge of track should follow code word of engine, if practicable to give it. It is desirable also to add code words for fuel and other features which affect the details of construction.

†Number required to be stated, or left unfilled if number is not decided upon.

††Name of point of delivery desired should follow code word of message and precede code word for size and design of locomotive.

Questions, Quotations, and Orders—*Continued*

Code Word	MESSAGE
THIASO.......	What locomotives have you on hand 30 inches gauge of track?
THINLY.......	What locomotives have you on hand 36 inches gauge of track?
THIRST.......	What locomotives have you on hand 39⅜ inches gauge of track?
THISOA.......	What locomotives have you on hand 56½ inches gauge of track?
THOASA.......	What locomotives have you on hand gauge of track as per code word ††———?
THORAX.......	What locomotives have you on hand gauge of track in inches *———?
THOREN.......	What locomotives have you on hand gauge of track 24 to 36 inches?
THRENO.......	What locomotives have you on hand gauge of track 36 to 42 inches?
THRICE.......	What locomotives have you on hand gauge of track 36 to 56½ inches?
THRUSH.......	{ Have you / We have } on hand 30 inches gauge locomotive(s), code word †———.
THUABA.......	{ Have you / We have } on hand 36 inches gauge locomotive(s), code word †———.
THUBAN	{ Have you / We have } on hand 56½ inches gauge locomotive(s), code word †———.
THYMEA.......	{ Have you / We have } on hand 36 or 56½ gauge locomotive(s), code word †———.
THYMOL.......	Locomotive(s) to be completed at factory within 10 days of receipt of order. †††
THYRSE.......	Locomotive(s) to be completed at factory within 15 days of receipt of order. †††
TIALCO.......	Locomotive(s) to be completed at factory within 20 days of receipt of order. †††
TIBIOS........	Locomotive(s) to be completed at factory within 25 days of receipt of order. †††
TIBIZO.	Locomotive(s) to be completed at factory within 30 days of receipt of order. †††

* Any code designated on page 204 may be used to express figures.

† See code words designating each locomotive, pages 19 to 139.

†† See code words for various gauges, page 211.

††† If two code words are used they are to be understood as if connected by the word *to*— i. e., TIERRA TIESOS signifies 90 days to four months. The expression "receipt of order" covers receipt of instructions as to gauge, couplings, and fuel, and as to any special features of construction which must necessarily be understood clearly before work can be commenced. For export locomotives 10 to 15 days' additional time is required for taking apart and boxing and for transit to vessel in New York harbor.

Questions, Quotations, and Orders—*Continued*

Code Word	MESSAGE
TICIDA......	Locomotive(s) to be completed at factory within 40 days of receipt of order. ††
TIDBIT......	Locomotive(s) to be completed at factory within 50 days of receipt of order. ††
TIDILY......	Locomotive(s) to be completed at factory within 60 days of receipt of order. ††
TIERCE......	Locomotive(s) to be completed at factory within 70 days of receipt of order. ††
TIERNO......	Locomotive(s) to be completed at factory within 80 days of receipt of order. ††
TIERRA......	Locomotive(s) to be completed at factory within 90 days of receipt of order. ††
TIERCON.....	Locomotive(s) to be completed at factory within 100 days of receipt of order. ††
TIERSAN.....	Locomotive(s) to be completed at factory within 110 days of receipt of order. ††
TIERTU......	Locomotive(s) to be completed at factory within †—— days of receipt of order. ††
TIESOS.......	Locomotive(s) to be completed at factory within 4 months of receipt of order. ††
TIESURA.....	Locomotive(s) to be completed at factory within 5 months of receipt of order. ††
TIFACEAS....	Locomotive(s) to be completed at factory within † —— months of receipt of order. ††
TIFATA......	Locomotive(s) to be completed at factory within 6 months of receipt of order. ††
TIFFED......	Enter our order on terms quoted for ONE locomotive, designated by code word *——.
TIFICA.......	Enter our order on terms quoted for TWO locomotives, designated by code word *——.
TIFONE......	Enter our order on terms quoted for THREE locomotives, designated by code word *——.
TIGELA......	Enter our order on terms quoted for FOUR locomotives, designated by code word *——.
TIGRIS.......	Enter our order on terms quoted for locomotives designated by code word *——, number of locomotives covered by this order is ——.

* See code words designating each locomotive, pages 19 to 139. (Unless already advised, or sent by mail, code words should be added for gauge of track, fuel, height of drawbar, and lettering, to facilitate quick completion.)

† Any code designated on page 204 may be used to express figures.

†† If two code words are used they are to be understood as if connected by the word *to* —*i.e.*, TIERRA TIESOS signifies 90 days to four months. The expression "receipt of order" covers receipt of instructions as to gauge, couplings, and fuel, and as to any special features of construction which must necessarily be understood clearly before work can be commenced. For export locomotives 10 to 15 days' additional time is required for taking apart and boxing and for transit to vessel in New York harbor.

Service Requirements and Conditions

Code Word	MESSAGE
TIJOLO	Radius of sharpest curve is 20 feet.
TIKOOL	" " " 20 to 25 feet.
TIKVAH	" " " 25 to 30 "
TILGEN	" " " 30 to 40 "
TILLAC	" " " 40 to 50 "
TILODE	" " " 50 to 60 "
TILOMO	" " " 60 to 75 "
TIMBRE	" " " 75 to 100 "
TIMEAS	" " " 100 to 125 "
TIMMEN	" " " 125 to 150 "
TIMUCU	" " " 150 to 200 "
TINACO	" " " 200 to 300 "
TINAGE	" " " 300 to 500 "
TINAIS	" " " over 500.
TINKLE	Steepest grade does not exceed ½ of 1 per cent.
TINOTE	" " " 1 per cent.
TINSEL	" " " 1½ "
TIPITI	" " " 2 "
TIPTOE	" " " 2½ "
TIPULA	" " " 3 "
TIRAPE	" " " 3½ "
TIRCIS	" " " 4 "
TIRRIA	" " " 4½ "
TIRYNS	" " " 5 "
TIRZAH	" " " 6 "
TISANE	" " " 7 "
TISARD	" " " 8 "
TISICO	" " " 9 "
TISSUS	" " " 10 "
TISTRE	Length of grade not more than 100 feet.
TITULO	" " " " 200 "
TITYOS	" " " " 500 "
TIZNAR	" " " " 1,000 "
TIZONA	" " " " 2,000 "
TOANAH	Length of grade not determined, but probably not over 500 ft.
TOBAJA	Length of grade in feet *———.
TOBBEN	Length of grade in miles *———.
TOCADO	Ruling grades are in favor of loaded trains.
TOCAGE	Ruling grades are against loaded trains.

* Any code designated on page 204 may be used to express figures.

Service Requirements and Conditions—*Continued*

Code Word	MESSAGE
TODDLE	Length of railroad does not exceed 1 mile.
TODTES	" " " " 1½ miles.
TOEHEK	" " " " 2 "
TOENEN	" " " " 2½ "
TOESAS	" " " " 5 "
TOFORE	" " " " 10 "
TOGATA	" " " " 15 "
TOGGEL	" " " " 20 "
TOLANE	Length of railroad in miles *———.
TOLOSA	Length of railroad.
TOLTEC	Weight of rail in pounds per yard *———.
TOLUOL	Approximate weight of rail per yard is 16 pounds.
TOMAUN	" " " " 20 "
TOMONE	" " " " 25 "
TONLOS	" " " " 30 "
TONOUS	" " " " not less than 35 lb.
TOPAIS	" " " " " " 40 "
TOPCHI	" " " " " " 45 "
TOPFUL	" " " " " " 50 "
TOPHIN	" " " " " " 60 "
	NOTE.—For comparison of weights in pounds per yard and kilograms per metre see page 194.
TOPICA	Speed in miles per hour *———.
TOPMAN	Total weight of freight to be carried one way per day of 10 hours, in tons of 2,000 pounds *———.
TORADA	Weight of cars and lading to be hauled at one time up grade, in tons of 2,000 pounds *———.
TORBOK	Weight of empty train to be hauled up grade (cars loaded only when coming down grade), in tons of 2,000 pounds *———.

Tank

Code Word	MESSAGE
TOTUMA	Saddle-tank over boiler.
TOUFAN	Side tanks, one each side of boiler.
TOUFFU	Side tanks, one each side at rear end of locomotive.
TOUTOU	Rear tank.
TOZUDA	Tank on 4-wheel tender.
TRABEO	Tank on 6-wheel tender.

(*Continued on next page.*)

* Any code designated on page 204 may be used to express figures.

Tank—*Continued*

Code Word	MESSAGE
TRAHIR	Tank on 8-wheel tender.
TRAHOB	Tender with sloped style of tank.
TRAJAR	Locomotive to have both saddle and rear tanks.
TRAJET	Locomotive to have both side tanks and rear tank.
TRAPEZ	Locomotive to have both saddle-tank and tender-tank.
TRASHY	Capacity of tank to be *―― gallons of 231 cubic inches.
TRASPE	Capacity of tank to be increased 50 gallons.
TRASTO	" " " " 100 "
TRAUFE	" " " " 150 "
TREBAC	" " " " 200 "
TREBOL	" " " " 250 "
TRECHO	" " " " 300 "

Tractive Force

TRECIN	Tractive force (as per formula on page 140) in pounds *――.
TRECOV	Tractive force to be increased *―― pounds.
TRECUS	Tractive force to be decreased *―― pounds.

Weight

TREFLE	(What is) Limit of weight per axle in pounds *――.
TREGOA	(What is) Limit of weight per axle in kilograms *――.
TREKOS	(What is) Total weight of locomotive in full working order *―― pounds.
TREPPE	(What is) Total weight of locomotive in full working order *―― kilograms.
TRESCATA	(What is) Weight on driving wheels in full working order *―― pounds.
TRESLER	(What is) Weight on driving wheels in full working order *―― kilograms.
TRESNAN	(What is) Weight on locomotive truck in full working order *―― pounds.
TRESOR	(What is) Weight on locomotive truck in full working order *―― kilograms.
TRESSES	(What is) Weight of tender in full working order *―― pounds.
TRETEAU	(What is) Weight of tender in full working order *―― kilograms.
TRETEN	(What is) Weight of one locomotive set up on car, without fuel or water, in shipping order, in pounds *――.
TRICHE	(What is) Weight of one locomotive and tender set up on car(s), without fuel or water, in shipping order, in pounds *――.

*Any code designated on page 204 may be used to express figures.

Weight—*Continued*

Code Word	MESSAGE
TRICON.......	(What is) Estimated weight of one locomotive (including tender, if any) taken apart and boxed for vessel shipment, in pounds *——.
TRIEGE.......	(What is) Estimated cubic tonnage (including tender, if any) of one locomotive taken apart and boxed for vessel shipment, in tons of 40 cubic feet *——.
TRIFUN	(What is) Estimated cubic feet (including tender, if any) of one locomotive taken apart and boxed for vessel shipment *——.
TRIGAR......	(What is) Estimated total tonnage (including tender, if any) of one locomotive taken apart and boxed for vessel shipment, reckoning on basis of vessel's option of calculating 2,000 pounds weight or 40 cubic feet measurement per ton on each separate piece, in tons *——.
TRIGGER.....	(What is) Estimated total tonnage (including tender, if any) of one locomotive taken apart and boxed for vessel shipment, reckoning on basis of vessel's option of calculating 2,240 pounds weight or 40 cubic feet measurement per ton on each separate piece, in tons *——.
TRILHO......	(What is) Weight of heaviest single piece in pounds *——
TRINCO.......	(What is) Cubic feet measurement of bulkiest single piece *——.

Wheels

Code Word	MESSAGE
TROUXA......	Diameter (outside) of driving wheels measured in inches *——.
TROVAO......	Diameter of driving wheels to be increased by *—— inches.
TROYANA....	Diameter of driving wheels to be decreased by *—— inches.
TROZOS.......	Driving wheels cast-iron centers with steel tires.
TRUAND......	Driving wheels solid cast iron with chilled flange and tread.
TRUFAR......	Driving wheels extra-wide tread.
TRUISM.......	Driving wheels steel centers with steel tires.
TRUJAL......	Engine truck wheels cast-iron centers with steel tires.
TRULLA......	Engine truck wheels steel centers with steel tires.
TRUMPF......	Engine truck wheels solid cast iron with chilled flange and tread.
TRUNFO......	Tender wheels cast-iron centers with steel tires.
TRUPPA......	Tender wheels steel centers with steel tires.
TRUWOR.....	Tender wheels solid cast iron with chilled flange and tread.
TRYGON.....	Cast-iron centers and steel tires for all wheels.
TRYLLE......	Steel centers and steel tires for all wheels.
TUBFUL......	Shallow flange for flat street rail.

*Any code designated on page 04 may be used to express figures.

INDEX

	PAGE
Animal Haulage, Cost of Operating	184
Cable Correspondence Code	204
Cable Address and Codes Used	3
Cars, Weights and Capacities	189, 190
Classification of Locomotives	16
Compressed-Air Haulage, Industrial, Underground (Advt.)	2
Conditions of Service	17
Cost of Operating Animals and Locomotives	184
Cost of Railroads per Mile	186
Crossties per Mile	193
Curves	173, 181
Compensation for, on Grade	178
Degrees of Curvature	173, 174
Elevation of Outer Rail	180
Gauge Widened on	178
Laying Out	176
Measurement of	175
Resistance of	177
Table of Degrees and Feet Radius	174
Cylindrical Tanks, Contents of	200
Duplicate System	7
Elevation of Outer Rail on Curves	180
Friction, Resistance and Test of	152, 153
Fuel, Smoke-Stacks for Different Kinds	11, 12
Gauge of Track	179
Stated in Inches and Millimetres	197
Wheel Clearance for	179
Widened on Curves	178
Gauges for Wire and Plates, Inches and Metric	201
Grades	170-172
Hauling Capacity on	152-169
Measurement of	171
Resistance of	152
Table of	172
Guaranty of Our Locomotives	6
Hauling Capacity and Rule for Calculation	152
Influenced by Speed	182
Tables, Various Weights Locomotives on Grades at Different Frictional Resistances	158-169
Tables of Percentages	156, 157
Table of Times Its Weight Locomotive Can Haul	158
Historic Data	5-8
Horsepower of Locomotives	203
Locomotives, Classification of	16
Cost of Operating	184
Horsepower of	203
Repairing of	8
Repair Parts for	7
Second-Hand	7
Selection of	17
Specifications of	10
Tables of Tractive Force of	142-151
Locomotives, "American" Design	18
"Back-Truck" Designs, Four Driving Wheels	50, 58, 60, 90, 96, 124, 126, 128
" " Six Driving Wheels	52, 62, 94, 100, 132, 134

INDEX—*Continued*

	PAGE
Locomotives—*Continued*	
For Coke-Oven Service	80
Consolidation Design	30
For Contractors' Service	64, 66, 68, 70, 72, 76, 86, 88, 110, 112, 114, 116, 118, 120
"Double-Ender" Designs	42, 44, 136, 138
Eight-Driving-Wheel Designs	30, 40, 74, 122
"Eight-Wheel-Passenger" Design	18
For Export	9
"Forney" Designs	44, 48, 54, 56, 92, 98
For Freight Service	26, 28, 30, 36, 38, 40, 44, 46, 48, 54, 56, 58, 60, 62, 70, 72, 74, 118-134, 138
For Furnace Service	64, 66, 68, 82, 84
For Industrial and Special Service:	
Four-Wheel-Connected	32, 34, 64, 66, 68, 76, 78, 86, 110, 112, 114, 116
Six-Wheel-Connected	36, 38, 70, 72, 88, 118, 120
Back-Truck	50, 52, 54, 56, 58, 60, 62
For Logging Service:	
Saddle-Tank Designs	54, 56, 58, 60, 90, 62-76, 86, 88, 98, 100
Separate Tender Designs	26, 28, 30, 36, 38, 40
For Mine Service, Steam	106, 108
Mogul Design	26, 28
Motors for Steam Street Railways	102, 104
For Passenger Service:	
With Separate Tender	18, 20, 22, 24
" Saddle or Side Tanks	42, 54, 124, 126, 136
" Rear Tanks	46, 50
For Plantation Service:	
With Wooden Cab with Tender	26, 28, 30, 32, 34, 36, 38, 40
" " " without Tender	46-74, 110, 112, 118, 120, 124, 12, 132, 134
" Open Canopy " "	76, 86-100, 114, 1168, 128, 130
For Shifting Service	32, 34, 36, 38, 40, 64, 66, 68, 70, 72, 74, 110, 112, 116, 120, 122
For Steel-Works Service	82, 84
Logs and Lumber, Weight of	192
Materials, Physical Tests of	13
Measures and Weights, American and Metric	195, 196
Miscellaneous Items of Information	189
Pipes, Cubic Contents of	200
" Weight and Contents	199
Pressures, Atmospheric	199
" Metric and Pounds	198
Rails	186
Tons per Mile	193
Weights of, American and Metric	194
Weight per Yard for Any Locomotive	192
Repair Parts for Locomotives	7
Resistances of Gravity and Friction	152, 182
" of Curves	177
Revolutions of Driving Wheels	201, 202
Specifications of Locomotives, Standard	10
Speed	182
On Curves	180
Resistance of	182
And Wheel Revolutions	202
Per Hour, Miles and Kilometres	196
Spikes, per Mile	193
Splice-Joints, per Mile	193
Stacks, Different Kinds	11, 12
Stock Locomotives Kept on Hand	7
Tables, Contents of Pipes and Tanks	199, 200
Curves, Degrees, and Feet Radius	174

INDEX—*Continued*

Tables—*Continued*   PAGE
- Curve Deflections... 177
- Curves, Elevation of Rail on...................................... 181
- Crossties per Mile... 193
- Distances, American and Metric................................. 196
- Grades... 172
- Hauling Capacity.. 162-169
- Hauling Capacity Percentages............................. 155-157
- Hauling Capacities in Times Engine's Weight............... 158
- Measurements, American and Metric........... 197, 195-199
- Pressures,   "   "   ".................................. 198
- Speeds per Hour, "   "   "........................... 196
- Thickness,   "   "   "................................. 201
- Tractive Force.. 143-151
- Weights of Cars and Loads................................ 190, 191
- "   " Logs and Lumber............................... 192
- "   " Rails, per Mile............................. 192, 193
- "   " Spikes,   "................................... 193
- "   " Splice-Joints................................ 193, 194

Telegraph Correspondence Code.............................. 204-221
Tractive Force, Formula for...................................... 140
    "   " Tables of.. 143-151
Underground Haulage (See Advt. page 2)................... 106, 108
Weights and Capacities of Cars.............................. 190, 191
    " of Logs and Lumber............................. 192
    " American and Metric............................ 196, 194
    " Miscellaneous...................................... 189
    " of Pipe... 199
    " of Rail, per Mile............................... 192, 193
    " of Railroad Spikes................................ 193
    " of Splice-Joints................................ 193, 194
Wheel Revolutions, per Minute.................................. 202
  "   "   " Mile....................................... 201
  " Section of Flange and Tread............................... 179

1908

Advertisement

Our Compressed-Air Locomotives are described in our new catalogue

Compressed-Air Haulage

which will be mailed free on request of mine or industrial operator or others interested

Compressed-Air Locomotives are preferable for underground haulage and for surface use at various industrial operations. They are wholly free from danger of fire, no dirt or smoke, easy to handle, free from breakdown, compare favorably with any other mechanical haulage as to economy, last longer with less repairs

In writing for Air Catalogue, please add "as advertised in Steam Catalogue"

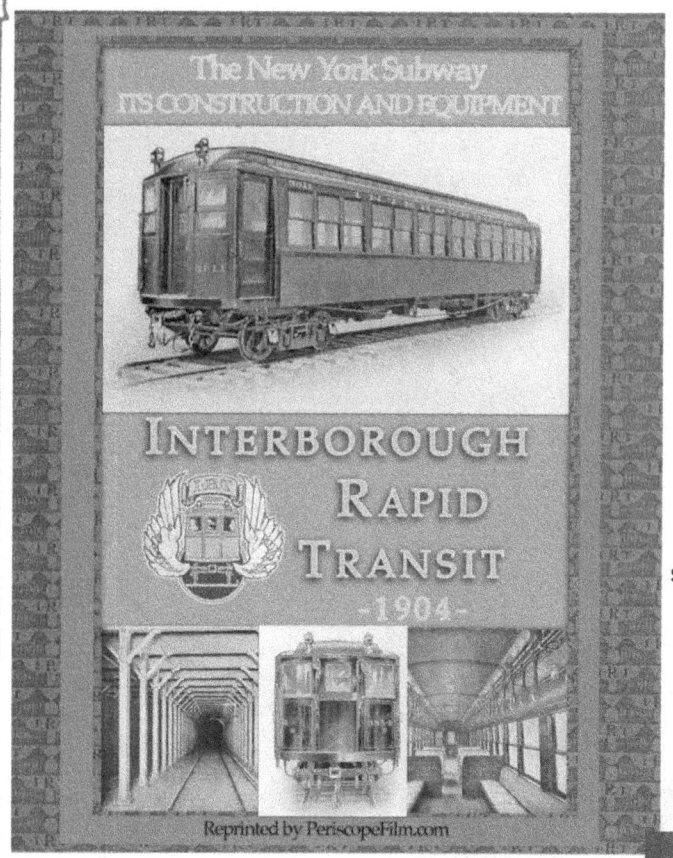

On October 27, 1904, the Interborough Rapid Transit Company opened the first subway in New York City. Running between City Hall and 145th Street at Broadway, the line was greeted with enthusiasm and, in some circles, trepidation. Created under the supervision of Chief Engineer S.L.F. Deyo, the arrival of the IRT foreshadowed the end of the "elevated" transit era on the island of Manhattan. The subway proved such a success that the IRT Co. soon achieved a monopoly on New York public transit. In 1940 the IRT and its rival the BMT were taken over by the City of New York. Today, the IRT subway lines still exist, primarily in Manhattan where they are operated as the "A Division" of the subway. Reprinted here is a special book created by the IRT, recounting the design and construction of the fledgling subway system. Originally created in 1904, it presents the IRT story with a flourish, and with numerous fascinating illustrations and rare photographs.

Originally written in the late 1900's and then periodically revised, A History of the Baldwin Locomotive Works chronicles the origins and growth of one of America's greatest industrial-era corporations. Founded in the early 1830's by Philadelphia jeweler Matthais Baldwin, the company built a huge number of steam locomotives before ceasing production in 1949. These included the 4-4-0 American type, 2-8-2 Mikado and 2-8-0 Consolidation. Hit hard by the loss of the steam engine market, Baldwin soldiered on for a brief while, producing electric and diesel engines. General Electric's dominance of the market proved too much, and Baldwin finally closed its doors in 1956. By that time over 70,500 Baldwin locomotives had been produced. This high quality reprint of the official company history dates from 1920. The book has been slightly reformatted, but care has been taken to preserve the integrity of the text.

NOW AVAILABLE AT
WWW.PERISCOPEFILM.COM

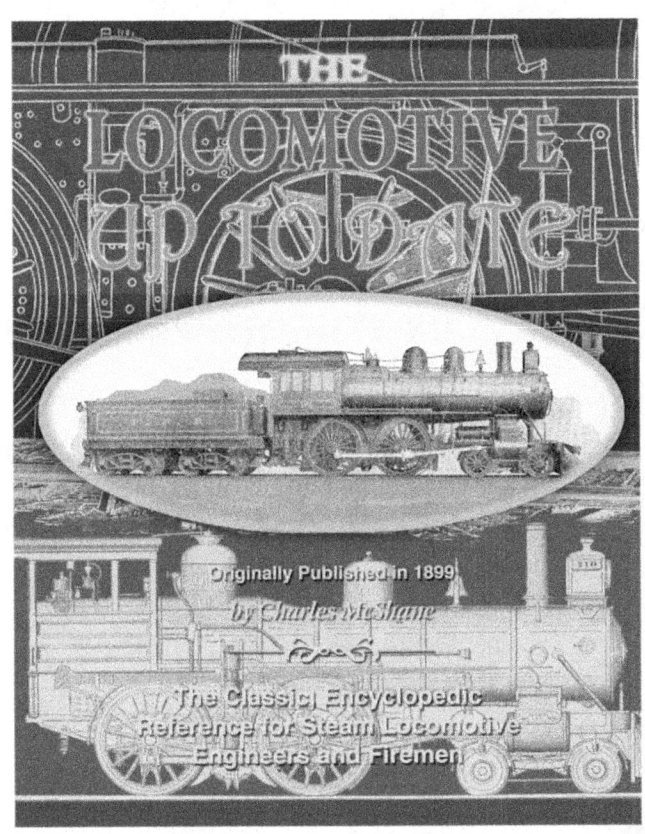

When it was originally published in 1899, **The Locomotive Up to Date** was hailed as "...the most definitive work ever published concerning the mechanism that has transformed the American nation: the steam locomotive." Filled with over 700 pages of text, diagrams and photos, this remains one of the most important railroading books ever written. From steam valves to sanders, trucks to side rods, it's a treasure trove of information, explaining in easy-to-understand language how the most sophisticated machines of the 19th century were operated and maintained. This new edition is an exact duplicate of the original. Reformatted as an easy-to-read 8.5x11 volume, it's delightful for railroad enthusiasts of all ages.

Originally printed in 1898 and then periodically revised, **The Motorman...and His Duties** served as the definitive training text for a generation of streetcar operators. A must-have for the trolley or train enthusiast, it is also an important source of information for museum staff and docents. Lavishly illustrated with numerous photos and black and white line drawings, this affordable reprint contains all of the original text. Includes chapters on trolley car types and equipment, troubleshooting, brakes, controllers, electricity and principles, electric traction, multi-car control and has a convenient glossary in the back. If you've ever operated a trolley car, or just had an electric train set, this is a terrific book for your shelf!

ALSO NOW AVAILABLE FROM PERISCOPEFILM.COM!

THE CLASSIC 1911 TROLLEY CAR BUILDER'S REFERENCE BOOK

ELECTRIC RAILWAY DICTIONARY

By Rodney Hitt
Associate Editor, Electric Railway Journal

REPRINTED BY PERISCOPEFILM.COM

www.ingramcontent.com/pod-product-compliance
Lightning Source LLC
Chambersburg PA
CBHW080454170426

43196CB00016B/2802